The Uncertain Crusade

Jimmy Carter and the Dilemmas of Human Rights Policy

By Joshua Muravchik

Foreword By Jeane Kirkpatrick

American Enterprise Institute for Public Policy Research
Washington, D.C.

Distributed by arrangement with
National Book Network
4720 Boston Way
Lanham, MD 20706
3 Henrietta Street
London, WC2E 8LU England

Library of Congress Cataloging-in-Publication Data

Muravchik, Joshua.
The uncertain crusade : Jimmy Carter and the dilemmas of human
rights policy / Joshua Muravchik ; foreword by Jeane Kirkpatrick.
p. cm.
Reprint. Originally published: Lanham, MD : Hamilton Press.
c1986. With new pref.
Includes bibliographies and index.
1. United States—Foreign relations—1977–1981. 2. Civil rights
(International law) 3. Carter, Jimmy, 1924–   —Views on human
rights. I. American Enterprise Institute for Public Policy
Research. II. Title.
E873.M87   1988
327.73—dc 19   88–1097 CIP
ISBN 0–8447–3648–1 (pbk. : alk. paper)

Contents

Acknowledgements

Many people gave me help in the research and writing of this book. Sylvia Gear of the Montgomery County Library and Rachel Van Wingen, Carolyn Colwell and Gail Flatness of the Georgetown University Library all were generous with their time and energies. Vita Bite of the Congressional Research Service helped me to locate some important materials and answered numerous questions for me. Karlyn Keene of *Public Opinion* magazine and John Rees of *Information Digest* and Susan Morris then of Senator Moynihan's staff took pains to provide me with source materials, as did John Haynes, a friend and former Congressional staff member to whom I turned repeatedly for advice. I had several valuable conversations with Charles Fairbanks, then the Deputy Assistant Secretary of State for Human Rights. Four people read the manuscript in different stages and offered valuable advice: William V. O'Brien, Midge Decter, Michael Jackson, and Bruce Cameron. To all these people I express a warm thank you.

I am indebted as well to the Institute for Educational Affairs for a generous research grant.

I am grateful to my daughters, Stephanie, Madeline, and Valerie, for their patience, and especially to my wife, Sally, to whom I dedicate this book.

Foreword

In retrospect it seems nearly inevitable that human rights should have become a central issue in American Foreign Policy once the U.S. became really involved in the world. The rights of individuals, whose protection we have always viewed as the purpose of a government, has always been a central preoccupation of America in politics.

Unlike older societies which have gone through diverse political transformations and have an identity that transcends any regime, the U.S. was born at a particular time out of a struggle over the rights of citizens. Our identity is inextricably involved with the Declaration of Independence and Constitution. The notion that policy should *not* reflect concern with human rights and democracy is as far-fetched as the notion that foreign policy should not express the nation. In the American view, human rights are universal and the very purpose of government is their protection. American politics ring with declarations that our rights are inextricably intertwined with the rights of others, and assertions that no one's rights are safe while others' rights are violated.

Still, the protection of human rights has been regarded by almost all nations as an internal matter—to be settled between a government and its citizens. Englishmen wrested their rights to representation, free speech and religion from reluctant English monarchs. Americans and French protect our rights through *our* constitutions and courts and so forth. The protection of human rights has never loomed large as a motive of governments in dealing with one another. Instead, governments have given priority to such factors as trade, aid, balance of power and alliances. It was Adolf Hitler's aggression, not his treatment of Jews, gypsies and dissidents, that provoked democratic nations into World War II. In the conventional view the purpose of foreign policy is to serve the national interest. The national interest does not include trying to shape other governments' treatment of their citizens.

Our national origins and our political culture assured that our approach to foreign affairs would not be routine *realpolitik*, but would have an explicit moral purpose. This requirement has sometimes led us to avoid the world, and other times to try to remake it.

Louis Hartz, the historian of American liberalism, noted that the American concern with morality in foreign policy had dual results. It stimulated both isolationism and meliorism. From the time of Jefferson onward, it was characterized by very strong isolationist impulses. "The sense that America's very liberal joy lay in the escape from a decadent old world that could only infect with its own disease," Hartz noted, "drove our isolationism." And this spirit pervaded our culture even during the revolutionary age of American history. "Yet," said Hartz, "in the 20th Century Americanism has also crusaded abroad in a Wilsonian way. It has been driven onto the world stage by events. It is inspired, willy-nilly, to reconstruct the very alien thing that is the world it had tried until then to avoid." "Its messianism," said Hartz, "is the polar counterpart of its isolationism. An absolute national morality is inspired either to withdraw from alien things or to transform them."

Woodrow Wilson's interpretation of the founding fathers led alternately to isolationism and internationalism.

In his speech, "Patriotism and the Sailor," for example, Wilson said, "It was not merely because of passing and transient circumstances that Washington said that we must keep free of entangling alliances, it was because he saw that no country had yet set its face in the same direction in which America had set her face. We cannot form alliances with those who are not going our way, and in our might and majesty and in the confidence and definitiveness of our own purpose, we need not and we should not form alliances with any nation in the world. Those who are right, those who study their consciences in determining their policies, those who hold their honor higher than their advantage do not need alliances. You do not need alliances when you are strong. You are weak only when you are not true to yourself. You are weak only when you are in the wrong. You are weak only when you are afraid to do the right thing. You are weak only when you doubt your course."

Abraham Lincoln believed we had a vocation to secure the rights of others asserting, "While man exists, it is his duty to improve not only his own condition, but to assist in ameliorating that of mankind."

Because these national characteristics are profoundly rooted in our political culture, it was probably inevitable that once the objective facts of international interdependence had been created—had "driven us into the world," in Hartz' term—the United States should seek ways of acting in the world compatible with our national predispositions. The notion that foreign policy should be guided by balance of power politics, or *realpolitik*, is utterly foreign to the American tradition and foreign to the American scene today. All our wars, beginning with the Revolutionary War, were justified in terms of the protection, the extension of universal human rights. Thus, the United States approached its participation in international affairs as an opportunity and a duty to achieve moral goals—preservation of democracy, respect for human rights, the peaceable settlement of disputes and elimination of war. We entered the world's center stage to make the world safe for democracy. And no sooner did we become seriously involved in global politics than our presidents—first, Woodrow Wilson, then Franklin Roosevelt—undertook to guarantee permanent peace and democracy through a world organization. We authored a universal declaration of human rights and secured its adoption in the global institution which we brought into being.

None of these efforts worked as expected, so, in the nineteen seventies, the U.S. undertook a new approach to foreign policy—the deliberate use of American policy to influence the internal policies of other nations with regard to the respect for human rights. Although that approach is associated with the Carter presidency and found its clearest and broadest expression in that administration, it is worth noting that the essential elements of "linkage" had other sources and were present before the Carter inauguration. These sources of linkage are, I believe, three.

The first legislation to systematically link U.S. economic policy to human rights of another country was the Jackson-Vanik amendment to the 1972 trade agreement. This amendment, authored by the late "Scoop" Jackson, made trade concessions to the Soviet Union contingent on a liberalization of immigration policies for Christians, Jews and others.

A quite different source of "linkage" is found in the anti-war movement, one of whose principal charges was that South Vietnam's human rights abuses made that government morally unworthy of survival. Similar charges were pressed against other Third World friends and allies—especially Iran and South Korea. These charges were most often made against traditional, not Marxist dictatorships by liberals who argued that we should form alliances only with those who share our values and goals and that we need not worry about a purist policy weakening us because strength depends on moral clarity and integrity. By definition, doing the "right thing" could not be inconsistent with our national interest.

The Carter approach to human rights had a third antecedent which was not home grown. The Soviet Union was by the mid-seventies pushing world wide a new doctrine of national liberation which denies legitimacy to governments targeted for incorporation into the Soviet bloc, defines armed opposition to these governments as a legitimate response to oppression, and defines a government's defense as a violation of human rights. More and more of those who advocated linking U.S. foreign policy to "human rights" seemed to accept these definitions without much thought.

The new doctrines of "linkage" struck root in American soil because they were compatible with essential strains of our political culture. They reflected our concern with our own virtue and with making the world more virtuous. They expressed the familiar conviction that we should seek universal altruistic goals, not "mere" national advantage, and they assumed that being true to ourselves meant making our foreign policies consistent with universal moral goals.

Yet, despite its manifest compatibility in the dominant strain of the American tradition and culture and the wide consensus in the U.S. concerning the role of human rights, the Carter approach to human rights was controversial from the start. This controversy, which continues still today, revealed that alongside the consensus on the importance of human rights in foreign policy existed important disagreements:

—Disagreement about what human rights are and which are more important among them—political, civil, legal, economic, social?

—Disagreement about how to promote respect for human rights in other countries—by persuasion, coercion, destabilization, example or what?

—Disagreement about the relations among our moral and strategic goals.

—Disagreement about what we should do and could do.

—Disagreement about politics and history.

Can we have strategic interests in countries with poor human rights records? Are traditional autocracies doomed to fall in any case? Should the U.S. take the risk of supporting Marxist/Leninist regimes in the hope of establishing good relations?

These disagreements illuminate several of the great issues that divide not only America but the world, and they raise serious questions about how far the Marxist/Leninists had succeeded in substituting their conceptions of human rights for the liberal, democratic conception and establishing a *presumption* that groups associated with them are the carriers of respect for human rights.

Carter policy confronted us head on with all the questions and problems latent in a serious effort to link human rights and foreign policy.

Do we want to deny food to people who already suffer under bad government *because* they suffer under bad government? Do we want to deprive of material assistance people already deprived of self-government? Do we want to turn over to efficient communist dictators people who already suffer under inefficient, home bred autocracies? Do we have the power to force reform on other nations? Do we have the wisdom to do so? Do we have the obligation?

The intellectual and practical problems of linking human rights and foreign policy are difficult and complex. Their analysis requires skill, balance, and a broad, sophisticated knowledge of the contemporary ideological and political world.

Josh Muravchik brings just such learning, balance and sophistication to the examination of the Carter Administration's record, and to the analysis of the broader problems.

Muravchik's life and work make clear his strong personal commitment to the use of American power to enhance human rights. Neither his analytical spirit nor his negative conclusions concerning the consequences of the Carter Administration's efforts diminish his solidarity with the struggle for human freedom and well being.

Muravchik's analysis of the dilemmas of human rights policy faces without compromise the full complexities of the relations among political, legal, social, and cultural rights, acknowledges the claims of each, and explains why there are no "trade offs" between democracy and equality, between democracy and law, between democracy and development because only democracy finally ensures respect for human rights, the rule of law, and opportunity for all.

Few of us in or out of government are willing to think about the relations between trade, aid, banks, tanks, and repression in Iran, Poland, Romania, Nicaragua, and El Salvador before and after Carter. The reason, probably, is that thinking about them brings us face to face with difficulties and limits—limits of our power, limits of our interests, limits of our commitment, limits to our seriousness. It brings us face to face with what many liberals have sought above all to avoid: the appalling complexity of the relations between intention and action, between ideas and institutions, between moralilty, power and foreign policy. Muravchik knows that "As long as there are armed tyrants in the world, human rights must be defended not only in the realm of ideas but in the realm of arms, as well." And he might have added, they are finally dependent on our power, understanding and realism as well as our good intentions.

This book eschews fashionable sentimentalities and simplifications, fashionable politics and ideology. It places its author solidly in the tradition of his mentor and friend, the late Scoop Jackson who might have been speaking to Muravchik, himself, when he said, "My friends, you and I fought for human rights before it became fashionable. I am confident that we will continue even after the fainthearted have tired of the struggle."

————— Jeane Kirkpatrick

Introduction

Soon after taking office in 1981, President Reagan appointed Ernest Lefever as his chief human rights official. Lefever was a distinguished academic who had spoken out against the very idea that the way other governments treat their own subjects should be an issue in U.S. dealings with them. Lefever had written: "we cannot export human rights....in dealing with Third World countries, their foreign policy behavior should be the determining factor, not their domestic practices."[1]

The Republicans had just won control of the Senate on Ronald Reagan's coattails, and thus the new president was enjoying a particularly cozy honeymoon with the senior chamber. But it rebelled against the appointment of Lefever, even though in his confirmation hearings he explained that he had changed his views.

Several different things fueled the opposition to Lefever, but at the core was Lefever's own expressed skepticism about President Carter's decision to give the subject of human rights a central place in U.S. foreign policy. Not that the senators approved of all that Carter had done in the name of human rights. On the contrary, most were deeply critical of Carter, and many shared some of the trenchant criticisms expressed in Lefever's writing, but few wanted to remove human rights from the agenda of American diplomacy.

Yet only eight years earlier, Henry Kissinger had, during his own confirmation hearings, expressed views identical to

Lefever's. "I do believe that it is dangerous for us to make the domestic policy of countries around the world a direct objective of American foreign policy," said Kissinger.[2] Kissinger was testifying to the same Foreign Relations Committee that later voted 13 to 2 against Lefever; indeed, in 1973 that committee, like the Senate as a whole, was more liberal than in 1981 (and controlled by the Democrats). Nonetheless, Kissinger's views evoked little objection. There were of course many differences between the Kissinger and the Lefever nominations, but it is hard to avoid the conclusion that one of them was that President Carter had wrought a lasting change in the prevailing view of the requisites of U.S. foreign policy. As the Reagan administration learned the hard way, the idea that the promotion of human rights throughout the world should be an important U.S. goal had taken hold.

In lieu of Lefever, President Reagan nominated Elliott Abrams, a former aide to senators Henry Jackson and Daniel Patrick Moynihan, two Democratic pioneers in the field of human rights. And soon thereafter the State Department declared, "Human rights is at the core of our foreign policy."[3]

But just as Republicans joined Democrats in upholding Carter's idea of having a "human rights policy," many Democrats joined Republicans in criticizing the way Carter had carried out that policy. After the Carter administration left office, Richard Holbrooke, Carter's assistant secretary of state for Asia, criticized the policy so harshly before a congressional committee,that the committee scheduled an additional day of hearings in order to afford Patricia Derian, Carter's assistant secretary for Human Rights, the opportunity to respond.[4] The fact that Holbrooke had been the author of the first speech ever delivered by Jimmy Carter on the subject of international human rights, a campaign speech before the B'nai B'rith in September 1976, made his subsequent disillusionment with the policy all the more significant.

Nor was Holbrooke alone. Carter's National Security Advisor Zbigniew Brzezinski has written in his memoirs of his unhappiness with the way the human rights policy was carried out.[5] Interestingly, similar sentiments have been given voice by former Under Secretary of State David Newsom, a State Department liberal much criticized by Brzezinski.

On the other hand, Patricia Derian, the chief human rights official of the Carter administration, often vented her frustrations with what she was and was not able to accomplish in her job. She testified on one occasion, for example, that: "Every night when I go home I think, 'I ought to quit this job.' Every morning when I get up I think, 'I will do it one more day.'"[6] And other Carter human rights officials, while defending the policy, volunteer that its presentation was "grandiose" or "overstated,"[7] a euphemistic way of saying that the policy did not live up to expectations.

In short, the Carter experience left in its wake a consensus on two points: first, emphasizing human rights in foreign policy is a good idea; second, implementing this idea is difficult and Carter's own efforts left much to be desired. This difficulty has two chief sources. First, too little is known about how to foment a lasting improvement in observance of human rights in societies where they are not widely observed. Experience teaches that this is at best a very difficult task, especially if the impetus comes from the outside. Second, even those who believe most strongly that the United States should have a human rights policy agree that it cannot be the only goal of U.S. foreign policy. Sometimes the pursuit of human rights may suggest actions that would disserve other goals.

The story of the Carter human rights policy is to a great extent the story of the discovery of the vexing dilemmas that arise in the course of trying to make human rights a central issue in the conduct of foreign policy. Carter had hit upon the human rights issue during the campaign, criticizing President Ford for refusing to invite Alexander Solzhenitsyn to the White House. Carter followed up by making human rights a central theme of his inaugural address. From that moment on, his administration was committed to an emphasis on human rights. Only in the ensuing months did administration officials come to appreciate the difficulty of constructing a human rights "policy."

This book aims, in part, to tell the story of the Carter human rights policy. Its more important aim is to identify the critical dilemmas of our human rights policy as they were revealed by the experience of the Carter administration. These dilemmas are of fundamental importance and will have to be confronted by any U.S. human rights policy. I have grouped these dilemmas into four major questions.

The first question concerns the relationship of human rights to political systems. Should a U.S. human rights policy endeavor to transcend the ideological conflict between the democratic and the Communist worlds, lest our policy seem self-serving or inspired by ulterior motives? Or is the struggle for human rights inseparable from that conflict?

The second question concerns the definition of "human rights." Which "human rights" should U.S. policy promote, those that are found in the American tradition or those that are embodied in international law and documents? Should U.S. policy recognize the category "economic and social rights"? Should it draw a distinction between civil and political rights, on the one hand, and rights of "integrity of the person," on the other? Should some rights receive priority over others, and if so which?

The third question concerns consistency. Should U.S. human rights policy aspire to respond in a similar manner or with similar severity to similar human rights violations irrespective of the identity of the offending government? If not, what are the justifiable bases for inconsistent responses? Should we treat countries differently based on our estimation of their "readiness" for human rights? Or based on other goals—strategic, economic, arms control—that might be at stake in our relations with them?

The fourth question concerns the use of punitive measures. Should the United States manipulate its economic aid, security assistance, credits and financing, trade, or other forms of resource transfers in the hope of coercing other governments into showing more respect for their subjects' rights? Do such measures work? If not, should we cut aid anyway in order to assure that the United States is not complicit in human rights violations? If the United States eschews such measures, what other tools can it use to promote human rights?

This book is organized into two major parts. Part One reviews the history of the Carter policy—its origins, its personnel, its goals, and its actions. Part Two consists of an explication of the critical dilemmas, the ways that the Carter administration responded to them, and possible alternative responses. The book has two concluding chapters, one devoted to a summary evaluation of the Carter policy, the other setting forth recommendations for a future U.S. human rights policy.

NOTES

1. U.S., Congress, House, Committee on Foreign Affairs, Human Rights and U.S. Foreign Policy, Hearings Before the Subcommittee on International Organizations, 96th Cong., 1st sess., 1979, pp. 230-231.

2. U.S., Congress, Senate, Committee on Foreign Affairs, Nomination of Henry A. Kissinger, 93rd Cong., 1st sess., p. 117.

3. William Clarke, Deputy Secretary of State, and Richard T. Kennedy, Under Secretary of State for Management, "Memorandum for the Secretary, Subject: Reinvigoration of Human Rights Policy," Oct. 26, 1981, p. 1, copy in author's file.

4. U.S., Congress, House, Committee on Foreign Affairs, Reconciling Human Rights and U.S. Security Interests in Asia, Hearings before the Subcommittees on Asian and Pacific Affairs and on Human Rights and International Organizations, 97th Cong., 2nd sess., 1982, pp. 3-81, 477-529.

5. Zbigniew Brzezinski, Power and Principle (New York: Farrar, Straus, Giroux, 1983), p. 128.

6. U.S., Congress, House, Committee on Foreign Affairs, Human Rights and the Phenomenon of Disappearances, Hearings before the Subcommittee on International Organizations, 96th Cong., 1st sess., 1979, p. 399.
7. Interview with Stephen Cohen, held in Washington, D.C., Nov. 14, 1983.

Preface to the
Paperback Edition

Jimmy Carter served only one term as president, and his human rights policy was in full voice for only half of that term. Yet it has left a lasting impress on U.S. policy. Probably few things would please Jimmy Carter less than the thought that he has contributed in a major way to the success of Ronald Reagan's presidency. And probably few things would please Ronald Reagan less than having to acknowledge such a debt to Carter. But for all the contrasts between their philosophies, Reagan's foreign policy developed in part on a base that Carter laid when he made human rights a principal issue in America's relations with the rest of the world.

True, Reagan has not emphasized human rights as Carter did. His principal theme has been the renewal of America's dignity—"standing tall again"—in contrast to the self-critical posture of the Carter years. At first the Reagan administration seemed inclined to treat the human rights issue as nothing more than another manifestation of Carterite wimpishness. But as it struggled to formulate foreign policy, the Reagan administration came to see that dignity entailed not only strength but purpose too. To stand tall America had not only to restock its arsenals but also to recapture its sense of mission as the world's engine of democracy, or human rights, or freedom—call it what you will. (Of course the terms "freedom," "democracy," and "human rights" are not synonymous, and their meanings may even conflict, as when a majority legislates restrictions on individual behavior, but the three concepts are closely related, all flowing from the idea that the individual morally precedes the state.)

After toying with the idea of emasculating the State Department's Human Rights Bureau, Reagan appointed two forceful and effective men to lead it—first Elliott Abrams and then Richard Schifter. He also inaugurated a "democracy project," which, with bipartisan support in Congress, blossomed into the National Endowment for Democracy. And in formulating policy toward such disparate places as Central America, the Caribbean, Eastern Europe, South Africa and East Asia, his administration came to emphasize America's values as well as its interests. As Charles Krauthammer has argued, it came to realize that America's values and its interests are not easily disentangled. In American foreign policy, idealism and self-assertion, far from being mutually contradictory, are mutually reinforcing. The growth of American power encourages the growth of democracy (and of human rights); the spread of democracy strengthens America's influence.

If this realization came slowly to Reagan's administration, it came no faster to Carter's. Although Carter and his aides sometimes intimated that one motive for his human rights theme was to enable America to regain the ideological initiative, Carter more often gave the impression that he saw a trade-off betwen power and idealism. Calling in his 1976 presidential campaign for a foreign policy "as good as the American people," Carter argued that the decline of America's prestige was the consequence of its misbehavior. Talking about human rights was a way of making America good again. Discontinuing aid to abusive governments was a way of cleaning our hands. Some in the Carter administration even seemed to accept the notion popularized during the Vietnam War that American influence in the third world was often malign and that those regions might benefit from its diminution.

The fall of Nicaragua's Somoza and of Iran's Shah—two targets of U.S. human rights pressures—had a sobering effect. The revolutionary governments that replaced these two dictators were soon recognized as being unfriendly not only to the United States, but also to human rights. The reduction of American influence proved no blessing for the peoples concerned. And the clean hands America could show for having remained above the fray yielded small comfort. Carter's response was to deemphasize the human rights issue for the remainder of his term (until resurrecting it rhetorically during his reelection campaign).

Carter's problem, however, was not that he had given human rights too much emphasis but that he had failed to work through the difficult choices to be made in translating a theme into a policy. In particular, he had failed to reconcile his human rights goals with two of his other main foreign policy themes: restraint in U.S. behavior abroad, and reconciliation with erstwhile foes in the Communist world and among Third World radicals. How could we cause other governments to modify their domestic behavior except by wielding a heavier, rather than a lighter, hand in our foreign relations? And how could we champion human rights while reconciling with radical govenments that were fierce abusers of human rights?

On these two subjects Reagan's impulses were diametrically opposed to Carter's. Reagan sought an expansion of American influence and a sharper confrontation with radical adversaries. These approaches were more compatible with vigorous human rights advocacy. Indeed, the extension of American influence and the effective confrontation of adversaries are enhanced if America hews to its role as carrier of the democratic revolution. (Reagan held office for some time, however, before he recognized this.) Reagan's attitudes on these subjects enabled him to resolve easily dilemmas that had dogged Carter's policy. Speaking of democracy more than of human rights spared his administration the tortuous task of defining human rights and the pitfall of trying to abstract human rights from political systems. (It has not, however, spared him the dilemma of whether to strive for a policy that is consistent from country to country.)

If Reagan has succeeded in reinvigorating American foreign policy, he has done so in part by reversing some of Carter's policies but also in part by nourishing a seed Carter planted. That seed was the conviction, lost in the course of the Vietnam War, that America is a force for good in the world.

Moreover, the unintended collaboration between these two mutually antagonistic presidents may be at the root of some of the major gains for human rights witnessed by the world in the 1980s. We are in the midst of a marked worldwide trend toward democratization. It is most pronounced in Latin America but is also notable in the Far East. One might argue that it can also be observed in small tremors in the Communist world as well. Both Reaganites and Carterites have credited their man for this progress. The Reaganites point out that most of the changes have occurred since Reagan took office. The Carterites point to the explicit credit given to Carter by such key figures in the democratic transition as Argentina's President Alfonsin. A good case can be made, however, at least with respect to the transitions in the non-Communist world, that Carter and Reagan together played a kind of unplanned "good-cop—bad-cop" routine. Carter came down hard on the old dictatorial regimes in many of these countries, convincing them that they faced a genuine danger of losing U.S. support. Then Reagan convinced them that a revivified United States would guard them against Communism and make them proud to be included in the free world. It may have been the combined effect of these two messages that induced the military establishments in so many of these countries to opt for a transition to democracy.

Whatever the validity of this speculation, the human rights issue now seems certain to remain an integral piece of U.S.

foreign policy far into the future. Carter, whose policies I often criticize in this book, is likely to be remembered more for raising this issue to prominence than for the errors he made in fashioning a policy out of it. Those errors were the consequence of the dilemmas that arise in reconciling human rights with other U.S. goals. Although progress has been made in resolving some of those dilemmas, a good deal more thought and experience will be needed to resolve all of them satisfactorily.

ONE
Prelude to Policy

ORIGINS

Where did the Carter human rights policy come from? It was, says former Carter speechwriter Hendrik Hertzberg, "pure Jimmy." "Jimmy Carter had a moral ideology but no political ideology and the human rights policy is very much a reflection of the strong moral impulses tethered somewhat loosely to a set of political goals," says Hertzberg.[1] Hertzberg's evaluation is echoed by Carter's other principal presidential speechwriter, James Fallows: "the moral theme was something right in Carter's soul...*realpolitik* was not what he wanted to do."[2]

But if the moral impulse was genuine, the issue of human rights, as an expression of that impulse, developed in Carter only slowly. In 1975, Jimmy Carter published a book, *Why Not the Best?*, designed to boost his then-nascent presidential campaign.[3] In part an autobiography and in part a discussion of issues, the book contains no mention of human rights. It does however contain this expression of the quest for morality in foreign policy: "As it has related to such areas as Pakistan, Chile, Cambodia and Vietnam, our government's foreign policy has not exemplified any commitment to moral principles....A nation's domestic and foreign policies actions [sic] should be derived from the same standards of

1

ethics, honesty and morality which are characteristics of the individual citizens of the nation."[4] Throughout 1975 and the following presidential primaries in 1976, morality in government and in foreign policy was a constant theme of Carter's, but "human rights" was rarely mentioned. Moreover, Carter made a point of his opposition to the "Jackson Amendment" on free emigration, the rallying point of one human rights crusade. At the 1975 Democratic Issues Conference Carter said: "I think that the so-called 'Jackson Amendment' was ill-advised....Russia is a proud nation, like we are, and if Russian Communist leaders had passed a resolution saying that they were not going to do this or that if we didn't do something domestically, we would have reacted adversely to it. That's exactly what happened."[5]

The human rights issue emerged not in any Carter speech, but in the writing of the 1976 Democratic Platform. "It was seen politically as a no-lose issue," says Patrick Anderson, Carter's chief speechwriter during the 1976 campaign. "Liberals liked human rights because it involved political freedom and getting liberals out of jail in dictatorships, and conservatives liked it because it involved criticisms of Russia."[6] But it was more than a "no-lose" issue, it was a rare point of unity in a bitterly divided party. The Democrats had fought their way through bruising internecine primary battles in each of the two previous presidential elections, in 1968 between Humphrey, Kennedy, and McCarthy, and in 1972 between McGovern, Humphrey, Muskie, and others. Each time the winners were left exhausted and the losers were left embittered. Each time the Republicans triumphed in November. And in the intervening years the Democrats continued their feuding, in the councils of the Democratic National Committee and in a procession of party commissions and conventions. These bodies wrangled over rules and representation and the party's charter, but the real source of division was foreign policy. The war in Vietnam, the most divisive issue in America's postwar history, ravaged the Democratic party, while leaving the Republicans relatively unscathed, since both sides in America's great schism were led by Democrats. It was Democrats who led America into the war, and Democrats who led the fight to get America out of it. Even as the war became increasingly the responsibility of a Republican administration, and finally drew to a close, polarization among the Democrats persisted. On one side were those to whom the war had taught the lesson that America needed above all to overcome what Senator J. William Fulbright called her "arrogance of power." On the other side were those who feared that America's failure in Vietnam would lead to a dangerous shift in the world's "correlation of forces" in favor of the Soviet Union.

In the presidential primaries of 1976, Senator Henry Jackson represented the latter of these groups, while several Democrats, most successfully Congressman Morris Udall, sought to speak for the former group, whose avatar, Senator George McGovern, did not enter the race that year. Jimmy Carter remained carefully aloof from these ideological battles, and it is likely that this helped him to win the nomination. Democratic primary voters were attracted to his "outsider's," "anti-Washington" pitch, not only because they were tired of big government, but also perhaps because they were tired of the relentless feuding among their party's leaders. Carter's "new face" may have looked more appealing for not having been scarred in these wars.

But if the split among the Democrats had been an asset to Carter's quest for the nomination, it was a liability to his prospects in the general election. As an "outsider" running against an incumbent, he badly needed the support of a united party. As the Democrats gathered to draft their platform in 1976, both of their well-defined factions were ready for battle. On the one side were the "Jackson Democrats," led by "Pat" Moynihan, Ben Wattenberg and Jeane Kirkpatrick, drawing staff support from the Coalition for a Democratic Majority (CDM). On the other side were the "McGovern Democrats," led by Sam Brown and Bella Abzug, and drawing staff support from Americans for Democratic Action (ADA). Each side had the goal of pulling the Democratic platform closer to its own convictions. The Carter

3

representatives, led by Carter's top "issues" man, Stuart Eizenstat, had the goal of keeping everybody else reasonably happy, and keeping the party intact. There were some differences on domestic issues, but the real dividing line was over foreign affairs. On that there was almost no agreement, except, as it turned out, about human rights. On this the two sides shared a humanitarian impulse, although they certainly didn't approach the issue in the same way. To the Jackson Democrats, the human rights issue brought to mind primarily the victims of Communism, and they thought of it as a way of maintaining the ideological struggle against Communism at a time when Americans were losing their stomach for the policy of containment. On the other side, the McGovern Democrats had in mind primarily the victims of rightist governments. Raising this issue was to them a way of scaling back America's foreign entanglements. But there was here, unlike most other foreign policy issues, enough common ground to allow a meeting of the minds. Moynihan has recalled it in these words:

> ...."We'll be against the dictators you don't like the most," I said across the table to [Sam] Brown, "if you'll be against the dictators we don't like the most." The result was the strongest platform commitment to human rights in our history. Whether or not it was this commitment which directly influenced the new President to take the offensive, he began doing so from the very first, in his inaugural address.[7]

Both factions went away satisfied. Bruce Cameron, then the foreign policy lobbyist for ADA, noted afterward with satisfaction that the platform's human rights language was based on an original ADA draft[8] while the next issue of CDM's newsletter boasted that the final human rights language adopted by the party was prepared with the help of CDM's staff.[9] Both were right.

The impact on Carter's campaign was probably greater and more immediate than Moynihan realized. The platform was adopted during the week of June 13. Ten days later, speaking before the Foreign Policy Association, candidate Carter placed more emphasis on human rights than in any previous campaign speech.[10] In early September, Carter, speaking before B'nai B'rith, gave his first major campaign speech whose principal theme was human rights.[11] According to Patrick Anderson, Carter's chief speechwriter during the campaign, "the impetus" for the B'nai B'rith speech and for the new emphasis on human rights "came from Stu" Eizenstat. Anderson attributes Eizenstat's interest in the issue to his being a "devout Jew" whose "main concern was the rights of Jews in Russia to leave."[12] Anderson may well be right in his description of Eizenstat's feelings; Eizenstat is active in various Jewish causes. But Eizenstat had been Carter's top issues man for a couple of years already, during all of which time Carter had ignored the issue of human rights, had forcefully opposed the Jackson Amendment, and had taken a position on Middle East issues that was less clearly pro-Israeli than that of the other Democratic candidates. This suggests that the emergence of the human rights issue as a Carter campaign theme was less the product of Eizenstat's Jewishness than of his firsthand observations at the Democratic platform meetings that this alone of all foreign policy issues united the Democrats.

It had this effect not only on the Democratic leaders and ideologues who wrote the platform, but among Democratic voters. Elizabeth Drew reported that "surveys by Patrick Caddell, Carter's campaign pollster, had shown that human rights was an issue that united liberals and conservatives— that it seemed to be, Caddell now says, 'a very strong issue across the board.'"[13] Carter's human rights theme served not only to draw support from various disparate constituencies, it also served to tie together a variety of criticisms of the incumbent. Drew reports being told by one Carter official: "Human rights was an issue with which you could bracket Kissinger and Ford on both sides....it was a beautiful campaign issue, an issue on which there was a real degree of public opinion hostile to the [Ford] Administration."[14]

This effect was magnified by President Ford's famous gaffe during the second presidential debate when he said:

"there is no Soviet domination of Eastern Europe, and there never will be under a Ford Administration." To which Carter deftly replied: "I would like to see Mr. Ford convince the Polish-Americans and the Czech-Americans and the Hungarian-Americans in this country that those countries don't live under the domination and supervision of the Soviet Union behind the Iron Curtain."[15] That exchange may well have been the campaign's turning point and for the remaining month of the campaign, human rights remained one of Carter's constant themes. He chided Ford for having rebuffed Alexander Solzhenitsyn and he pledged that "when I am elected and go to the White House next January, I'm going to invite Alexander Solzhenitsyn to come by and see me."[16]

Thus, by the time of Carter's election, human rights had become one of the key points of his campaign. It gave needed substance to his otherwise vacuous pet theme of restoring morality to foreign policy. And all of those who were around him say that he took the issue to heart. As Brzezinski puts it:

> The commitment to human rights reflected Carter's own religious beliefs, as well as his political acumen. He deeply believed in human rights and that commitment remained constant during his Administration. At the same time, he sensed, I think, that the issue was an appealing one for it drew a sharp contrast between himself and the policies of Nixon and Kissinger.[17]

Carter stressed the human rights issue in his inaugural address and took some other actions in this area during his first weeks in office. He discovered quickly that this issue could be as politically valuable to him as president as it had been as a candidate. He reports in his memoirs:

> Judging from news articles and direct communications from the American people to me during the first few months of my administration, human rights had become the central theme of our foreign policy in the minds of the press and public. It

seemed that a spark had been ignited, and I had no inclination to douse the growing flames.[18]

Actually, Carter had something more to go on than "news articles and direct communications." He had his private polls. Elizabeth Drew reported a few months after Carter took office: "Polls taken by Patrick Caddell in this country this spring indicated that of the issues Carter was given high approval on, this was among the highest. 'Just enormous,' Caddell says."[19]

The impetus for Carter's human rights campaign was that the issue had resonance, both in Carter's soul and in his polls. But, at the time he took office, this commitment had not been translated into a consciously formulated "policy." Brzezinski reports that two weeks before he took office, Carter's National Security Council held an initial unofficial meeting. "The broad scope of the new President's policies was reflected by the studies that were commissioned" at that meeting, he says.[20] None of the fifteen studies was about human rights. And the issue was far enough from the center of Secretary Cyrus Vance's thoughts that, in a message of greeting he issued to the rest of the department upon taking office, human rights was not included in the list of a half dozen "global issues" that he mentioned. Six months after Carter's inauguration, Drew was still able to report:

> throughout our government, officials have been struggling to wrestle an idea into a policy....one foreign-policy official recently told me [that] "No one knows what the policy is, yet it pervades everything we do." Another official, who has done a good deal of the wrestling, told me,"....There's no question that human rights was stated as a principle before anyone thought about it in operational terms as a concrete policy."[21]

PERSONNEL

If there was not at first a "policy," there began to be

7

assembled a staff—a group of officials whose job it would be to carry out the human rights "policy" as it became formulated, and to help formulate it. In assembling this staff, the Carter administration departed in one decisive way from the approach of the Carter campaign. To the campaign, the human rights issue had been a means of uniting both ideological wings of the Democratic party. This had been one of the salient features of that issue. And given Ford's debate gaffe about Eastern Europe, his rebuff of Solzhenitsyn, and his vulnerability on the issue of detente, candidate Carter probably gave more emphasis to the Jackson/Moynihan version of the human rights issue than to the McGovern/Sam Brown version. At least that was how it appeared to one knowledgeable and impartial observer, the *Washington Post*'s Stephen Rosenfeld, who wrote:

> Sen. Henry Jackson (D.-Wash.) may have lost the battle for the Democratic presidential nomination but—to judge by the foreign and defense chapters of the Democratic platform worked out in Washington this week—he has largely won the policy war....
>
> The result is a document that firmly (though not exclusively) asserts the basic Jackson & Co. principle that the linchpin of American foreign policy is the survival of freedom around the world.[22]

But when the Carter administration began to assemble its human rights staff, no person who approached the human rights issue from the Jackson perspective was included; all who were chosen were from the party's McGovern wing.

This slant in the composition of Carter's human rights appointments in part reflected the overall coloration of Carter's foreign policy team. Although candidate Carter had carefully straddled his party's two ideological wings, not just on human rights but on foreign and defense issues in toto— he let it be known, for example, that in preparation for the second debate he had been briefed by both Paul Warnke and Paul Nitze—when it came to staffing his administration, he included only the McGovernites. This group, to be sure, was leavened with some key figures from the foreign policy establishment who were seen as ideologically neutral, Secretary Vance, for example, but they were not balanced by any voices from the party's Jackson wing. And this despite the fact that Jackson had withdrawn from the presidential race relatively early—after losing the Pennsylvania primary—and had refused to be party to any "stop Carter" machinations, while such McGovernites as Udall and Senator Frank Church had insisted on battling Carter to the bitter end.

Why Carter chose this slant, for which his campaign gave no forewarning, remains something of a mystery on which neither his memoirs, nor those of Vance nor Brzezinski, shed any light. But that there was such a slant, although denied in a perfunctory way by Carter spokesmen, was widely recognized and commented upon by Democrats of both factions. Ben Wattenberg, advisor to Jackson and chairman of the Coalition for a Democratic Majority, complained that his was a "missing point of view" in the Carter foreign policy team,[23] while Alan Baron, advisor to McGovern and organizer of the McGovernite faction in the Democratic National Committee, enthused: "George McGovern told friends that he considers the majority of Secretary of State Cyrus Vance's appointments to date to be 'excellent...quite close to those I would have made myself.'"[24] In the human rights area, this slant was especially pronounced, and it was all the more galling to the Jacksonites who felt that they had made an especially important contribution to the Carter campaign on the issue.

As his chief human rights official, Carter appointed Patricia Derian, whose title was soon upgraded to that of assistant secretary of state. Like UN Ambassador Andrew Young, another official who had an important part in Carter's human rights policy, Derian came to her post as a result of her political ties to Carter and was without any experience in foreign policy. Derian had served as deputy director of Carter's campaign, and on the Carter transition team planning policy for the Department of Health, Education and

9

Welfare. Despite her inexperience in international affairs, there was a certain logic to her appointment. It made sense to choose for the human rights field someone of stature in the American civil rights movement, and Derian was such a person. She had been, in the 1960s, one of the few white Mississippians to assume a prominent position in the overwhelmingly black "loyalist" Democratic party which was formed when the regular Democratic party of that state refused to acquiesce in racial integration.

To have stood with Mississippi's blacks in that situation proved that Derian had much raw courage. It did not prove that she was very far to the liberal side of the political spectrum. The Mississippi "regulars" were sufficiently reactionary and bigoted that even a moderate or conservative, by northern standards, might have stood with the "loyalists." But, in fact, Derian did stand rather far to the liberal side of the spectrum. In the councils of the Democratic National Committee, Derian was counted regularly in the "McGovernite" faction. She was a member of the Executive Committee of the American Civil Liberties Union, a member of the Steering Committee of the National Prison Project, and a member of the Board of Directors of the Center for Community Justice.[25]

In addition, Derian has lectured at the "Washington School" of the Institute for Policy Studies (IPS), and served as a member of an IPS delegation that met at a week-long conference held in Minneapolis in 1983 with a delegation of Soviet officials on the subject of peace and disarmament.[26] IPS describes itself as a center for "radical scholarship,"[27] but its most important role is acting as a transmission belt for conveying certain kinds of radical ideas to the liberal political establishment.[28] Derian's association does not prove that she herself is a "radical." It does, however, reveal a blindness to certain subjects critically important to her work as a human rights official.

IPS is distinctive not so much for being "radical," but because its ideological center of gravity is unmistakablyly sympathetic to various Communist governments, and apologetic for the human rights abuses of those governments. IPS's two founders and dominant figures, Richard Barnet and Marcus Raskin, were pungently critical of those human rights activities of the Carter administration that aimed at the Soviet Union. Raskin wrote that "Carter's administration hoped to recapture the world image of moral champion...while continuing the same imperial mischief. Its political objective was to split the Soviet elite."[29] And Barnet wrote that "watching the Soviets squirm as world attention is focused on the Ginsberg, Bukovsky and Sakharov scandals is in the tradition of the propaganda wars of the past."[30] It is hard to imagine that Derian would have associated in any way with a group apologetic for right-wing dictatorships, say in South Korea or Chile, or that she would have kept silent had her successors in the Reagan administration done so.

Derian herself has never evinced a trace of sympathy for Communism, but she has sometimes shown what seems to be an impatience with anti-Communism. She praised President Carter for having "raise[d] some fallen banners and illuminate[d] some values that had grown dim while we were busy containing communism, arms racing, selling America abroad, and devastating our nation's morale with war."[31] And she has described revolutionary guerrillas as a lesser evil than repressive governments: "the citizenry, faced with official terrorism, and guerrilla terrorism, wisely decides to go with something that hasn't got the force of law behind it."[32]

Derian's principal deputy was Mark Schneider, who came to the Human Rights Bureau from the staff of Senator Edward Kennedy, and who was well known on capitol hill as a liberal activist. During the years that Schneider served as Kennedy's foreign affairs aide, the senator established an uneven record in the human rights area, characterized by a militant, punitive stance toward rightist dictators and a restrained one toward leftist dictators.[33]

The other deputy assistant secretary in the human rights bureau during the first years of the Carter administration was Stephen Cohen, who is of an ideological bent similar to

Derian's and Schneider's. Cohen says that his involvement in politics began in the Vietnam antiwar movement and in the 1968 Eugene McCarthy presidential campaign. A teacher of tax and corporate law by profession, Cohen says "I got my job" in the Carter administration as a result of "the people I knew from liberal Democratic Party politics."[34]

Schneider and Cohen, as well as John Salzberg, who came to the Human Rights Bureau in 1979 from the staff of Congressman Donald Fraser (D.-Minn.), were mentioned by Carter's Under Secretary of State David Newsom as among those "people at the Bureau of Human Rights who, I don't think it is putting it too strongly, came into the Department dedicated to the idea of seeing the overthrow" of rightist dictators in such countries as Indonesia, Nicaragua, Iran and the Philippines.[35]

In addition to Schneider and Cohen, two other people held the title of deputy assistant secretary in the human rights bureau, albeit only briefly, toward the end of the Carter years. One was Roberta Cohen, who came to the bureau from one of the mainstream human rights organizations, the International League for Human Rights. The other was Stephen Palmer, a career foreign service officer, who was, he says, brought into the bureau at the urging of Deputy Secretary Christopher during Carter's last year "in order to have a senior professional in the bureau should there be a need for transition to another kind of administration" and to bring more "professionalism" to the bureau.[36]

Given its mission and its political composition, it is not surprising that the human rights bureau was often embroiled in heavy bureaucratic conflict with other parts of the government. But it did not always stand alone. It often found allies among officials in other parts of the executive branch whose political philosophies were similar to those of Derian, Cohen, Schneider and Salzberg.

The official in charge of human rights issues on the National Security Council staff was Jessica Tuchman, who had worked at developing policy positions for the Udall presidential campaign. Tuchman was one of those whom

Brzezinski says he hired in part in order to give himself political cover. He explains in his memoirs:

> I intentionally recruited several individuals whose views were
> more "liberal" than mine, but whose expertise on foreign affairs
> I very much respected. I knew that at some point I would
> be attacked from the left...and that the attack would focus on
> my alleged reputation as a "hawk." I felt, therefore, that a
> liberal presence on the staff would give me a more diversified
> perspective and would also be politically helpful.[37]

Another NSC staff member whom Brzezinski lists in
this group is Robert Pastor, who served as his chief Latin
American specialist. Pastor, who joined Brzezinski after serving as staff director for the so-called "Linowitz Commission"
on U.S.-Latin American relations, had also been one of the
seven members of IPS's Ad Hoc Working Group on Latin
America, a role which Pastor says was of little importance.[38]

The State Department's Policy Planning staff was designated as the "buffer" between the human rights bureau and
the department's other bureaus. Its Latin American specialist
was Richard Feinberg, who came to State from the Treasury
Department, which Feinberg had left following an embarrassing disclosure about him in papers recovered by the FBI
from the briefcase of Orlando Letelier. Letelier, a former top
official of the Allende government of Chile, was in exile in
Washington, working for IPS, when he was brutally murdered by agents of the Chilean secret police. In his briefcase at the time of his death was a letter to him from an
official of the North American Congress on Latin America
(NACLA), an openly Castroite offshoot of the 1960's New
Left, organized to mobilize support for Communist guerrillas in Latin America. The letter asked Letelier to cooperate
with Feinberg in some research for a report he was writing
for NACLA, and asking Letelier to "not tell anyone else that
he is working on the project, please. It wouldn't help his
work at Treasury (obviously)."[39]

Another important figure in Carter's human rights
campaign with strong ideological proclivities was UN

Ambassador Andrew Young. Numerous observers have described Young's role as that of a militant on human rights issues in the administration's internal debates. But if this was so, it was only with respect to nations friendly to the United States, for the special role that Young carved out for himself was that of defending governments hostile to the United States, including the defense of their human rights records. Thus, Young praised the role of Cuban troops in Angola as "bring[ing] a certain stability and order" and he praised Ayatollah Khomeini as "some kind of saint."[40] In regard to human rights Young said: "before we take the road to criticize others, we should rather see what we can ourselves do. In the area of human rights, for example, it is we, among all the significant countries, who have not yet ratified the three most important international instruments for the protection of human rights."[41] And to carry out this dictum, Young belittled Western criticisms of the trial and imprisonment of Anatoly Scharansky by arguing that there were "hundreds, perhaps thousands, of political prisoners" in the United States.[42] Young brought with him to the UN Brady Tyson, an original founder of the Castroite organization, NACLA, who used the opportunity of representing the United States at the UN Human Rights Commission to proclaim a public, though unauthorized, apology on behalf of his country for having overthrown the Allende government,[43] an accusation pressed by Communists, but which the Church Committee, after a probing investigation, had concluded was probably not true.[44]

In sum, the foreign policy team of the Carter administration included a network of individuals in key positions affecting human rights policy who shared a "McGovernite" or "left-liberal" worldview and whose human rights passions were focused on the depredations of rightist regimes. It included no one, at least among its political appointees, who shared the "Jacksonite" worldview and whose human rights passions were directed to the acts of Communist governments.[45]

This distinct political character of the human rights staff

appointed by Carter was reinforced by, or perhaps was
a reflection of, the approach of Secretary of State Vance.
Although Vance was very much the apotheosis of the foreign
policy establishment, and certainly no ideologue, he was not
politically neutral. His style was bland and professional, but
his opinions were strong. He says in his memoirs that: "I
hoped that I would be asked to become Secretary of State
because I had strong views about what should be done in
foreign policy."[46] And his record as secretary gives much
reason to credit the sincerity of that statement. Buttoned-
down establishmentarian that he was, Vance resigned his
office over a matter of principle, an act all the more remark-
able because the issue involved was a trivial one on which
his stance was surely not popular either with his colleagues
or with the public.

Nor is there any reason to doubt the sincerity of Vance's
declarations of support for the human rights policy, although
it is obvious that he was much less gripped by the issue than
was Carter. This comes through when Vance says in his
memoirs that Carter "felt particularly strong about the need
for the United States to make human rights a central theme
of its foreign policy. I was in accord. I pointed out, however,
that we had to be flexible and pragmatic..."[47] What did grip
Vance, as shown in almost his every act as secretary, was
a driving urge to effect a reconciliation between the United
States and its Communist and Third World antagonists, especially the Soviet Union.

Vance said in an interview with *Time* magazine that he
thought that Carter and Brezhnev "have similar dreams and
aspirations about the most fundamental issues."[48] In a letter
to the president quoted in Brzezinski's memoirs, Vance said:
"we can help encourage a more cooperative attitude on the
part of Soviet leaders by conspicuous attention to the sense of
equality to which they attach so much importance."[49] When
Soviet international behavior incited a surge in anti-Soviet
sentiment within the United States, Vance preferred to place
the blame on Americans rather than Russians. "It is true
that there was [in 1978] growing public and congressional

concern about Soviet international behavior," he wrote. "But I felt that much of it arose from background press sessions held by staff members of the national security advisor and was self-inflicted."[50] To arrest the deterioration in relations, Vance says he urged a number of steps, most of them conciliatory, including this one: "We should review the application of our human rights policies toward the Soviet Union. It was clear there was a critical point beyond which our public pressure was causing the Soviets to crack down harder on Soviet dissidents."[51]

To fill the post of chief advisor to the State Department on Soviet affairs, Vance chose Marshall Shulman, one of the most conciliatory and optimistic of American Sovietologists. If Vance was at most lukewarm about human rights actions aimed at the Soviet Union, Shulman was ice-cold. At the time he assumed his position in the Department of State, Shulman published an essay arguing that "the effort to compel changes in Soviet institutions and practices by frontal demands on the part of other governments is likely to be counterproductive." He urged that U.S. human rights efforts be limited to statements by private "individuals and groups."[52]

Vance's and Shulman's approach to U.S.-Soviet relations was counterbalanced to some extent by that of Brzezinski. Although Brzezinski seems to have been more attuned to countering the Soviets through geostrategic power politics—playing the "China card," shoring up the Shah—than through the ideological politics of human rights, he says in his memoirs that he "felt strongly that in the U.S.-Soviet competition the appeal of America as a free society could become an important asset, and I saw in human rights an opportunity to put the Soviet Union ideologically on the defensive."[53]

But in his views on the Soviet Union, Brzezinski was one against many within the Carter administration. The philosophical composition of the Carter team was weighted toward a human rights policy that focused on the abuses of rightist rather than Communist governments. This impulse warred against the legacy of the Carter election campaign, in which the human rights issue was frequently and effectively expressed in terms of criticisms of détente, the Helsinki Accords, the Solzhenitsyn rebuff, and Ford's debate gaffe about Eastern Europe. It took a few months before the Carter team's philosophical impulses effectively braked the policy momentum from the campaign. In its early weeks the Carter human rights policy aimed just as strongly at the Soviet bloc as at rightist governments. But as time passed the focus came to rest much more heavily on the latter.

GOALS

Because the human rights campaign began as something less than an explicitly formulated policy, no one seems in the beginning to have asked what exactly Carter hoped it would accomplish. Only gradually did the administration come to articulate explicit goals for the policy. In addition to the most obvious one—"to enhance respect worldwide for internationally recognized human rights"[54] —three other distinct themes emerged in the statements of administration officials. One was essentially inward looking. Carter said: "I really felt when I came into office that something needed to be done just to raise a banner for the American people to admire and of which they could be proud again."[55] An important implication of this goal, as explained by Brzezinski, was that human rights policy would help "to sustain domestic support for our policies by rooting them clearly in our moral values."[56]

Another was to strengthen America's position in the international arena. As Deputy Secretary Warren Christopher put it, the human rights policy "gives us a way of taking the ideological initiative, instead of merely reacting."[57] This, said Carter, "might possibly reverse the tide that has been going against democracies in the past."[58] A fourth goal was, in the words of the president, to "strengthen our influence among some of the developing nations."[59] The way to do this was to get on the side of "change." Secretary Vance said: "Change

was and is sweeping through Africa, and those who identify with it will be able to influence its direction."[60] By getting on the side of change, America could have friendly relations with incoming governments as they overthrew existing
governments. As Derian put it: "If we ignore oppression,
we may obtain closer relations with a particular regime over
the short run. But there is significant risk that its successor
will be hostile to our interests."[61]

There may have been a fifth, ulterior goal. This was of
course not publicly proclaimed by the administration, but it
was reported by a sufficiently impressive array of journalists
to lend credence to the inference that it was indeed on the
administration's mind. Elizabeth Drew wrote: "one of the
(at least privately) acknowledged points of speaking out on
human rights in the Soviet Union was to give the President
'running room' on the right in the United States so that he
could get approval of a SALT agreement."[62] *U.S. News and
World Report* wrote that "by vigorously backing human rights,
the Administration seeks to mobilize solid support among
the American people and in Congress for its foreign policy—
in particular, the policy of seeking a new treaty with Russia
to curb the nuclear-arms race."[63] And columnist Anthony
Lewis wrote:

> The Soviets forced an early and awkward test of the
> Carter policy when they expelled an American correspondent,
> threatened Andrei Sakharov and arrested other dissidents. If
> the President had not responded clearly, he would in effect
> have given his position away at the start. He would also have
> looked weak, and he would have hurt his chances of selling
> any future arms control agreement to the Senate.[64]

NOTES

1. Interview with Hendrik Hertzberg held in Washington, D.C.,
   Nov. 2, 1983.
2. Interview with James Fallows, held by telephone, Dec. 8, 1983.

3. Jimmy Carter, *Why Not the Best?* (Nashville: Broadman Press, 1975).

4. Ibid., p. 123.

5. U.S., Congress, House, Committee on House Administration, *The Presidential Campaign 1976*, Vol. 1, Pt. 1, Jimmy Carter (Washington, D.C.: U.S.G.P.O., 1978) pp. 83-84.

6. Interview with Patrick Anderson, held by telephone, Feb. 7, 1984.

7. Daniel P. Moynihan, "The Politics of Human Rights," *Commentary*, Vol. 64, No. 2 (August 1977) p. 22.

8. Interview with Bruce Cameron, held in Washington, D.C., Nov. 4, 1983.

9. *Political Observer*, July 1976., p. 3.

10. *The Presidential Campaign 1976*, ibid., p. 270.

11. Ibid., pp. 709-714.

12. Anderson interview.

13. Elizabeth Drew, "Reporter at Large: Human Rights," *The New Yorker*, July 18, 1977, p. 37.

14. Ibid., p. 38.

15. U.S., Congress, House, Committee on House Administration, *The Presidential Campaign 1976*, Vol. 3, The Debates (Washington, D.C.: U.S.G.P.O., 1979), p. 100.

16. Ibid., Vol. 1, Pt. 2, Jimmy Carter, p. 1043.

17. Zbigniew Brzezinski, *Power and Principle* (New York: Farrar, Straus, Giroux, 1983), p. 49.

18. Jimmy Carter, *Keeping Faith* (New York: Bantam Books, 1982), p. 145.

19. Drew, "Reporter at Large," p. 61.

20. Brzezinski, *Power and Principle*, pp. 51-52.

21. Drew, "Reporter at Large," p. 36.

22. Stephen Rosenfeld, "Secretary of State Scoop Jackson?" *Washington Post*, June 18, 1976.

23. Rowland Evans and Robert Novak, "A Complaint From The Democratic Center," *Washington Post*, Jan. 31, 1977.

24. *The Baron Report*, No. 12, Pt. 2, Jan. 25, 1977, p. 1.

25. U.S., Department of State, *Biographical Sketches of Speakers*, National Foreign Policy Conference on Human Rights, Feb. 27-28, 1978. Copy in author's files.

26. Arch Puddington, "The New Soviet Apologists," *Commentary*, Vol. 76, No. 5 (November 1983), pp. 29-31.

27. "Institute for Policy Studies Annual Report, 1979-1980," p. 3.

28. See Joshua Muravchik, "The Think Tank of the Left," *New York*

Times Magazine, April 26, 1981, pp. 36-122.
29. Marcus Raskin, *The Politics of National Security* (New Brunswick: Transaction, 1979), p. 11.
30. Richard Barnet, "U.S. Needs Modest, Uniform Stand on Human Rights," *Los Angeles Times*, March 13, 1977, Pt. VII, p. 2.
31. U.S., Department of State, Office of the Historian, *American Foreign Policy Basic Documents 1977-1980*, Pub. 9330, 1983, p. 437.
32. U.S., Congress, House, Committee on Appropriations, *Foreign Assistance and Related Agencies Appropriations for FY1978*, Pt. 3, 95th Cong., 1st sess., 1977, p. 308.
33. See Joshua Muravchik, "Kennedy's Foreign Policy: What the Record Shows," *Commentary*, Vol. 68, No. 6 (December 1979), pp. 34-40.
34. Interview with Stephen Cohen, held in Washington, D.C., Nov. 7, 1983.
35. Interview with David Newsom, held in Washington, D.C., June 22, 1982.
36. Interview with Stephen Palmer, held in Washington, D.C., June 13, 1983.
37. Brzezinski, *Power and Principle*, p. 75.
38. Interview with Robert Pastor, held in Washington, D.C., Nov. 10, 1983.
39. Quoted in *A.I.M. Report*, Vol. IX, No. 19 (Oct. 1980), pub. by Accuracy in Media, Inc., Washington, D.C.
40. "The Cuban Presence: Into the African 'Vacuum'," *Washington Post*, Feb. 1, 1977; "The Turbulent Times of an Outspoken Ambassador," *Time*, Aug. 27, 1979, pp. 12-13.
41. *Department of State Bulletin*, June 1979, p. 49.
42. "Turbulent Times," pp. 12-13; "Outspoken Interpretor of U.S. Policy at U.N.," *New York Times*, Aug. 16, 1979, p. 14.
43. *New York Times*, March 9, 1977, p. 1.
44. U.S., Congress, Senate, Select Committee to Study Governmental Operations with Respect to Intelligence Activities, *Covert Action in Chile, 1963-1973*, Staff Report, 94th Cong., 1st sess., 1975.
45. Samuel Huntington, who served on the NSC staff might be said to be of the Jackson camp, but he was not involved with human rights policy. It is, of course, possible that some of the foreign service officers assigned to human rights work under Carter privately held such views.
46. Cyrus Vance, *Hard Choices* (New York: Simon and Schuster,

1983), p. 31.
47. Ibid., p. 33.
48. "'People Want to See Coonskins'," *Time*, April 24, 1978, p. 20.
49. Brzezinski, *Power and Principle*, p. 221.
50. Vance, *Hard Choices*, p. 84.
51. Ibid., p. 102.
52. Marshall D. Shulman, "On Learning to Live with Authoritarian Regimes," *Foreign Affairs* Vol. 55, No. 2 (January 1977), p. 334, p. 333.
53. Brzezinski, *Power and Principle*, p. 149.
54. Warren Christopher, testimony before House, Committee on Foreign Affairs, *Human Rights and U.S. Foreign Policy, Hearings before the Subcommittee on International Organizations*, 96th Cong., 1st sess., 1979, p. 340.
55. "Interview With the President," *Weekly Compilation of Presidential Documents*, Dec. 19, 1977, p. 1848.
56. Zbigniew Brzezinksi, "The United States and Japan," *Department of State Bulletin*, June 1978, p. 1.
57. Warren Christopher, Speech to the American Bar Association, Aug. 4, 1980, quoted in Vita Bite, "Human Rights and U.S. Foreign Policy," Issue Brief No. IB77056, Congressional Research Service, Library of Congress, Archived Feb. 23, 1981, p. 31.
58. "Moral Policeman to the World?", *U.S. News and World Report*, March 14, 1977, p. 18.
59. Carter, *Keeping Faith*, p. 143.
60. Vance, *Hard Choices*, p. 313.
61. U.S. Congress, House Committee on Foreign Affairs, *Arms Trade in the Western Hemisphere, Hearings before the Subcommittee on Inter-American Affairs*, 96th Cong., 1st sess., 1979, p. 284.
62. Drew, op. cit., p. 56.
63. "Moral Policeman to the World?", *U.S. News and World Report*, March 14, 1977, p. 18.
64. "A Question of Humanity," *New York Times*, Feb. 28, 1977, p. 27.

TWO
The Policy in Practice

LAUNCHING A POLICY

Carter was inaugurated on January 20, 1977. Before the month was over, his human rights campaign, even if not yet a "policy" to those who insist on a rigorous use of the term, was at the center of diplomatic activity. On January 26, State Department spokesman Frederick Z. Brown read a statement criticizing the government of Czechoslovakia for arresting and harassing Czech dissidents who had circulated a statement, "Charter 77," calling for Czech observance of the terms of the Helsinki accords.[1] At the same time, the department criticized Rhodesian Prime Minister Ian Smith for his stance in negotiations over the future of that country.[2] Also at that briefing, a reporter asked the department, had it "any comment concerning the warnings the Soviets have given to Sakharov about his activities?"[3] Peter Osnos, Moscow correspondent for the *Washington Post*, speculated that those warnings may have been intended to test the willingness of the new administration to risk straining U.S.-Soviet relations over human rights matters.[4]

The department did not respond to the query about Sakharov until the next day, when this statement was given to reporters:

We have long admired Andrey Sakharov as an outspoken

champion of human rights in the Soviet Union. He is, as you know, a prominent, respected scientist, a Nobel laureate, who, at considerable risk, has worked to promote respect for human rights in his native land.

Any attempts by the Soviet authorities to intimidate Mr. Sakharov will not silence legitimate criticism in the Soviet Union and will conflict with accepted international standards in the field of human rights.[5]

The statement was moderate in tone and contained no threats. It is hard to imagine that the department could have said much less in response to the Sakharov question. Nonetheless, Soviet Ambassador Dobrynin called Secretary Vance to protest,[6] and two days later Tass, the Soviet press agency, issued a statement denouncing the State Department's words about Sakharov as an "unsavory ploy" and criticizing Western correspondents stationed in Moscow for giving too much attention to Soviet dissidents.[7] A visible tremor went through the administration. The next day, Carter told reporters that the Sakharov statement had not been cleared with him.[8] He said that the statement correctly reflected his "attitude" about the Sakharov matter, but that he wanted to avoid "aggravating" relations with the Soviet Union, leading the *New York Times* to infer that "his intent seemed to be to emphasize that while criticism of the Soviet Union was by no means unthinkable, it should be made only after consideration at the highest level."[9] The following day, Vance announced that the Sakharov statement hadn't been cleared with him, either. "I did not see it," said Vance.[10] And he made a statement that seemed designed to reassure the Soviet government that the Carter administration had no wish to engage in an ideological battle. He said:

We will speak frankly about injustice both at home and abroad. We do not intend, however, to be strident or polemical, but we do believe that an abiding respect for human rights is a human value of fundamental importance and that it must be nourished. We will not comment on each and every issue, but we will from time to time comment when we see a threat to human rights, when we believe it constructive to do so.[11]

The administration also took action on some human rights issues during those first few days that were directed at smaller countries, and these created fewer problems. On January 28, the administration asked a Chilean government official, who was here as a guest of the State Department, to leave the United States, following charges by human rights groups that he had been responsible for the torture of some prisoners in Chile.[12] The Chilean denied the charges, but complied with the request.[13] Also during January, according to Stanley Karnow, "the administration subtly communicated its displeasure to a totalitarian client by spurning a request by South Korea that Vice President Mondale visit that country after his visit to Japan."[14] And at the same press conference at which Vance labored to reassure the Soviets about the Sakharov statement, he resumed the offensive against Rhodesia's Ian Smith. "The so-called 'internal settlement' will not produce a peaceful settlement and therefore will not have the support of the United States," said Vance. And he announced that "to reemphasize our opposition to the maintenance of minority-imposed control of the government of Rhodesia, this administration will strongly support repeal of the Byrd amendment."[15]

Carter's and Vance's efforts to distance themselves from the State Department's Sakharov statement prompted CBS correspondent Marvin Kalb to ask whether the administration was "not running the danger...of setting up what amounts to a double standard [by] the manner in which you respond to violations of human rights in the Soviet Union and in smaller countries where there is not a direct, vital interest conflict?"[16] But whether or not it wished to back off from confrontation with the Soviet Union, neither the Soviet government nor the dissidents it was persecuting would give the administration the chance to do so. On January 28, the State Department received a letter addressed to President Carter from Andrei Sakharov that had been smuggled out of the Soviet Union by two American human rights activists. The letter described Soviet government violations of the Helsinki Accords, detailed the persecution of fifteen leading dissidents, and called on Carter "to raise your voice" on their behalf.[17] In the first days of February, the Soviet government arrested the noted dissident, Alexandr Ginzburg, and expelled Associated Press correspondent George Krimsky from the Soviet Union because of his contacts with dissidents.[18] The day before the Soviet expulsion of Krimsky, Czech authorities had detained NBC correspondent Leslie Collitt as he was trying to leave that country.[19] The Krimsky and Collitt incidents, coming only a day apart and within a week of Tass's warnings to Western correspondents, suggested an orchestrated campaign to cut the nexus between Soviet bloc dissidents and the Western press.

Whatever the feelings of Carter or Vance, the administration could scarcely have avoided responding to any of these events. Having made a campaign issue of Ford's rebuff of Solzhenitsyn, Carter could not ignore a letter from Sakharov, the Soviet Union's other most prominent dissident. Nor could he, in view of the close connection between Solzhenitsyn and Ginzburg, easily ignore the arrest of Ginzburg. Solzhenitsyn had used the proceeds from *The Gulag Archipelago* to create a fund for the relief of the families of persecuted Soviet dissidents. Ginzburg had been arrested for his work as the executor of this fund. Nor could the administration easily ignore Soviet abuse of Western reporters.

It may be unfair to speculate about whether the administration had any hesitations, for the essential point is that it responded in a clear way to all three events. After getting off what may have been the best quip of his presidency—he said he was tempted to respond to the expulsion of the AP correspondent in Moscow by expelling the AP correspondent in Washington—Carter did retaliate by expelling a Soviet correspondent.[20] On February 4, Vance conveyed to Ambassador Dobrynin the administration's concern about Ginzburg, and three days later, apparently having received no positive response, the State Department issued a public statement calling the incident "a matter of profound concern for all Americans."[21] Most important, Carter sent a return letter to Sakharov.

Carter's letter was drafted jointly by Vance and Brzezinski, says Brzezinski, and it was "couched in language that made it clear that the President's concern was global in character and not focused specifically on the Soviet Union."[22] The letter said: "You may rest assured that the American people and our government will continue our firm commitment to promote respect for human rights not only in our own country but also abroad."[23] However gently the message was couched, the mere fact that Carter sent it evoked strong reactions among both Soviet dissidents and their persecutors. According to Freedom House's Ludmilla Thorn, a leading American contact for Soviet dissidents, "that one letter, dissidents told me later, gave enough spiritual food for them for three months."[24] On the other side, Ambassador Dobrynin this time did not just phone, but came to the State Department to deliver his protest. More ominously, the Soviet government, according to Brzezinski, demonstrated its defiance by "stepp[ing] up sharply their suppression of human-rights activists."[25]

At about the same time, the administration discovered that even with regard to small countries, its outspokenness about human rights could cause it difficulties. On February 16, the Anglican Archbishop of Uganda and two cabinet ministers were reported by the Ugandan government to have been engaged in an insurrectionary plot and to have died in an "automobile accident."[26] A week later, after evidence mounted that the three had been murdered, perhaps by Idi Amin's own hand, amidst a bloody campaign against Uganda's Christians, the State Department released a statement deploring the "massive violations of human rights in Uganda" and the "violent death" of the three men.[27] The same day, President Carter said at a press conference that events in Uganda "have disgusted the entire civilized world."[28] Ugandan dictator Idi Amin responded by ordering the two hundred Americans then living in that country to come to Kampala to meet with him and decreeing that none of them could leave the country until they complied.[29] This left the administration worrying about what the sanguinary and none-too-stable Amin might have in store for these Americans, almost all missionaries and their dependents, who were now in effect hostages. After a few days of intense behind-the-scenes diplomatic maneuvering, as well as the movement of a U.S. naval task force to the African coast, the Americans were allowed to depart. In the end, Carter publicly thanked Amin for assuring the safety of the Americans, a spectacle that led reporters to ask whether this "does not...underline a certain weakness in the whole policy of speaking out on human rights?"[30]

On February 24, Vance appeared before the Senate Subcommittee on Foreign Operations Appropriations and announced that the administration planned to reduce foreign aid to Argentina, Uruguay, and Ethiopia because of human rights violations.[31] Officials explained that the new administration had cut in half the Ford administration's figure for military credits for Argentina, that it had entirely eliminated credits for Uruguay, and that Ethiopia would retain its credits, but would no longer receive grants.[32] Vance also said that in cutting aid, the United States had to "balance a political concern for human rights against economic or security goals," citing South Korea as an example where our "security commitments" made it unwise to cut aid "despite the fact that we have great concern—and have so stated— with respect to the human rights situation in that country."[33]

Within a week Uruguay and Argentina delivered diplomatic notes in protest. Uruguay said that it had not asked to be included in any future program of military assistance from the United States, and Argentina rejected whatever military credits the administration had left in the budget.[34]

On March 12, the State Department released the first of what were to become annual reports on human rights practices in other countries. These reports were required by an amendment to the Foreign Assistance Act adopted in 1976. Since 1979 these reports have covered all independent countries in the world, but in 1977, pursuant to the law at that time, they covered only those countries receiving security assistance from the United States. As a courtesy, prior to releasing them publicly, the department distributed to each subject country the report about its practices. On reading theirs, Brazil, Guatemala, and El Salvador followed the lead of Uruguay and Argentina, and announced their rejection "in advance" of any military aid from the United States.[35]

Meanwhile, the Kremlin kept up its campaign against dissidents. On February 7, two members of a small Ukrainian group seeking to monitor Soviet compliance with the Helsinki Accords were arrested. On February 10, Yuri Orlov, the leader of the main group of "Helsinki monitors," was arrested. On February 12, an editorial in *Pravda* accused the dissidents of engaging in "a carefully planned and coordinated act of sabotage" against the Soviet Union.[36]

On the question of human rights in the Soviet Union, the administration seemed to have a tiger by the tail. The overriding priority of its foreign policy was to reach a new SALT agreement. The harshness of the Soviet reaction to the American human rights campaign began to create fears that SALT could be in jeopardy. On the other hand, Carter knew, as Anthony Lewis pointed out, that to back down in the face of this Soviet reaction could jeopardize the support he would need at home to get a treaty ratified by the Senate.[37] Trying to navigate SALT betweeen this Scylla and Charybdis, the administration zigged and zagged.

Appearing on "Face the Nation" on February 27, Secretary Vance once again tried to reassure the Russians. "Insofar as speaking out on human rights issues abroad is concerned," said Vance, "we will speak out when we consider it desirable to do so. We will try to do it in a nonstrident, nonpolemical way; and would expect others, if they see things happening in the United States, to criticize us, because this is not a one-way street."[38]

Two days later, the president received at the White

House the celebrated Soviet dissident Vladimir Bukovsky. Bukovsky had been released into exile in the West in a trade for an imprisoned Chilean Communist leader during the last weeks of the Ford administration. When Bukovsky sought an audience with President Carter, an appointment was made for him with Vice President Mondale instead, while the president hesitated about whether he, himself, should receive Bukovsky. The Russians, as Marvin Kalb put it, "indicated that they would very much appreciate it—and I am understating it now—if the President did not receive Vladimir Bukovsky."[39] The president hesitated until the last minute—Vance said only two days before the meeting that he was unaware of the president's intentions[40] —and when he finally received Bukovsky, he refused to allow reporters to photograph them together.

Following the Bukovsky meeting, Soviet recalcitrance deepened. On March 4, *Izvestia* accused some leading Jewish dissidents of working for the CIA.[41] On March 13, *Pravda* said that Carter's human rights policies were "bringing about an atmosphere of distrust."[42] On March 15, Soviet authorities arrested the most prominent Jewish dissident, Anatoly Shcharansky. And on March 21, Brezhnev, in a speech to the Trade Union Congress, said: "Washington's claims to teach others how to live, I believe, cannot be accepted by any sovereign state....we will not tolerate interference in our internal affairs by anyone and under any pretext. A normal development of relations on such a basis is, of course, unthinkable."[43]

In response, the administration sought to allay Soviet anger but without abandoning its human rights campaign. On March 17, Carter addressed the United Nations General Assembly. There he declared: "All the signatories of the U.N. Charter have pledged themselves to observe and respect basic human rights. Thus, no member of the United Nations can claim that mistreatment of its citizens is solely its own business."[44] He added that this issue "should not block progress on other important matters affecting the security and well-being of our people and of world peace. It is obvious that the reduction of tension, the control of nuclear arms, the achievement of harmony in troubled areas of the world, and the provision of food, good health, and education will independently contribute to advancing the human condition."[45] The key point was that the administration rejected what had come to be called "linkage." It would protest Soviet misbehavior, such as violations of the Helsinki Accords, but it would not make any other aspect of U.S.-Soviet relations conditional on improvements in Soviet behavior.

The administration pinned its hopes for overcoming the initial bumps in its relations with the Kremlin on Secretary Vance's mission to Moscow in late March. Vance's goal was a breakthrough on the issue of strategic arms limitation. If the way could be cleared to a SALT agreement, other aspects of U.S.-Soviet relations would also improve. In order to stress its rejection of "linkage," Vance told a Moscow press conference on the eve of his first meeting with Brezhnev that he would not see any dissidents while in Moscow, and although he said he was prepared to discuss human rights if the subject came up, he dodged the question of whether "you plan on your own behalf to raise the issue." He would only reply that "I do not plan in my opening statement to touch on it."[46]

But Vance's good manners were not reciprocated. He recalls in his memoirs his first session with Brezhnev: "I had hoped we would move directly to SALT, but Brezhnev launched into a diatribe in which he catalogued alleged human rights abuses in the United States."[47] Apparently Brezhnev took to heart Vance's invitation on "Face the Nation" to others "to criticize us." Of course everyone understood that Brezhnev's concern was not with the state of human rights in the United States. He was trying to make a point. The point was that the Russians insisted on a kind of linkage of their own. We might not make U.S.-Soviet relations conditional on rectifications of their domestic misconduct, but they would make U.S.-Soviet relations conditional on our not complaining about their misconduct.

The Vance mission ended in acrimony and complete

failure, and although it was evident that the human rights issue was not the sole cause of this failure—the Soviets were also unhappy with the American SALT proposals—it was clear, as Adam Ulam put it, "that the rather rude reception accorded Mr. Vance was not unconnected with the President's recent utterances on behalf of the Soviet dissidents."[48]

From that moment, the administration was much more cautious in the application of its human rights policy to the Soviet Union. A month later, on April 30, Vance delivered a speech, the purpose of which, he says in his memoirs, was "to define the elements of a sound human rights policy."[49] Without explicitly criticizing the Sakharov letter or the Bukovsky meeting, Vance recalls that these two events especially "concerned" the Soviet leaders, thereby complicating the quest for SALT II, "the most pressing issue in U.S.-Soviet relations." Then Vance adds, in suggestive contrast: "My preference in dealing with human rights issues was to emphasize quiet diplomacy, saving public pressure for those occasions that called for a strong and forthright public statement."[50] At the time, President Carter, asked by *Newsweek* in April whether the fact that he seemed "less outspoken lately on human rights" meant that he was "having any second thoughts," replied, "No, I think we've made a point."[51] In July, the administration announced the creation of an interagency committee, chaired by Marshall Shulman, to "coordinate" policy toward the Soviet Union. Shulman, an unfailing advocate of a conciliatory approach to the Soviet Union, had categorically opposed allowing human rights issues to enter into the government-to-government relations between the United States and the Soviet Union. Thus Brzezinski, in his memoirs, seems either naive or disingenuous when he chides the *New York Times* for its "amazing interpretation that this was a further public signal to the effect that the Administration was moving toward a more conciliatory attitude toward the Soviet Union."[52]

In January of 1978, the *Washington Post* reported that the State Department had instituted a new rule requiring that members of the staff of the U.S. embassy in Moscow and their spouses give twenty-four hour notice of any meetings to be held with Soviet dissidents. This rule, said the *Post*, "marks a shift in the Carter Administration's policy toward dissent in the Soviet Union" in favor of "quiet diplomacy similar to that pursued by former Secretary of State Henry Kissinger" and has resulted in a decline in the "quality and volume of information" exchanged between dissidents and American diplomats.[53]

Administration spokesmen were at pains to deny that they were backing down from pressing the human rights issue in regard to the Russians. Asked late in 1977 whether the United States had "backed away in our support of human rights in the Soviet Union," Vance replied that we were not "backing off in any way whatsoever."[54] And Brzezinski, in response to a similar question, complained that the administration was "accused of having compromised and of having backtracked" merely because it had emphasized "the global character of our interest."[55] But other observers were virtually unanimous in perceiving a retreat. Arthur Schlesinger, Jr. wrote:

> The Soviet resentment, for some utterly mysterious reason, astonished Carter himself; he spoke in June 1977 of the "surprising adverse reaction in the Soviet Union to our stand on human rights." But he accepted it as a fact of life and moderated his campaign accordingly.[56]

Sandra Vogelgesang, who served as the human rights officer on the State Department's Policy Planning Staff during the first months of the Carter administration, wrote after leaving the government:

> Carter by his own admission was "surprised" [by the Soviet reaction]. He shifted gears by mid-1977—because of pressure from moderates within his administration, concern expressed by important allied leaders such as West German Chancellor Helmut Schmidt, and the belief that a point, once publicly and forcefully made, need not be repeated at every occasion.[57]

And the Congressional Research Service of the Library of Congress said:

> It is commonly believed...that human rights initiatives will prejudice—at least in the short term—the full range of other interests that the United States has with another country....Early experience with the Soviet Union most impressively demonstrated this principle. The complications with respect to many aspects of bilateral relations that resulted from U.S. human rights initiatives led to a rapid limitation of those initiatives.[58]

In sum, from the time of the March 1977 Vance mission to Moscow, the Carter administration pulled back from outspoken criticism of Soviet human rights violations. It renewed those criticisms, to some degree, in the summer of 1980, when, under the combined impetus of events in Afghanistan and the electoral challenge posed by Ronald Reagan, Carter again spoke sharp words about Soviet abuses.[59] In the interim its voice was muted, although not silent. It did insist on speaking about some of those abuses at the Belgrade conference to review the Helsinki Accords, albeit, as Vance recommended, in a "nonstrident, nonpolemical" way. And, as the Soviets continued throughout the late seventies their determined drive to crush the dissident movement, the administration did, as Vance had advocated, issue an occasional public statement in response to some particularly egregious events. But these were far fewer and gentler than the dissident movement had been led to hope for by the heady events of Carter's first five weeks. Ludmilla Thorn summarized their feelings: "What we all found was disappointing was that Carter...sort of ceased his public stance, at least vis-a-vis the Soviet Union. So I think it began very well,...but somehow, he was intimidated, perhaps by his colleagues and associates and subordinates, into this quiet stance, and Russian dissidents became quite openly disappointed in him."[60]

The human rights policy did not, however, end with the retreat from confrontation with the Soviet Union. In a sense that was only the beginning. But its focus turned to less costly directions. Prime among these were Latin America and white Africa. In March of 1977, both the Soviets and several Latin governments were angry at Carter's human rights pronouncements, but their anger had unequal results. The difference was that the Russians had a big stick—they could and did threaten not to cooperate in reaching a SALT agreement, thereby depriving Carter of the central goal of his foreign policy. The Latins, on the other hand, could only fume and reject American aid. What kind of threat was that? And the white Africans, Smith and Vorster, didn't even have any aid to reject. All they could do was fume.

In March, at the very moment that Vance was in Moscow, being lectured by Brezhnev on human rights, Patricia Derian was in Buenos Aires lecturing the government of Argentina on the same subject.[61] And throughout the spring of 1977, as the administration was retreating on the Soviet human rights front, it was advancing steadily on Latin America. In June, Secretary Vance addressed the General Assembly of the Organization of American States, and spoke in uncharacteristically blunt words. He said:

> If terrorism and violence in the name of dissent cannot be condoned, neither can violence that is officially sanctioned. Such action perverts the legal system that alone assures the survival of our traditions.

> The surest way to defeat terrorism is to promote justice in our societies—legal, economic, and social justice. Justice that is summary undermines the future it seeks to promote. It produces only more violence, more victims, and more terrorism. Respect for the rule of law will promote justice and remove the seeds of subversion. Abandoning such respect, governments descend into the netherworld of the terrorist and lose their strongest weapon—their moral authority.[62]

At a press conference at the OAS meeting two days later, Vance commented on "the attention which is being paid to the issue of human rights. There is no question that the issue is dominating the discussion in the OAS itself and in the bilaterals which each of us is having. There can be no doubt that whatever way the actual concrete steps eventuate from this meeting, the sensitivity of all the parties at this meeting has been greatly raised."[63]

Another important landmark in human rights policy toward Latin America was passed during June. Human rights officials within the administration fought to cancel three agricultural loans to Chile proposed by the Agency for International Development.[64] Because the loans were for projects that would benefit poor farmers, they fell under the rubric of aid directed to meeting "basic human needs." Under the terms of all relevant human rights legislation, foreign aid projects that were specifically designed to meet "basic human needs" were exempt from the restrictions imposed on aid to repressive governments. Under this exemption even the Khmer Rouge regime in Cambodia had received some aid from the United States—DDT to help control malaria—on the theory that it made no sense to deprive those Cambodians who escaped Pol Pot's executioners of the chance also to escape disease.[65] To declare Chile ineligible even for aid that fell in the "basic human needs" category was to stamp it with an anathema applied virtually to no other government. Yet some administration officials found the Pinochet government to be so reprehensible that they wished to add this fillip to the other human rights sanctions already in place against Chile. The outcome of the administration's internal battle over Chile was a compromise that turned into a victory for the human rights officials. The administration announced that the loans were being "deferred" for thirty to sixty days because of human rights violations in Chile. Two day later an indignant President Pinochet announced his rejection of the aid money.[66]

The administration took a tough stance yet again toward Latin American governments in November 1977, when Vance, accompanied by Derian, traveled to Brazil and Argentina, where he is reported to have put human rights at the top of his diplomatic agenda. He presented to the

Argentine government a list, prepared by Argentine human rights groups, of names of people who had "disappeared," presumably as the result of illegal, violent acts by the authorities.[67]

As the human rights issue came to dominate U.S. policy toward Latin America, as toward no other region, it evoked mounting resistance from those U.S. diplomats responsible for relations with Latin America. In February 1978, Terence Todman, assistant secretary of state for Inter-American Affairs, delivered a speech that was widely interpreted as criticizing the human rights policy. In it, Todman said:

> Our experiences over the past year have shown clearly that we must be careful in the actions we select if we are truly to help and not hinder the cause of promoting human rights and alleviating suffering.)

> We must avoid speaking out before learning all the facts, or without calculating the likely reaction and responses to our initiatives.

> We must avoid expecting other governments to achieve overnight fundamental changes in their societies and practices in response to our bidding and without regard to historical circumstances.

> We must avoid assuming that we can deal with one issue in isolation without considering the consequences for other aspects of our relationships.

> We must avoid believing that only the opposition speaks the truth, the whole truth and nothing but the truth about conditions in their country.

> We must avoid presuming to know so much more about another society than any of its own citizens that we can prescribe actions for them without bearing any responsibility for the consequences.

We must avoid punishing the poor and already victimized by denying them assistance to show our dissatisfaction with their governments.

We must avoid pointing to some and not to others. Selective morality is a contradiction in terms.

We must avoid condemning an entire government for every negative act by one of its officials.

We must avoid holding entire countries up to public ridicule and embarrassment, trampling on their national dignity and pride.

Finally, we must avoid being so concerned with declaring the rightness of our course that we lose sight of our true objective—to alleviate individual suffering.[68]

The speech was criticized by the administration's human rights activists as too solicitous of the sensibilities of governments that violate human rights.[69] Some in the human rights movement had opposed Todman's nomination from the start; for example, the Council on Hemispheric Affairs had urged the Senate not to confirm him.[70] And throughout the first year of the Carter administration, Todman, a career foreign service officer, pressed for a more diplomatic and conciliatory approach to Latin American governments. He was often among those arrayed on the opposite side from the department's human rights bureau in disputes like the one over the agricultural loans for Chile. Within weeks of his speech, Todman was demoted. He was removed from his post as assistant secretary and named ambassador to Spain.

Making public his concerns about the direction of the human rights policy may have been an insubordinate action on Todman's part, but Andrew Young and his deputy, Brady Tyson, had already proved that loose and insubordinate talk was not in itself cause for being removed from one's post in the Carter administration. (It may be argued that being black gave Young a certain political immunity for his insubordination, but, then, Todman is also black.) The real reason for Todman's removal was that he was out of step. As Cedric W. Tarr, Jr., an academic sympathetic to the human rights movement, described it:

> Initially, many members of the Carter administration seemed not to have received the message that human rights are to be promoted aggressively. However, an active alliance between nongovernmental human rights groups and human rights activists within the Administration is perhaps responsibile for conveying the message to persons such as the former Assistant Secretary of State for Inter-American Affairs, Terence A. Todman, who was moved to the U.S. embassy in Madrid.[71]

The ouster of Todman consecrated the ascendance of the human rights bureau in formulating policy toward Latin America. This makes an interesting contrast to the evolution of the administration's policy toward the Soviet Union. Todman was not nearly as strongly opposed to injecting human rights issues into U.S. dealings with Latin governments as Marshall Shulman was to injecting them into U.S. dealings with the Soviet government. Richard Feinberg, the Latin American specialist of the Policy Planning Staff, who was usually on the opposite side from Todman in policy debates, says Todman "did carry on private diplomacy in the sense that when he would visit a country and meet with government officials he would talk extensively about human rights."[72] Shulman, on the other hand, opposed any official human rights policy toward the USSR. Yet, after an initial shake-down period of the human rights policy, Shulman's authority over policy toward the Soviets was augmented while Todman was removed from his responsibility for policy toward Latin America. As the Carter administration wore on, no one would say about U.S.-Soviet relations what Jo Marie Griesgraber, a scholar who served during the Carter years as associate director of the Washington Office on Latin America, said of U.S.-Argentine relations during those years: "Human rights issues came to dominate the United States-Argentina agenda, prompted by the enormity of the violations and U.S. domestic pressure."[73]

INSTITUTIONALIZING A POLICY

In the middle years of the Carter administration, the president's own role and rhetoric on human rights became less pronounced. But by then the administration's human rights policy had become institutionalized.

A network of offices and personnel had been created within the government whose business was human rights. The position of "Coordinator for Human Rights and Humanitarian Affairs" in the State Department was upgraded by Congress at the request of the administration to that of assistant secretary. The Bureau of Human Rights and Humanitarian Affairs was created to replace what had merely been an "office" for human rights. The size of the bureau quickly grew to about twenty staff, [74] from an initial seven or eight.[75] "This newly strengthened human rights office inserted itself into the established Department of State procedures with vigor," wrote Stephen Cohen who served as one of its deputy assistant secretaries.[76] According to Lars Schoultz, it had "demanded and obtained the right to review all [foreign] aid proposals,"[77] which embroiled it, in Cohen's words, in "intense bureaucratic warfare"[78] both within the State Department and with other agencies, such as the Departments of Defense, Treasury, Agriculture, and Commerce. The role of the bureau consisted largely of trying to stop other parts of the U.S. government from assisting or maintaining normal relations with foreign governments that were guilty of human rights violations.

These bureaucratic wars required the creation of a variety of coordinating bodies which served as arenas in which the disputes between the Human Rights Bureau and its intragovernmental adversaries were thrashed out. The most important of these was the Interagency Group on Human Rights and Foreign Assistance, created pursuant to a

National Security Council Directive issued on April 1, 1977, and chaired by Deputy Secretary Warren Christopher, after whom it came to be known as the "Christopher Group."

In addition, full-time human rights officers were appointed in every one of the State Department's regional bureaus, and in each U.S. embassy one officer was designated as the human rights officer,[79] although this was not a full-time responsibility.[80] On the National Security Council staff, a "cluster" was created with responsibility for "global issues," which included human rights.

It is possible to detail the activities of this network of human rights officials and bodies, but its importance was greater than the sum of its various activities. It created within the government a lobby with a "vested interest" in human rights or at least in the human rights issue. The very existence of this lobby sent a message to the outside world about the administration's goals and forced other parts of the U.S. government to weigh the likely reactions of the lobby to any activities that might bear on its interests.

One of the major activities of the new Human Rights Bureau was the preparation of annual "Country Reports" on human rights around the world. These reports, which were required by Section 502(b) of the Foreign Assistance Act, were originally intended as a congressional weapon with which to cut back military aid to repressive governments and hence initially covered only those countries receiving military aid. The reports, however, soon outgrew their original purpose, becoming primarily a vehicle for focusing attention on human rights conditions around the world; therefore the Congress amended the law to require reports on all members of the United Nations. The first edition of these reports was issued in March 1977 and was a mere 137 pages long. The last edition prepared by the Carter administration was issued in February 1981 and consumed 1,140 pages.

In addition to becoming a vital source of information about human rights and focusing public attention on the issue, the process of preparing the reports had an important effect within the government. As Jessica Tuchman put it: "having to do them...transformed the whole apparatus inside the Department. When we began there were few countries about [whose human rights situations] we knew a great deal....Having to do these things really helped to get the embassies informed and get the information back to the Department."[81]

Despite the various dramatic and well publicized highlights of the Carter human rights campaign, the administration's principal human rights activity consisted of what is prosaically called "quiet diplomacy." Patricia Derian said that "such diplomacy is the workhorse of a human rights policy....It is the most effective tool, though not the only one."[82]

It is in the nature of "quiet diplomacy" that its frequency or quantity, and even more so its quality or effectiveness, remains essentially unknown to those outside the government and even to many inside it. So there is no easy way to verify the claims of the Carter administration that its use of quiet diplomacy was, as Warren Christopher put it, "a dramatic change from past practice."[83] "In past years," said Christopher, "diplomats tended to shy away from high-level dialogue on sensitive human rights issues....Now those issues....are brought to the center of the diplomatic interchange."[84] Whether or not the diplomatic activity was as intense, or the change from past practice as dramatic, as Christopher claims, there is no reason to doubt that the Carter administration did engage in much of this kind of diplomacy.

The opposite side of the coin of quiet diplomacy is, of course, public diplomacy, or symbolic acts designed to broadcast American concern about human rights violations. The State Department explained in 1978: "Meetings with opposition leaders from countries with human rights problems can...be used to send signals to the governments of these countries. U.S. officials have met with several such leaders in Washington, including some living in exile. And abroad, U.S. Ambassadors regularly meet with opposition leaders."[85] In addition to meetings in Washington, the Carter administration frequently used trips to foreign countries as a means of dramatizing its human rights concerns. This involved the travels of the President himself, and those of Vance, Derian and other officials. Thus, when Vance visited Argentina in 1977, he brought with him a list of names of the "disappeared." When Carter visited Brazil in March of 1978, he met not only with officials, but also with Paolo Cardinal Arns, a human rights activist and critic of the government.[86] And when he visited South Korea in 1979 he insisted that the final joint communique that he issued with President Park say: "President Carter expressed the hope that the process of political growth in the Republic of Korea would continue commensurate with the economic and social growth of the Korean nation."[87] Within Derian's first year in office, Vance reported that she "has visited Argentina, El Salvador, Bolivia, Brazil, Uruguay, Indonesia, Singapore, the Philippines, Thailand, and Yugoslavia, and has held discussions with the highest government officials in those countries."[88] Those discussions were private and thus may have constituted "quiet diplomacy," but the very announcement that Derian was visiting a country was a kind of public statement about American concerns regarding the behavior of its government.

Occasionally, also, symbolic acts of a public but low-key nature were undertaken by American embassies abroad, such as when the embassy in South Korea invited several prominent dissidents to a diplomatic reception in 1977 or when the embassies in Thailand and the Soviet Union sent officers to observe legal proceedings against dissidents.[89]

The other main part of the "human rights policy" consisted of various material sanctions exacted in terms of aid and trade against countries whose governments were guilty of human rights violations. New guidelines were developed by the Agency for International Development to govern the disbursement of bilateral economic aid. These directed that wherever "there is a serious question about the recipient government's human rights status" U.S. economic aid would be limited to projects that "will directly benefit" the "needy people."[90] No aid for general development purposes would be given.

Security assistance was terminated to at least eight countries because of human rights violations. The eight listed by Stephen Cohen, who served as deputy assistant secretary for Human Rights in charge of security assistance, were Argentina, Bolivia, El Salvador, Guatemala, Haiti, Nicaragua, Paraguay, and Uruguay.[91] Other administration officials, including Brzezinski, Christopher, and Derian have cited other countries as having suffered military aid cuts on grounds of human rights, including Indonesia, the Philippines, Thailand, Afghanistan, Morocco, Tunisia, and perhaps Zaire, South Korea, and Ethiopia.[92] (It seems strange that there should be confusion and disagreement about something that seems as straightforward as the question of which countries did or did not suffer cuts in aid on human rights grounds. The explanation is that in various cases aid was cut for a confluence of reasons, leaving those who had participated in the bureaucratic debates with differing views about which considerations had been decisive.) The administration also instituted rather strict prohibitions on the transfer of police equipment to repressive governments, not only excluding such items from military aid packages, but prohibiting private sales of these items as well.[93]

In addition to cuts in bilateral aid, human rights criteria were applied to guide the votes that were cast by U.S. representatives on the boards of the multilateral development banks through which an increasingly large share of American foreign aid came to be channeled. The representatives were directed to abstain or vote "no" on proposed loans to repressive governments, except where the loans were for projects that would directly meet "basic human needs." There was significant opposition within the Congress and the administration to applying similar criteria to the activities of the Export-Import Bank and the Overseas Private Investment Corporation (OPIC), because these were regarded as agencies whose main purpose was to assist American businesses. Nonetheless, certain restrictions were legislated by Congress and enforced by the administration. In the case of the Ex-Im Bank, these ended up affecting only four countries—South Africa, Argentina, Chile, and Uruguay. In the case of OPIC, the only country affected by a formal action was El Salvador, although others may have been affected informally by discouraging investment.

In addition to its bilateral diplomacy on behalf of human rights, the administration also worked on human rights in international arenas. President Carter signed the UN-sponsored International Covenants on Civil and Political Rights and on Economic, Social and Cultural Rights, as well as the OAS-sponsored American Convention on Human Rights, and tried in vain to secure Senate consent for the ratification of these and two other treaties that had been signed by previous administrations—the Genocide Convention and the Convention on the Elimination of All Forms of Racial Discrimination.

The administration also took some domestic actions that the State Department said would "improve the U.S. human rights record."[94] It lifted the restrictions on travel by Americans to those few countries to which it had been curbed and it eased the restrictions on entry into this country by foreign Communists. These steps were necessary, said the State Department, because Americans had "to recognize that unless U.S. domestic actions reflect a firm commitment to human rights, the message being sent to others will ring hollow."[95]

THE POLICY IN DECLINE

By mid-1979, after the fall of the governments of Iran and Nicaragua, the human rights policy seemed to have lost its central place in the administration's outlook. Brzezinski says in his memoirs: "....some of our goals in the global issues area [the rubric that encompassed human rights] contradicted our strategic objectives. In the first two years of the Administration, these global concerns tended to overshadow the pressing requirements of strategic reality. In the last two, we had to make up for lost time, giving a higher priority to the more fundamental interests of national security."[96] In June of 1979, Griesgraber complained in congressional testimony on behalf of the Washington Office on Latin America that "human rights is increasingly being shunted aside in the administration's decision-making process."[97] And in August the *Washington Post* reported that the Sandinista victory in Nicaragua had ignited a major debate within the administration over removing its prohibitions based on human rights on military aid to other Central American governments.[98]

Griesgraber later wrote that "Derian's influence was waning" and that her "access to the President declined."[99] In May 1980, Derian publicly threatened to resign in protest against the administration's plans to seek closer relations with the government of Argentina.[100]

Griesgraber attributed Derian's decline to growing "hostility" toward her on the part of target governments such as that of Argentina, but this explanation is unconvincing. There is no reason to believe that the hostility of Argentina or other Latin governments was greater in 1980 than it had been in 1977 when they responded in shocked indignation to the first dramatic public criticisms and material sanctions that were imposed for human rights reasons. What had changed by 1980 was that the overall foreign policy of the administration, of which its human rights policy had been one pillar, was in shambles. The new governments in Iran and Nicaragua had proved implacably hostile to the United States, dashing the hopes of those Americans who had believed that a rapprochement with them would be possible. And the Soviet Union had invaded Afghanistan, snuffing out the last hope for Senate ratification of Carter's prized SALT treaty. Reeling under these blows, it seems hardly surprising that the president would have turned away from someone as strongly identified as Derian with the bold gambles that characterized the administration's early days.

At the Democratic National Convention in 1980, where he was renominated, Carter said: "The new Republican leaders oppose our human rights policy. They want to scrap it. Just what do they think our country should stand for?"[101] Carter was right in feeling that the American public still liked the idea of advocating human rights. But in his defensiveness he was creating a straw man. The question was not whether America should stand for something other than human rights. The question was whether his human rights policy had effectively served the interests either of America or of human rights.

NOTES

1. *New York Times*, Jan. 27, 1977, p. 1.
2. *Washington Post*, Jan. 27, 1977, p. 2.
3. "Secretary Vance's News Conference of January 31," *Department of State Bulletin*, Feb. 21, 1977, p. 138.
4. *Washington Post*, Feb. 1, 1977, p. 4.
5. "Secretary Vance's News Conference of January 31," p. 138.
6. Ibid.; also, *New York Times*, Jan. 29, 1977, p. 1.
7. *New York Times*, Jan. 30, 1977, p. 1.
8. *New York Times*, Jan. 31, 1977, p. 1.
9. Ibid.
10. "Secretary Vance's News Conference of January 31," p. 141.
11. Ibid., p. 138.
12. *Washington Post*, Jan. 29, 1977, p. 13.
13. *New York Times*, Jan. 30, 1977, p. 11.
14. Stanley Karnow, "Carter and Human Rights," *Saturday Review*, April 2, 1977, p. 7.
15. "Secretary Vance's News Conference of January 31," p. 137.
16. Ibid., p. 140.
17. *New York Times*, Jan. 29, 1977, p. 2.
18. *New York Times*, Feb. 6, 1977, p. 1.
19. *New York Times*, Feb. 14, 1977, p. 6.
20. *New York Times*, Feb. 8, 1977, p. 1.
21. "U.S. Concerned at Treatment of Aleksandr Ginzburg," *Department of State Bulletin*, Feb. 28, 1977, p. 161.
22. Zbigniew Brzezinski, *Power and Principle* (New York: Farrar, Straus, Giroux, 1983), p. 156.
23. Quoted in William Cooper, "Soviet-American Relations in 1977," Report No. 79-60 S, Congressional Research Service,

Library of Congress, March 1, 1979, p. 23.
24. Interview with Ludmilla Thorn, held in New York City, Jan. 5, 1984.
25. Brzezinski, *Power and Principle*, p. 156.
26. *New York Times*, Feb. 17, 1977, p. 17.
27. "U.S. Concerned at Violations of Human Rights in Uganda," *Department of State Bulletin*, March 21, 1977, p. 250.
28. *New York Times*, Feb. 24, 1977, p. 22.
29. *New York Times*, Feb. 26, 1977, p. 1.
30. "Secretary Vance's News Conference of March 4," *Department of State Bulletin*, March 28, 1977, p. 280.
31. U.S., Congress, Senate, Committee on Appropriations, *Foreign Assistance and Related Programs Appropriations for FY1978*, 95th Cong., 1st sess., 1977, pp. 149-205.
32. *New York Times*, Feb. 25, 1977, p. 1.
33. Senate Committee on Appropriations, *Foreign Assistance and Related Programs Appropriations for FY1978*, p. 186.
34. U.S., Congress, House, Committee on Appropriations, *Foreign Assistance and Related Agencies Appropriations for FY1978, Pt. 1, Hearings before the Subcommittee on Foreign Operations Appropriations*, 95th Cong., 1st sess, 1977, p. 760.
35. Ibid.
36. Quoted in Cooper, "Soviet-American Relations in 1977," p. 22.
37. See infra, Chap. 1, fn. 64.
38. "Secretary Vance Interviewed on 'Face the Nation'," *Department of State Bulletin*, March 21, 1977, p. 246.
39. Ibid., p. 247.
40. Ibid.
41. Cooper, "Soviet-American Relations," p. 26.
42. Quoted in ibid., p. 27.
43. Quoted in Joseph G. Whelan, "Human Rights in Soviet-American Relations," Issue Brief IB77031, Congressional Research Service, Library of Congress, Archived May 8, 1978, p. 4.
44. "United Nations," *Weekly Compilation of Presidential Documents*, March 21, 1977, p. 401.
45. Ibid., p. 402.
46. "Secretary Vance Visits Moscow and Western Europe," *Department of State Bulletin*, April 25, 1977, p. 391.
47. Cyrus Vance, *Hard Choices* (New York: Simon and Schuster, 1983), p. 53.
48. Adam Ulam, "U.S.-Soviet Relations: Unhappy Coexistence,"

Foreign Affairs, Vol. 57, No. 3 (1979), p. 558.

49. Vance, *Hard Choices*, p. 46.
50. Ibid.
51. "'I Don't Intend to Lose'," *Newsweek*, May 2, 1977, p. 37.
52. Brzezinski, *Power and Principle*, p. 174.
53. *Washington Post*, Jan. 5, 1978, p. 23.
54. "Where U.S. Is Gaining In the World," *U.S. News and World Report*, Nov. 7, 1977, p. 27.
55. "What's Right With Our Foreign Policy: Interview With Zbigniew Brzezinski," *U.S. News and World Report*, Feb. 13, 1978, p. 31.
56. Arthur Schlesinger, Jr., "Human Rights and the American Tradition," *Foreign Affairs*, Vol. 57, No. 3 (1977), pp. 516-517.
57. Sandra Vogelgesang, *American Dream: Global Nightmare* (New York: W.W. Norton, 1980), pp. 103-104.
58. U.S., Congress, Senate, Committee on Foreign Relations, *Human Rights and U.S. Foreign Assistance*, report prepared by the Foreign Affairs and National Defense Division, Congressional Research Service, November 1979, p. 63.
59. See *New York Times*, July 30, 1980, p. 7; and "Continuing the CSCE Process," *Department of State Bulletin*, September 1980, p. 50.
60. Ludmilla Thorn interview.
61. *Washington Post*, March 31, 1977, p. 17.
62. "Secretary Vance Attends OAS Assembly at Grenada," *Department of State Bulletin*, July 18, 1977, p. 70.
63. Ibid., p. 73.
64. *New York Times*, June 24, 1977, p. 5.
65. "Human Rights Situation in Cambodia," *Department of State Bulletin*, Sept. 5, 1977, p. 324.
66. *New York Times*, June 29, 1977, p. 3, and July 1, 1977, p. 4.
67. U.S., Congress, House, Committee on International Relations, *Human Rights Conditions in Selected Countries and the U.S. Response*, Prepared by the Foreign Affairs and National Defense Division, Congressional Research Service, Library of Congress, 95th Cong., 2nd sess., 1978, pp. 32-33.
68. Printed in U.S., Congress, House, Committee on Banking, Finance and Urban Affairs, *U.S. Participation in Multilateral Development Institutions*, 95th Cong., 2nd sess., 1978, p. 334.
69. *Christian Science Monitor*, March 2, 1978, p. 3.
70. Lars Schoultz, *Human Rights and United States Policy toward Latin America* (Princeton: Princeton U. Press, 1981), p. 79.

71. "Human Rights and Arms Transfer Policy," in Ved P. Nanda, James P. Scarritt, and George W. Shephard, Jr., eds., *Global Human Rights: Public Policies, Comparative Measures, and NGO Strategies* (Boulder: Westview, 1981), p. 91.

72. Interview with Richard Feinberg, held in Washington, D.C., Dec. 14, 1983.

73. Jo Marie Griesgraber, "Implementation by the Carter Administration of Human Rights Legislation Affecting Latin America," (Ph.D. dissertation, Georgetown University, 1984), p. 228.

74. Stephen B. Cohen, "Conditioning U.S. Security Assistance on Human Rights Practices," *American Journal of International Law*, Vol. 76 (1982), p. 262n.

75. U.S., Congress, House, Committee on International Relations, *Foreign Relations Authorization for FY1978, Pt. 1, Hearings before the Subcommittee on International Operations*, 95th Cong., 2nd sess., 1978, p. 171.

76. Cohen, "Conditioning U.S. Security Assistance," p. 262n.

77. Schoultz, *Human Rights and United States Policy*, p. 143.

78. Cohen, "Conditioning U.S. Security Assistance," p. 256.

79. U.S., Department of State, "Report of the Secretary of State to Congress Regarding the Operations and Mandate of the Bureau of Human Rights and Humanitarian Affairs," reprinted in *Congressional Record*, Senate, Feb. 6, 1978, p. 2311.

80. Testimony of Stephen B. Cohen in U.S., Congress, House, Committee on Foreign Affairs, *Human Rights in Africa, Hearings before the Subcommittees on Africa and on International Organizations*, 96th Cong., 2nd sess, 1980, p. 17.

81. Interview with Jessica Tuchman held in Washington, D.C., Dec. 29, 1983.

82. U.S., Congress, House, Committee on Foreign Affairs, *Implementation of Congressionally Mandated Human Rights Provisions, Hearings before the Subcommittee on Human Rights and International Organizations*, Vol. I, 97th Cong., 1st sess., 1981, p. 69.

83. House Committee on Foreign Affairs, *Human Rights and U.S. Foreign Policy*, p. 7.

84. Ibid.

85. U.S., Department of State, "Human Rights and U.S. Foreign Policy," Pub. No. 8959, December 1978, p. 12.

86. Bite, "Human Rights and U.S. Foreign Policy," Issue Brief, NO. IB77056, Congressional Research Service, Library of Congress,

p. 35.

87. "Seoul, Republic of Korea," *Weekly Compilation of Presidential Documents*, July 9, 1979, p. 1209.
88. "Report of the Secretary of State," p. 2311.
89. House Committee on International Relations, *Human Rights Conditions in Selected Countries*, pp. 236, 289.
90. U.S., Agency for International Development, "Human Rights Review Procedures for AID Projects," pp. 5-7, copy in author's files.
91. Cohen, "Conditioning U.S. Security Assistance," p. 270.
92. Brzezinski, *Power and Principle*, p. 127; Christopher testimony before House Committee on Foreign Affairs, *Human Rights and U.S. Foreign Policy*, p. 329; Derian testimony before U.S., House Committee on Appropriations, *Foreign Assistance and Related Agencies Appropriations, FY1979, Part 2*, 95th Cong. 2nd sess., 1978, p. 1223.
93. U.S., Congress, House, Committee on Appropriations, *Foreign Assistance and Related Agencies Appropriations for FY1979, Part 2*, 95 Cong., 2nd sess., 1978, p. 442.
94. Department of State, "Human Rights and U.S. Foreign Policy," p. 10.
95. Ibid.
96. Brzezinski, *Power and Principle*, p. 145.
97. House Committee on Foreign Affairs, *Human Rights and U.S. Foreign Policy*, p. 387.
98. *Washington Post*, Aug. 2, 1979.
99. Griesgraber, "Implementation of Human Rights Legislation," op. cit., p. 70.
100. *New York Times*, May 31, 1980, p. 16.
101. "New York, New York," *Weekly Compilation of Presidential Documents*, Aug. 18, 1980, p. 1536.

THREE
Human Rights and Political Systems

Perhaps because of the unplanned way in which human rights emerged as a focus of Carter's foreign policy, little advance thought was given to how human rights might fit in with the administration's other major foreign policy goals. Prime among these was the administration's deep yearning for reconciliation, even friendship, with the traditional antagonists of the United States, a yearning given voice in the president's declaration that we had as a people overcome our "inordinate fear of communism."[1] The administration was not sympathetic to Communism, it merely sought to reduce what it saw as the excessive role that anti-Communism had traditionally played in shaping U.S. foreign policy.

During his campaign for the presidency, Carter had said: "The greatest challenge we Americans confront is to demonstrate to the Soviet Union that our good will is as great as our strength until, despite all obstacles, our two nations can achieve new attitudes and new trust, and until, in time, the terrible burden of the arms race can be lifted from our peoples."[2]

True, Carter had criticized President Ford for giving away too much to the Soviets in the name of detente and for acquiescing in Soviet human rights violations. But the broad criticisms of detente seem to have been more polemical than real: a more important thrust of Carter's campaign was that he would be less willing than Ford and Kissinger to use force to challenge the expansion of Soviet influence, as in Angola. As Carter put it in his inaugural address: "we will fight our wars against poverty, ignorance, and injustice, for those are the enemies against which our forces can be honorably marshalled."[3] On the other hand, his criticisms of Ford and Kissinger on the specific issue of Soviet human rights violations were undoubtedly sincere. But Carter had hoped that the human rights issue would not be an impediment to good relations with the USSR. "This issue is important in itself," he said. "It should not block progress on other important matters."[4] When the Soviets demonstrated a contrary view, Carter confessed this "was a surprise" to him.[5]

In response to this "surprise," the administration took special pains to emphasize that its human rights policy was not an anti-Soviet policy. "It is not done in response to the Soviet Union, to try to position ourselves better," insisted Derian.[6] The State Department, in an outline of U.S. policy toward the Soviet Union in 1977, declared that "the United States is firmly committed to promoting respect for human rights around the globe," but added that "we do not seek to change the Soviet political system, nor do we wish to single out the USSR for special criticism."[7]

The Carter administration was dedicated to achieving friendlier relations not only with the USSR, but with all Communist countries, and in general with countries with which the United States had had strained relations. In his first month in office Carter held a question-and-answer session with employees of the Department of Agriculture at which he listed his foreign policy priorities. The list did not include promoting human rights, but it did include this: "to normalize relationships with countries with whom we don't have a present friendship."[8] A few months later, the president told interviewers that he wished "to aggressively challenge...the Soviet Union...for influence in...places like Vietnam and places like Iraq and Somalia and Algeria and places like the People's Republic of China and even Cuba. I don't have any hesitancy about these matters," he said.[9] These well-chosen words show Carter at his politically most adept. The phrase "aggressively challenge" conveys toughness, but the substance was that Carter intended to court favor with Communist and pro-Communist governments in the hope of outbidding the USSR for their affections.

In his memoirs, Vance recalls that "we had generally agreed at the outset of the new administration that we should seek to establish normal relations with all nations regardless of the fact that we had differing ideologies: hence our initial contacts with Cuba, Vietnam and the PRC, as well as Angola."[10] Richard Fagen has written that the two items "at the head of the list" of the administration's initial goals in Latin America were the Panama Canal treaty and improving relations with Cuba.[11] In his memoirs, Brzezinski reports rather contemptuously: "In the pre-inaugural 'informal' NSC meeting, held to define our immediate priorities...State focused on such peripheral issues as relations with Vietnam." He later adds that he "could never quite understand [this] from a policy standpoint, but [it] perhaps may be better explained by the psychologically searing impact of the Vietnamese war tragedy."[12]

But even Brzezinski, the administration's "hard-liner," did not in principle oppose seeking warm relations with Communist governments. On the contrary, his own principal achievement was the establishment of normal diplomatic relations with the People's Republic of China, a process begun by Henry Kissinger, but that had stalled over the issue of Taiwan. That issue was of deep importance to the Chinese, but it also touched on long-standing commitments of the United States. Brzezinski broke the deadlock by accepting terms more self-effacing for the United States than Kissinger had been willing to accept.

In his memoirs, Brzezinski gives the impression of having been well charmed by China's Deng Xiao Ping. In a jocular tone, he relates the following anecdote:

> ....At one stage, when Carter registered his concern for human rights, requesting Deng to be flexible on emigration from China, Deng leaned forward toward Carter and said, "Fine. We'll let them go. Are you prepared to accept ten million?"[13]

The anecdote is supposed to illustrate both Deng's sparkling sense of humor and the inherent futility of pressing the human rights issue with China. What it in fact illustrates is Brzezinski's cavalier attitude toward the human rights issue when it came to Communist regimes that were in his good graces. His bland acceptance of Deng's retort ignores the obvious distinction between, on the one hand, the unwillingness of the Chinese government to permit its citizens to emigrate and, on the other hand, the difficulty that many of these individuals might have finding places of refuge if they were allowed to go. The latter problem is far from unique. Many Third World countries have more citizens wishing to emigrate than can find countries willing to admit them, but few use that as an excuse to deny the right to emigrate.

Brzezinski's weakness for Deng is but a small example of a large dilemma. How could U.S. policy address itself with new zeal and determination to the quest for human rights worldwide and at the same time pursue new understanding and reconciliation with regimes traditionally at odds with the United States? The Soviet government was not the only traditional adversary with which the human rights issue was bound to cause friction. All of America's traditional adversaries are dictatorships; there was not one democracy with which we stood in need of "reconciliation."

Thus the administration felt impelled to go beyond denying merely that its policy was aimed at the Soviet Union. It sought a convincing way to deny in general that its policy was aimed at the traditional antagonists of the United States. The solution it found was to assert again and again that it perceived no connection between human rights and "ideology," between human rights and political systems.

Vice President Mondale said in June of 1977: "We believe that human rights transcend ideology. We believe all nations, regardless of political systems, must respect those rights."[14] As a normative or prescriptive statement this is unarguable, but the administration seemed to mean something more. Patricia Derian, when asked in a congressional hearing, "why do we spend so much time worrying about human rights violations in right-wing governments...?" replied:

> ....it is always a surprising question to me, although...I get it often, because human rights violations do not really have much to do with the form of government or the political ideology or philosophy. What is a gross violation in one place is not [sic] a gross violation in another.[15]

Subsequently in a speech, Ms. Derian elaborated on this point. "Suffering and oppression can take place in any society—totalitarian, authoritarian, democratic, or other," she said, "and...it is our obligation to work to obliterate human rights abuses wherever they occur."[16] When Jeane Kirkpatrick spoke of the distinction between authoritarian and totalitarian regimes, Derian retorted: "What the hell is 'moderately repressive'—that you only torture half of the people, that you only do summary executions now and then? I don't even know what 'moderately repressive' is."[17]

Another top Carter administration official who saw no human rights significance in ideological differences among nations was UN Ambassador Andrew Young. Indeed, Young apparently saw no important distinction at all in the different systems. He sought, he said, to "break the sterile impasse between 'capitalism' and 'Socialism' that has for several generations served as an anesthetic to imagination as we are all caught up in one rigidity or another."[18]

In this, Young and Derian were only echoing the president who proclaimed upon his arrival in Poland in December 1977 that "old ideological labels have lost their meaning."[19] The next day First Secretary Gierek seemed to go out of his way to refute this assertion. Referring to Poland's "alliances with the Soviet Union and other friends," Gierek said:

> Our nation has made a choice...which provides for the best premises for development....Today Poland belongs to the group of countries of the world which are having the greatest development scale as far as production in industry is concerned ....We have created just, democratic, socio-political conditions....we are enriching contemporary life of Poles by new, profoundly humanistic contents.[20]

Polish shipworkers in Gdansk could have done just as good a job as First Secretary Gierek of disabusing Carter of the notion that "old ideological labels" have grown meaningless. Although surely there has been some evolution in the meanings of such labels as "Communism" (for example, it no longer carries the connotation of monolithism that it did in the heyday of the Comintern), one area in which there has been precious little loss of meaning is precisely that of human rights.

The Gdansk workers could have explained to Carter that under "Communism" workers may not form unions. They may of course belong to "unions" formed for them by the state, unions whose purpose it is to assure political and labor discipline, but they may form no organization of their own. The official reason is that because they live in and are employed by a "workers' state," any organization that would be set up to represent their interests as against those of their employer would be "objectively" antiworker.

The right to form labor unions is only one of many rights that are inherently denied by Communist governments. And Communism is only one of many political systems that inherently deny rights. All dictatorships do.

Human rights violations may of course occur in democracies as well, but what Carter and his colleagues seemed to miss, indeed to deny, is that the distinction between democracy and dictatorship is the "great divide" when it comes to human rights.

Democracy is premised on some idea of human rights, at least on that most basic right, the right of self-government (or, as that right is necessarily translated, of participation in the periodic selection of the goverment). The starting point for American democracy, as the Founders put it, was that men were "endowed with unalienable rights."

Dictatorship, on the other hand, begins with the premise that some adults properly have authority over others without any consent being given. The system itself is an inherent denial of human rights. In addition, in contrast to democracy, it ordinarily offers little course for redress of specific abuses.

The very vocabulary of the Carter human rights policy served to obscure this distinction. It focused insistently on individual abuses rather than systemic deformities. It spoke always of "violations" of human rights, rather than of their "denial." What does it mean to say, for example, that the Soviet government "violates" the right of free speech? The Soviet government simply does not recognize that right. It denies it both in theory[21] and in practice, and has done so for the better part of a century.

To speak in terms of "violations" in the Soviet Union or in many other countries is implicitly vastly to understate the problem, because the word "violation" suggests something that contradicts a norm. But in the USSR and much of the rest of the world, the vast majority have long since learned that they dare not give voice to unapproved ideas. Silence and obedience are the norm.

The struggle for human rights, far from being, as Carter and his aides proclaimed, indifferent to political systems, is fundamentally a struggle about political systems. It cannot sensibly be merely an endless chase after an infinite number of individual "violations." It must aim instead to erect political systems which have the idea of human rights, and the means for their protection, built in.

Recognition that the struggle for human rights is basically a struggle about political systems leads to consideration of another struggle. To say that the distinction between democracy and dictatorship is the "great divide" as far as human rights are concerned does not mean that all forms of dictatorship are equally bad. On the contrary, dictatorships vary greatly in form and severity. In today's world, one form of dictatorship stands out as the most virulent enemy of human rights—Communism.

There are several arguments for this. The first argument is simply quantitative. Of the vast amounts of innocent blood shed in the course of human persecution, the mightiest rivers belong to the Communists. Only Hitler can be counted as a rival to Stalin or Pol Pot in the sheer dimensions of the suffering imposed on the people within their respective grips. Hitler, however, is long dead and the National Socialist system he created died with him. Pol Pot, on the other hand, is alive and kicking and bidding for a return to power, and he enjoys the support of thousands of armed men. Stalin is dead, but the system he created lives on, more powerful than ever before and with an ever growing number of clones. This is not to deny that some non-Communist regimes have spilled more innocent blood or done more grisly things than some Communist regimes. One might well prefer to live in, say, Tito's Yugoslavia than in Amin's Uganda. But the grim toll that may be attributed to government forces in Uganda or Argentina or Guatemala or other such places would have to be multiplied many times over before it would approach the level of carnage exacted by Stalin or Pol Pot or Mao. Moreover, although non-Communist dictatorships in certain countries are bloodier than Communist dictatorships in certain other countries, in any one country Communism has almost always been more sanguinary. No Communist regime has been more benign than the regime that it replaced, except in East Germany.

The second argument is that, as Peter Berger has put it, Communist regimes "must be seen as an assault on human rights in their very structure, over and beyond the particular outrages they habitually engage in."[22] Here we are talking neither about gallons of blood nor about numbers of beatings or incarcerations nor any other quantifiable (at least in our imaginations) acts of brutality. We are talking rather about the extent to which a government attempts to make every moment or every action in the individual's life its own. The salient case in point is not that of the dissident, but that of the individual who in no way challenges the regime. If he leaves it alone, will the regime be content to leave him alone? The answer for Communist regimes is no. Robert Nisbet has put it this way:

> What identifies the totalitarian country and stamps it with far greater menace to human freedom than any other state known to us in history is its systematic and relentless effort to destroy every possible form of the past and present that in any way might militate against the formation of "the New Soviet Man," or whatever his counterpart may be in other totalitarianisms.[23]

Other kinds of dictatorships may exploit people or rob them, may neglect their needs and deny them many freedoms, may abuse those seen as opponents of the established order, but none except the totalitarian regime seeks to mold each of its citizens according to its own model. (The term "totalitarian" as used here and "Communist" are not synonyms, but since World War II the only extant totalitarian regimes have been Communist. It is of course far from inconceivable that other forms of totalitarianism could again arise, and some of the apparent goals of Khomeini's "Islamic Republic" seem to suggest this very characteristic of totalitarianism.)

A third argument for the view that Communism is an especially virulent enemy of human rights is that Communist regimes are often expansionist. The Soviet Union gobbled up Estonia, Latvia, Lithuania, as well as parts of Poland and Finland, conquered an empire in Eastern Europe and seeks more of the same in Afghanistan. The People's Republic of China swallowed Tibet and attacked India. North Korea invaded South Korea. North Vietnam conquered South Vietnam, Laos and Cambodia, and Cuban troops are today serving the cause of repression on three continents. There are of course many non-Communist governments that engage or have engaged in acts of aggression, but none has shown that it has the combination of means and inclination that the Communist governments have. This discussion may seem more relevant to the problems of preserving peace than to human rights, but the point here is that Communist governments more than others not only violate the rights of their own subjects, but also aspire to violate those of other surrounding and even distant peoples.

A fourth argument is that no Communist government has ever evolved into a democracy or been ousted by domestic opposition (except by other Communists). All manner of other dictatorships have given way to democracy, for example in Spain, Portugal, Greece, and recently all over Latin America. Even the Fascist government of Italy, the first self-proclaimed "totalitarianism," was overthrown by domestic forces, albeit not by democrats.

The fifth and most important way in which Communism is distinct from most other forms of dictatorship is that Communism is not merely a form of government; it is also an ideology. As Senator Moynihan has put it: "authoritarian regimes of the Right....commit abominations in practice; the Communist countries commit abominations on principle."[24] Is this an exaggeration? Do Communists really violate rights "on principle?" Let us consider Lenin, the inventor of Communism. Lenin explained that the seizure of power by Communists constitutes not the conclusion, but in a sense only the beginning of the struggle to build Communism. "The proletariat does not cease the class struggle after it has captured political power, but continues it until classes are abolished."[25] This *continuation* of the class struggle of the proletariat" after it has seized power, he explained, is what is meant by the term "the dictatorship of the proletariat."[26]

Kautsky and other interpreters of Marx in the social democratic tradition have argued that Marx used the term, "dictatorship of the proletariat," without really meaning what is normally meant by the word "dictatorship." But this view so enraged Lenin that he was inspired to write his classic pamphlet, "The Proletarian Revolution and the Renegade Kautsky." In it, Lenin declared: "The revolutionary dictatorship of the proletariat is rule won and maintained by the use of violence by the proletariat against the bourgeoisie, rule that is unrestricted by any laws."[27] Obviously, rule that is "unrestricted by any laws" is also unrestricted by any notion of human rights.

Nor did Lenin's idea of the "dictatorship of the proletariat" necessarily embody any majoritarian implications, as some of his apologists have claimed. Lenin argued that the term "dictatorship" didn't necessarily mean rule by a single individual, but he did not rule out that the proletariat's dictatorship could be exercised that way. "In the history of revolutionary movements the dictatorship of individuals was very often the expression, the vehicle, the channel of the dictatorship of the revolutionary classes," he said, adding that "there is...absolutely *no* contradiction in principle between Soviet (that is, socialist) democracy and the exercise of dictatorial powers by individuals," and that "the...revolution demands...that the people *unquestioningly obey the single will* of the leaders of labor."[28]

Even so, does this really, as Moynihan claims, distinguish Communism from other dictatorships? Isn't Lenin in these passages merely prescribing repression as a means to some higher goal, and don't the others often claim that their repression is similarly instrumental? Perhaps, but there is a vast difference in the nature of the goals proclaimed and therefore in the time and exertion required to fulfill them. Other dictatorships characteristically justify themselves in terms of the need to restore order or to salvage the economy or to root out corruption or similar transitory goals. But Communists are after something much loftier—the abolition of classes, which in itself requires at least large steps toward the creation of a "new man."

Here again Lenin is instructive. "In order to abolish classes completely," he said, "... it is necessary to abolish the distinction between town and country, as well as the distinction between manual workers and brain workers" and "it is necessary to overcome the enormous force of habit and conservatism which are connected with" the survival of small-scale production.[29]

Until this is achieved, the class struggle—which means the dictatorship of the proletariat, which means rule by violence and without law—must continue. To achieve all this, added Lenin, acknowledging the obvious, "requires a very long period of time."[30]

Lenin could scarcely have foreseen that only seventeen years after he uttered these words, the Soviet government would proclaim the achievement of a classless society, which it did in the new constitution promulgated by Stalin in 1936. But, alas, the unforeseen rapidity with which the class struggle was brought to completion in the USSR did not serve to shorten the duration of justified repression in Communist theory, for it turned out that Lenin, and before him Engels, had considered the problem too narrowly. They had treated the class struggle only in its national, but not its international, dimension. The dictatorship of the proletariat was supposed to lead to the withering away of the state. But no sooner had Stalin proclaimed victory in the class struggle than at the Eighteenth Congress of the Communist Party of the Soviet Union in 1939, he modified the doctrine of the withering away of the state.

Stalin explained that when Engels had postulated the withering away of the state he had been considering only an abstract socialist state existing in isolation, but the Soviet state could not be dispensed with because it was surrounded by enemies. It, too, might wither, but only "if the capitalist encirclement is liquidated and is replaced by a socialist encirclement."[31] Stalin's "cult of personality" was denounced by Khrushchev at the Twentieth Party Congress in 1956, but this doctrine has never been repudiated. Carried to its logical end, it means that coercion and dictatorship must continue not only until a new Soviet man has been created, but until that creature constitutes the only form of human life left on earth.

It has been three generations since the Bolsheviks seized power and this goal is not yet in sight. To estimate the toll of suffering that might be inflicted before it is reached may be beyond the powers of the human imagination.

But are there no limits to what Communist theory will allow in pursuit of its goals? Stalin and Pol Pot have shown us that there are virtually no limits in practice to what Communist rulers will do, but, and this is the crux of Moynihan's point, Lenin and Trotsky have told us that there are no such limits *in principle*, either. The two key founders of Communism both made a point of repudiating any standard of morality by which it would be possible to condemn as excessive any action serving the cause of Communism. Lenin said in his 1920 speech to the Komsomol:

When people tell us about morality, we say: to a Communist all morality lies in...conscious mass struggle against the exploiters. We do not believe in eternal morality....

...Communist morality is based on the struggle for the consolidation and completion of Communism.[32]

In the same vein, Trotsky wrote:

Civilization can be saved only by the socialist revolution. To accomplish the overturn, the proletariat needs all its strength, all its resolution, all its audacity, passion and ruthlessness. Above all it must be completely free from the fictions of religion, "democracy" and transcendental morality—the spiritual chains forged by the enemy to tame and enslave it. Only that which prepares the complete and final overthrow of imperialist bestiality is moral, and nothing else. The welfare of the revolution—that is the supreme law![33]

It is hard to see how Lenin's and Trotsky's view can be disputed if one accepts Marx's premise that "Communism is the riddle of history solved."[34] It is also hard to see how, given this view, Trotsky could object, for example, to his own assassination, except to argue that the ice-axe landed in the wrong cranium.

This view, moreover, is closely linked to another important tenet of Soviet morality, that which governs the relationship of the individual to society. It has been put this way by

A. F. Shishkin, the author of the major Soviet text on Marxist-Leninist ethics:

> The new society cultivates the individual in such fashion as to cause him...to see the fullness of human existence to lie in struggle for a common cause and, in that struggle, to be able to resolve in favor of society any contradiction arising between the needs of society and his personal ambition.[35]

It is important to note that here Shishkin is speaking not of a society in transition but of "the new society." Thus, not only is the revolution a supreme value to which the well-being of the individual is completely subordinate, but even when the revolution has reached its goal the individual must remain subordinate to "society." He possesses no "rights" that he may assert over and against the interests of society. In theory, this does not necessarily contradict the idea of a stateless society: each individual might learn to be voluntarily self-subordinating, making coercion unnecessary. But until that happens, the use of coercion against deviants or dissidents would be not only necessary, but a positive good, a way of teaching the individual to be a good person. In this we can see the full meaning of Moynihan's formulation that Communists violate human rights "on principle."

But even this does not reveal the full scope of Communism's challenge to human rights. It must be combined with the recognition that Communism makes what Henry Kissinger calls "universal ideological claims."[36] Communism offers itself, by means of persuasion and coercion, as a model to all mankind. What other form of tyranny has such pretensions? Surely not Pinochet's, nor Botha's, nor Fahd's. Even Khomeini's or Hitler's schemes offer or offered models only for selected groups or races.

Significantly, one other system that *does* claim universal applicability is liberal democracy. "Working men of *all* countries unite," said Marx: "*All* men are created equal and endowed by their creator with certain unalienable rights," said Jefferson.

As models, these two systems have been remarkably

successful. If one counts by country, most countries of the world are neither Communist nor democratic, but if one counts people, more than two-thirds of the world's people live either in democracies or under Communism, more than a billion and a half in each category out of a world population of approximately four and a half billion. This is the result of a very rapid transformation of the world: all of the Communist nations and almost all of the democratic ones have become so since 1917.

When it comes to human rights, these two models are polar opposites. Democracy, in its modern, American-born sense, is predicated on the idea that human beings have innate or "natural" or "unalienable" or God-given rights. A main purpose of government is to protect these rights. In accepting the authority of government, individuals surrender a certain portion of their rights in exchange for the protection of the better part of them. This exchange is made voluntarily: governmental authority is justly derived only from the consent of the governed. And democracy is the method of government by which that consent may be formally and repeatedly ascertained.

Communism, in contrast, is predicated on the denial that individuals have innate rights. Communists will sometimes speak of "human rights," especially in international settings, but they profess a unique definition of the term. As Shishkin makes clear, in Communist theory rights inhere not in individuals but in "society." The individual is obliged to accommodate himself to "society," and society may grant him certain "rights" that do not conflict with its own. But there is no notion here of a voluntary exchange or of consent of the governed.

The individual under this system is free to say whatever he is not forbidden to say. He is, for example, free to praise Stalin...until Stalin dies. Then he is no longer free to praise Stalin, but is free to praise Khrushchev...until Khrushchev is deposed. Then he is no longer free to praise Khrushchev, but is free to praise Brezhnev. To look upon this as a different form, or even a lesser form, of "rights" is to miss the point: this is the negation of rights. The right of free speech means that the individual may say whatever *he* wishes to say. This right is not only unknown to Communism but is contradictory to its basic principles.

Alas, the problem does not end there, for the struggle betweeen democracy and Communism is entwined in a conflict between two power blocs. Much of world politics is shaped by the actions and competition of two superpowers, each of which was the original model for its system. In such a conflict the actions of each side will inevitably be motivated by a mixture of idealism and self-interest. Naturally, in its perceptions and descriptions of its own motives, each side will tend to emphasize the idealistic component, while outsiders will be more skeptical, tending to see that of self-interest.

Concern over such skepticism led President Carter to say: "The cause of human rights will be all the stronger if it remains at the service of humanity, rather than at the service of ideological or partisan ends."[37]

But a few weeks later he said something quite different: "America did not invent human rights. In a very real sense, it's the other way around. Human rights invented America...The fundamental force that unites us is not kinship or place of origin or religious preference. The love of liberty is the common blood that flows in our American veins."[38]

These two statements are hard to reconcile. If human rights is the essence of Americanism, how can the advocacy of human rights not serve partisan ends, if by "partisan" we mean advancing America's cause? Any victory for freedom is a victory for America—perhaps not of her "imperial" interests, but always of her ideological interests. Indeed, it is hard to think of any case where a victory for freedom or human rights did any damage even to America's "imperial" interests, although there have been a few instances in which some U.S. officials feared such damage.

Samuel P. Huntington has put it thus:

....any increase in the power or influence of the United States in world affairs generally results—not inevitably, but far more often than not—in the promotion of liberty and human rights in the world. The expansion of American power is not synonymous with the expansion of liberty, but a significant correlation exists between the rise and fall of American power in the world and the rise and fall of liberty and democracy.[39]

Huntington's claim is not absolute. There have been instances in which the United States has intervened against democracy, such as in Iran or Guatemala in the early 1950s, but these have been few. It can also be argued against Huntington that the United States often gives aid support to governments that are not democratic. But this argument carries little weight. In almost all such situations the United States finds itself in a position not of wishing to sustain undemocratic rule, but of not knowing how to engender a shift to democratic rule in countries without democratic traditions. U.S. influence in such countries is generally a force for liberalization but is insufficient to bring about full-scale democratization. In situations where the United States has been free, by virtue of conquest, to work its will with another country, as in Germany, Japan, the Dominican Republic or Grenada, it has consistently used that power to "impose" democracy and freedom.

In addition, though much of the world looks skeptically upon claims that Soviet or American policy is idealistically motivated, it still does see the two superpowers as embodying contradictory models of civilization, and therefore tends inevitably to see the rise or fall of American or Soviet power as a critical measure of the "success" or "failure" of the respective system. In the eyes of Third World elites, few benefits are sufficiently appealing to recommend the adoption of a particular political system if it appears that that system will weaken their countries.

Huntington criticized what he labeled the "new moralism" in U.S. foreign policy for seeking "to effect a reduction in American power."[40] Just such a new moralism was at work in Carter's administration and in his own approach to world affairs. As a presidential candidate he had declared: "our foreign policy ought not to be based on military might nor political power nor economic pressure. It ought to be based on the fact that we are right and decent and honest and truthful and predictable and respectful."[41] Then, in an address to people of other nations delivered upon taking office, President Carter said: "We will not seek to dominate nor dictate to others....we Americans have...acquired a more mature perspective on the problems of the world. It is a perspective which recognizes the fact that we alone do not have all the answers to the world's problems."[42] Nonintervention became the hallmark of his presidency.

But who has ever claimed that "we alone" have "all the answers"? The real question is whether the United States and other democracies have *one key answer*, or, better yet, have the best system for arriving at answers. It is hard to see why one would favor a "human rights" policy unless one did believe something along these lines. Carter's assault on this straw man revealed the depths of the conflict between his human rights policy and his commitment to a policy of national self-effacement.

This conflict prevented him from ever seeing clearly the most important truths about the quest for human rights worldwide: that it is fundamentally a quest for the creation of political systems predicated on the belief in human rights; and that, at this moment in history, it is critically dependent upon the success of democracy in its conflict with Communism, and upon the power of the United States relative to that of the Soviet Union.

NOTES

1. "Notre Dame," *Weekly Compilation of Presidential Documents*, May 27, 1977, p. 774.
2. Jimmy Carter, "Relations Between World's Democracies," in U.S. , Congress, House, Committee on House Administration, *The Presidential Campaign 1976*, Vol. 1, Pt. 1, p. 272.
3. "Inaugural Address of President Jimmy Carter," *Weekly Compilation of Presidential Documents*, January 24, 1977, p. 88.

4. "United Nations," Ibid., March 21, 1977, p. 402.

5. "President's News Conference, June 30, 1977," ibid., July 4, 1977, p. 960.

6. U.S. , Congress, House, Committee on Appropriations, *Foreign Assistance and Related Agencies Appropriations for FY 1978, Part 3*, Hearings before the Subcommittee on Foreign Operations Appropriations, 95th Cong., 1st sess., 1977, p. 308.

7. "U.S.-Soviet Relations," *Department of State Bulletin*, Sept. 12, 1977, p. 356.

8. "Department of Agriculture," *Weekly Compilation of Presidential Documents*, Feb. 21, 1977, p. 209.

9. "Magazine Publishers Association Interviews President Carter," *Department of State Bulletin*, July 11, 1977, p. 46.

10. Cyrus Vance, *Hard Choices* (New York: Simon and Schuster, 1983), p. 275.

11. Richard R. Fagen, "The Carter Administration and Latin America: Business as Usual," *Foreign Affairs*, Vol. 57, No. 3, pp. 652-653.

12. Zbigniew Brzezinski, *Power and Principle* (New York: Farrar, Straus, Giroux, 1983), p. 197, p. 228.

13. Ibid., p. 407.

14. Walter F. Mondale, "Address to the World Affairs Council of Northern California," *Department of State Bulletin*, July 1977, p. 42.

15. U.S., Congress, House, Committee on Foreign Affairs, *Human Rights and the Phenomenon of Disappearances*, Hearings before the Subcommittee on International Organizations, 96th Cong., 1st sess., 1979, p. 330.

16. U.S., Department of State, *American Foreign Policy: Basic Documents 1977-1980*, Pub. 9330 (Washington, D.C.: GPO, 1983), Document 170, p. 438.

17. Quoted in Philip Geyelin, "Human Rights Turnaround," *Washington Post*, Dec. 12, 1980, p. A33.

18. Andrew Young, "Statement to UN Economic Commission for Latin America," *Department of State Bulletin*, May 30, 1977, p. 571.

19. "Warsaw, Poland," *Weekly Compilation of Presidential Documents*, January 2, 1978, p. 1958.

20. Ibid., p. 1968.

21. Article 39 of the Soviet Constitution guarantees the right of free speech so long as it is not exercised "to the detriment of the interests of society and the state."

22. Peter L. Berger, "Human Rights and American Foreign Policy: A Symposium,"*Commentary*, Vol. 72 No. 5 (November 1981), p. 28.
23. Robert Nisbet, ibid., p. 55.
24. Daniel P. Moynihan, "The Politics of Human Rights," *Commentary*, Vol. 64, No. 2 (August 1977), p. 24.
25. V. I. Lenin, "A Great Beginning," *The Lenin Anthology*, ed., Robert C. Tucker (New York: W.W. Norton, 1975), p. 478.
26. Lenin, "The Dictatorship of the Proletariat," ibid., p. 490.
27. Lenin, "The Proletarian Revolution and the Renegade Kautsky," ibid., p. 466.
28. Lenin, "The Immediate Tasks of the Soviet Government," ibid., pp. 454-455. All emphases as given.
29. Lenin, "A Great Beginning," ibid., p. 479.
30. Ibid.
31. J. Stalin, "Report on the Work of the Central Committee to the Eighteenth Congress of the CPSU," *A Documentary History of Communism*, ed., Robert V. Daniels (New York: Vintage Books, 1962), Vol. 2, p. 79.
32. Lenin, "The Tasks of the Youth Leagues," *The Lenin Anthology*, pp. 670-671.
33. "The Moralists and Sycophants Against Marxism," *Their Morals and Ours*, Essays by Leon Trotsky, John Dewey, George Novack (New York: Merit, 1969), pp. 49-50.
34. Karl Marx, "Economic and Philosophical Manuscripts," *The Marx-Engels Reader*, ed., Robert C. Tucker, 2nd ed. (New York: W. W. Norton, 1978), p. 84.
35. A. F. Shishkin, "On Moral Values in the Contemporary World," *Soviet Studies in Philosophy*, Vol. 17, No. 1 (Summer 1978), p. 73. Translated from *Vaprosy Filosofii*, 1977, No. 11.
36. Henry A. Kissinger, "Continuity and Change in American Foreign Policy," *Society*, Vol. 15 (November-December 1977), p. 101.
37. Jimmy Carter, "Address to the 10th General Assembly of the Organization of American States," *Department of State Bulletin*, January 1981, p. 34.
38. "President Carter's Farewell Address to the Nation," ibid., February 1981, p. 23.
39. Samuel P. Huntington, "Human Rights and American Power," *Commentary*, Vol. 72, No. 3 (September 1981), p. 38.
40. Ibid., p. 42.
41. U.S. , Congress, House, Committee on House Administration,

The Presidential Campaign 1976, Vol. 1, Pt. 1, Jimmy Carter, (Washington, D.C.: USGPO, 1978), p. 80.

42. Jimmy Carter, "Address to People of Other Nations," *Weekly Compilation of Presidential Documents*, January 24, 1977, p. 89.

FOUR
Defining "Human Rights"

INTERNATIONAL LAW OR AMERICAN TRADITIONS?

T he Carter administration recognized that the principal objection to its human rights program was that it was intervening in the internal affairs of other nations. What right, it was asked by America's adversaries as well as by some of its allies, has the United States to preach to the rest of the world how another nation ought to govern itself? And by virtue of what writ does the United States assume that its peculiarly Anglo-American notion of human rights is superior to that by which other nations conduct their affairs? Who has the authority to proclaim the American conception of "democracy" superior to the conception observed in the People's Democratic Republic of Yemen or the German Democratic Republic?

It was in response to this challenge that the Carter administration adopted the stance that U.S. human rights policy was based on international law. We were not trying to impose our way of doing things on other countries, the administration said, but only trying to make all countries live up to the standards enshrined in international treaties. "International law is our guide to the definition of human rights," testified Assistant Secretary Derian.[1]

Less than two months into his term, President Carter went before the UN General Assembly to present his human rights policy. He said there:

All the signatories of the U.N. Charter have pledged themselves to observe and to respect basic human rights. Thus no member of the United Nations can claim that mistreatment of its citizens is solely its own business. Equally, no member can avoid its responsibilities to review and to speak when torture or unwarranted deprivation occurs in any part of the world.[2]

This remained the constant theme of his human rights policy. Three days before leaving office, President Carter, in his last State of the Union message, said once again:

Rather than attempt to dictate what system or institutions other countries should have, the U.S. supports, throughout the world, the internationally recognized human rights which all members of the United Nations have pledged themselves to respect. There is more than one model that can satisfy the continuing human reach for freedom and justice.[3]

While the resort to international law and the references to UN documents helped the Carter administration to respond to one problem, it created another set of problems, problems that arise both from the nature of the relevant international institutions and from the relationship of the United States to them. Not least of these is that the content of international human rights law is uncertain. The charter of the United Nations, which is binding on all UN members, contains brief human rights provisions. Articles 55 and 56 pledge all members "to take joint and separate action in cooperation with the" UN to "promote....universal respect for, and observance of, human rights and fundamental freedoms for all without distinction as to race, sex, language, or religion." But the Charter contains nothing further; it obligates members to no specific actions.

The document that might serve in the international arena as the equivalent of the Bill of Rights in the United States is the Universal Declaration of Human Rights, but it was specifically adopted by the United Nations as nonbinding, as a "declaration" not a piece of law. The universal declaration is supplemented by two covenants, the International

Covenant on Civil and Political Rights and the International Covenant on Economic, Social, and Cultural Rights. These covenants are binding, but only on those who ratify them. Although the covenants have been open for ratification since 1966, only a minority of states have ratified them. Fewer still have acceded to the Optional Protocol or the Optional Article which are the only significant mechanisms through which a complaint may be brought against a signatory for noncompliance with the covenant.[4] An additional problem for U.S. policy is that the United States is not among the ratifiers of either covenant.

In addition to the charter and the covenants, there are several other pieces of international human rights law, but each has some significant limitation. There are some other conventions, but these either have been signed by only a minority of states or pertain only to a relatively narrow slice of human rights issues, such as the conduct of war or labor standards. There are some regional human rights treaties, but each of these covers only a few countries. The most effective, the European Convention on Human Rights, for example, applies only to the states of Western Europe. There are probably some isolated bits of customary law, such as the outlawry of slavery and the slave trade,[5] but again, these apply only to a single aspect of human rights. In short, there is no binding law, ratified by most states, that pertains to the central issues of human rights.

Some human rights activists among international lawyers have sought to rectify this defect by devising arguments aiming to prove that the Universal Declaration has become binding. These arguments, however, all tend to be as unconvincing as they are well intentioned. Eleanor Roosevelt, who was generally recognized as the guiding spirit behind the Universal Declaration, presented it to the General Assembly this way:

> In giving our approval to the declaration today it is of primary importance that we keep clearly in mind the basic character of the document. It is not a treaty, it is not an international agreement, it is not and does not purport to be a statement of

law or of legal obligation. It is a declaration of basic principles of human rights and freedom to be stamped with the approval of the General Assembly by formal vote of its members, and to serve as a common standard of achievement for all peoples of all nations.[6]

To argue that, despite statements such as this, the nations assembled were inadvertently adopting something contrary to their intentions is sheer casuistry.

In defense of such an approach it might be said that the cause of human rights is so morally compelling that it is justifiable to stretch the law in its behalf. But however good the cause, the question is, what will this stretched law achieve? International law rests essentially on voluntary compliance, a chancy business at best. It is unlikely that many nations will voluntarily comply with "laws" to which they have never consented. Thus the net effect of such stretching is likely to be not a strengthening of human rights, but a weakening of the already fragile tissue of international law, and with it a weakening of whatever prospects exist that international law can some day become a more effective instrument for the advancement of human rights. No act of casuistry will suffice to remedy the problem of the lack of a body of binding international human rights law, dealing with central issues, to which the United States is party.

The Carter administration, to its credit, did not rely primarily on casuistic arguments to deal with this problem. Its main approach was to try to secure United States ratification of five major human rights treaties: the two covenants, the Convention on the Prevention and Punishment of the Crime of Genocide, the International Convention on the Elimination of All Forms of Racial Discrimination, and the American Convention on Human Rights.

But despite Carter's exhortation that "no single action by this country would do more to advance the cause of human rights than Senate approval of these instruments,"[7] the Senate acted on none of them. Why was the Senate so recalcitrant? Was it reverting to isolationism and know-nothingism? Hardly. The treaties were stuck in the Foreign Relations Committee under Senator Frank Church, a bastian of liberal internationalism. They were stuck because the problems with them are real and vexing.

Article VI of the United States Constitution declares that treaties as well as federal law and the Constitution, itself, constitute "the supreme Law of the Land." This seems to mean that the authority of a treaty is equal to that of an act of Congress, and so the courts have held. Indeed, in some ways the Supreme Court has placed treaties above legislation.[8] This means that by signing treaties the American government is making law binding on the United States.

Most of the time this fact is of no domestic consequence because most treaties concern only our relations with other states. But the human rights covenants and conventions are primarily concerned with the domestic actions of states. It would hardly be surprising if the Senate felt that matters of this kind are properly left to the normal legislative and judicial procedures of the United States rather than insinuated into our law through treaties.

At the very least ratification of these treaties would raise ticklish legal questions. Article 1[1] of both the economic and social and the civil and political covenants proclaims that "all peoples have the right of self-determination." Not long ago self-determination for American blacks was a demand raised by some militant groups. Would this demand now find legal footing? Perhaps more plausibly, what if groups of American Indians asserted their independence from the United States? And could U.S. affirmative action laws and rulings survive the dictate of Article 7[c] of that covenant guaranteeing "equal opportunity for everyone to be promoted in his employment to an appropriate higher level, subject to no considerations other than those of seniority and competence"? At worst, parts of these treaties directly conflict with the U.S. Constitution, such as Article 4[a] of the convention on racial discrimination which requires that all parties "shall declare an offense punishable by law all dissemination of ideas based on racial superiority or hatred [or] incitement to racial discrimination."

In order to cope with this problem, President Carter's message to the Senate submitting the treaties included the statement: "Wherever a provision is in conflict with United States law, a reservation, understanding or declaration has been recommended" by the State and Justice Departments in order to remove any "constitutional or other legal obstacles to United States ratification." Altogether the administration proposed seventeen "reservations," "understandings," "statements," and "declarations."[9]

These reservations pose problems of their own. Their status under international law is ambiguous, except if no other signatory raises any objection, an unlikely eventuality. At a minimum, no treaty to which the United States appended a reservation would be considered in effect between the United States and any country that objected to the reservation.[10] Friendly governments might be disposed to acquiesce in these reservations, but surely some others would find themselves unable to resist the temptation to embarrass the United States by objecting to them. And these are likely to be the very ones that we would most wish to bring under some sort of international regime of human rights. Nonetheless, the Carter administration's proposed reservations might solve the essential legal problems.

They would not, unfortunately, touch the larger, practical problem, namely that the treaties are not enforceable. The basic enforcement mechanism of the treaties are periodic reports submitted by each party concerning its own compliance. Is it any surprise that the variations in these self- evaluations provide an analogue to Senator Moynihan's aphorism that you can land in any country in the world and if the newspapers are filled with good news, you can assume that the jails are filled with good people? The governments that most abuse human rights tend to file the most glowing reports. Compounding this problem, these governments are also heavily represented on the UN committees that receive the reports. The net effect, as one UN official acknowledged, has been that "the respective Committees have tended to accept at face value the anodyne self-congratulatory reports of states with notoriously poor human rights records, while examining in great detail and sometimes even with a certain hostility the honestly self-critical reports of manifestly democratic states."[11]

In addition to self-reporting, the Covenant on Civil and Political Rights has optional provisions that, although not constituting "enforcement," would at least allow for a freer airing of complaints. These are the Optional Protocol by which states authorize the Human Rights Committee to receive complaints about their alleged violations from aggrieved individuals, and the Optional Article by which states agree to submit to investigation of complaints brought against them by other states. As of December 1984, ninety-one states had ratified the covenant, forty-one of these had ratified the Optional Protocol and seventeen had accepted the Optional Article. Once again, those most willing to submit to outside complaints are those about whom there is least cause to complain.

In its eagerness to show that, as Derian's deputy Mark Schneider put it, "the rights we have promoted are not parochial American values,"[12] the administration professed to see in this UN record evidence of an "international consensus" on human rights. President Carter proclaimed that "the Universal Declaration of Human Rights is the cornerstone of a developing international consensus on human rights."[13] In the annual volume of country reports covering 1979 the State Department said:

> There now exists an international consensus that recognizes basic human rights and obligations owed by all governments to their citizens. This consensus is reflected in a growing body of international law: the Universal Declaration of Human Rights; the International Covenant on Civil and Political Rights; the International Covenant on Economic, Social and Cultural Rights; and other international and regional human rights agreements. There is no doubt that these rights are often violated; but virtually all governments acknowledge their validity.[14]

There is something a bit funny in the State Department's proclaiming that an international consensus is embodied in documents which the U.S. Senate refuses to accept, but the more serious point is that not nearly all governments "acknowledge the validity" of human rights. The UN documents are evidence less of consensus than of hypocrisy. The contrast between practice and preachment of human rights is not explained, as the State Department seemed to be suggesting, by the fact that governments violate their own beliefs (as if somehow the spirit was willing but the flesh was weak), but by the fact that many governments are quite willing to proclaim principles that they neither believe nor practice.

In truth, the United Nations exhibits growing discord on human rights, and that is the very nub of the problem of relating U.S. human rights policy to international law. The Universal Declaration was adopted by the General Assembly in 1948 by a vote of forty-eight in favor, none against, and eight abstentions.   Of the forty-eight positive votes, the majority were democracies. They were voting for something in which they genuinely believed. Most of the rest of the forty-eight, though not democracies themselves, looked to democracies as their models. The eight abstentions were also sincere votes, cast by states that knew they did not believe in human rights: the Soviet bloc, South Africa, and Saudi Arabia.

Today the number of UN members has trebled, but the number of democracies has not grown appreciably. They now constitute not a hegemonic majority, but a clear minority. Which is not to say that the Universal Declaration, if introduced anew, would have tougher sailing through today's General Assembly.   On the contrary, it would probably pass unanimously, this time without abstentions. Gorbachev's delegates would have a more clever strategy than Stalin's had, and so too would the Saudis and the South Africans. This points up two cardinal developments in the UN during these thirty-five years—on the one hand growing diversity, and with it discord; on the other growing hypocrisy. In regard to human rights questions the latter has to some extent masked the former.

The twin problems of discord and hypocrisy do not necessarily render all international human rights instruments useless, but the ones that have proved most effective are the ones that somehow diminish the effects of one or the other of these factors. The most effective international human rights agreement is the European Convention on Human Rights, which has been in effect for thirty years. The convention sets a demanding standard for observance of human rights and it contains a full-blown enforcement mechanism designed not merely to air complaints but to adjudicate them. Moreover, the mechanism allows for complaints to be initiated by either states or individuals. Hundreds of complaints have been processed over the years, and the convention is widely held in high repute. The key to this success is that the parties are all Western European states. They are all democracies, and they share a great degree of cultural homogeneity.

Another regional treaty, the American Convention on Human Rights, has only been in force for a few years, but it already has shown utility as an instrument with which the hemisphere's democracies can bring constructive pressure to bear on its tyrannies. Although all of its adherents are not democracies, they share an even greater degree of cultural homogeneity than do the West Europeans.

The other most effective international human rights instrument has been the Helsinki "Final Act." It has not brought about any concrete improvement in respect for human rights other than perhaps some humanitarian gestures involving family reunifications, and it seems that the level of respect for human rights in the Soviet Union is lower today than at the time the Final Act was signed in 1975. But in addition to providing a point of reference and a source of encouragement for East European dissidents, it has created an effective framework for bringing attention to human rights abuses. This effectiveness has resulted from three factors that distinguish the Helsinki Accords from the UN-sponsored human rights treaties and that serve to mitigate the noxious impact of hypocrisy. First, the human rights provisions of the Helsinki Final Act are more specific, more detailed, and less far-reaching than those of the UN treaties. Second, the Helsinki agreements include provisions that have allowed for regular, public review of their implementation. Third, and most important, the tyrannies constitute only a small minority of the Helsinki signatories, and the democracies constitute a clear majority, as they once did in the UN. The tyrannies lie and posture and prevaricate in the Helsinki review meetings just as they do at the UN, but because they are only a few against the many they do not succeed in creating the same miasma of lies and equivocations that so shrouds the human rights deliberations of the UN.

The European and American conventions and the Helsinki Final Act offer sorely needed evidence that international instruments can do some service for the cause of human rights, but their limitations and their special characteristics also reinforce the impression that international law is a disappointing instrument in the service of that cause. Law must rest either on consent or on some power of enforcement. International law has always rested, and in its very conception rests, on consent. But there is no likelihood at all that tyrannies will consent to respect human rights, which is equivalent to abolishing themselves, merely because they are told that international law requires it. The idea that abuses of human rights can in this manner be outlawed calls forth one historical analogy—in 1928 the nations of the world outlawed war.

If international human rights law cannot rely on consent, then is there some power that can enforce it? Patricia Derian once expressed the view that because "human rights is international law...there can be no other course for the U.S. Government but to apply and enforce that law."[15] But the United States has no authority, under the law, to act as the enforcer; indeed the effort to play enforcer might itself run afoul of other parts of international law, as witness the questions raised in connection with U.S. actions in Grenada. Nor has the United States, in an age when tyrants are armed with nuclear weapons, the power to enforce the law, except in isolated instances. Those who seek in international law the enforcement of human rights may have in mind a transformation of international law into something more supranational. As a prominent exponent of that approach, John Humphrey, has put it: "what has traditionally been known as international law should now be called world law."[16] But the advent of some kind of new "world law" that will force governments to respect human rights not only seems exceeding remote, its desirability has been cogently challenged by J.S. Watson. Watson writes:

> Unless we are talking about a revolution of the human spirit, the proposed system of regulating conduct will have to be by external means. This would mean that the only substitute for the horizontal international order is a vertical order, a super state of some kind...Precisely why this super state, however administered, will be free from the ills of the present smaller states is nowhere clarified. This centralized world government would have to be achieved either by a great political force the like of which has been, thankfully, unknown up to now, or else by means of a spiritual awakening. Needless to say, a spiritual revolution of the degree necessary to overthrow the nation-state would make law largely redundant.[17]

In short, international law offers no short cut to making abusive governments mend their ways. Its usefulness lies in whatever moral weight it can add to a broader political or ideological struggle to make those governments change or give way to better ones. But the very terms in which the Carter administration invoked international law served to make that struggle more difficult.

The administration was right in sensing that any U.S. human rights policy needs to confront the accusation of ethnocentrism. It must try to show that its objectives are values of universal validity. Carter's approach to this task was to adduce international law as evidence of an "international consensus," in other words to argue that human rights principles have already been universally accepted. But this is manifestly false, and everyone knows it to be false. The signatures of various states on UN human rights treaties are not proof of universal acceptance of those principles. Those treaties are not merely violated in practice, they are also explicitly contradicted in the pronouncements, the laws and even in the constitutions of signatory states. In this context, to speak of an "international consensus" is to gloss over both the profound hostility to human rights of many governments and their cynicism toward international treaties.

There is a firmer ground on which to answer the charge of ethnocentrism. It is to assert that human rights reside in the dignity of man. In the American tradition, this conception of the nature of man is consecrated in our most sacred documents, to wit, the declaration that "all men are created equal and are endowed by their creator with certain unalienable rights." We believe that these rights are each man's due by virtue of his membership in the species, whether he is an American or a Pole or a Tibetan or a Namibian. And we believe it irrespective of whether he believes it or whether it is acknowledged by his government or by the ancestral wisdom of his culture. Ultimately this is the only logically tenable foundation on which a U.S. human rights policy can be based.

If it is our purpose to impel or induce other governments to respect the human rights of their subjects, then we must face the fact that we are trying to get them to obey principles *in which most of them do not presently believe*; in short, that we are trying to impose, or at least to impart, "Western" ideas.

Such "cultural imperialism" alarms many, including many who are eager to spread to non-Western cultures such Western inventions as industrialization and other things that go under the name "modernization." It alarmed the Carter administration, whose deepest impulse in foreign policy was to lead the United States to a graceful acceptance of diminished influence in world affairs, or, as Carter put it, to "a more mature perspective....which recognizes the fact that we alone do not have all the answers." Perhaps it is wrong to seek to transplant Western ideas to cultures where they have not spontaneously taken root. But those who believe it is wrong cannot also believe in pursuing a human rights policy. It was probably this quandary that led the Carter administration to invoke an imaginary "international consensus" on human rights.

Though human rights policy consists of promoting Western ideas, these are not "parochial American" ideas. The American founders were important contributors to the development of human rights thinking, and the American experiment has given the idea of human rights its most powerful vindication, but the idea is not an American one. It was born, in its modern form, before the American republic, in the thinking of French and English Enlightenment philosophers. The notion of human dignity that underlies this tradition also has important medieval, classical and biblical roots.

Moreover, the goal of U.S. human rights policy is surely not to have others copy American institutions. A written constitution, a written bill of rights, federalism, the separation of powers, bi-cameralism, the two party system, the separation of church and state, and many other hallmarks of the "American system," are strictly optional from the point of view of human rights policy. Other successful democracies flourish without these institutions. Things that are *not* optional, that human rights policy aims to see adopted universally, are such principles as rule of law, rule by the consent of the governed, due process of law, and freedom of conscience and of expression and of emigration.

Even if these are "Western" ideas, what is wrong with trying to foist them on others? It may be empirically true that democracy has had difficulty taking root in Third World countries. But that does not make it wrong to try to transplant democracy to them. Is it possible to "force" people to be free? Is it wrong to do so? Although it has often been said that freedom can be frightening, there is no concrete example in which a free people has voluntarily relinquished its freedom. Where people have lost their freedom it has always been because others—whether compatriots or foreigners— have taken it away.

Although the task of fostering observance of human rights in non-Western cultures may be difficult, the argument against "imposing" human rights on others is logically untenable. If people have rights "imposed" on them that they would rather not have, they need only abstain from exercising those rights. No force on Earth can stop a person from subordinating himself to another, if that is his wish. Therefore, it is meaningless to speak of imposing human rights on unwilling people. The only possible "victims" of the "imposition" of human rights are dictatorial rulers whose subjects will gain the chance to choose whether or not they wish to continue to be so ruled.

The conviction that all people are entitled to that choice is the bedrock on which U.S. human rights policy must rest, not on the appeal to hypocritical signatures on UN treaties.

ECONOMIC AND SOCIAL RIGHTS

In his memoirs, Jimmy Carter confesses that "at first we were inclined to define human rights too narrowly," but he came to realize, he says, that "the right of people to a job, food, shelter, medical care, and education could not be ignored."[18] It is true that in Carter's inaugural address, where the human rights program was launched, and in the administration's early pronouncements, the rights of which it spoke were limited to the traditional Anglo-American conception of "rights."[19] But within its first hundred days the administration had decided that it would depart from that tradition and include "economic and social rights" in its working definition of human rights.

This was announced in Secretary Vance's Law Day speech of April 30, 1977, which set the guidelines for the administration's policy. Vance began by stating that he wished to "define what we mean by 'human rights.'" He listed three categories of rights. First came "the right to be free from governmental violation of the integrity of the person." Last came "the right to enjoy civil and political liberties." In between was "the right to the fulfillment of such vital needs as food, shelter, health care, and education."[20] Thus, not only were economic and social rights on the list, but they were listed ahead of the category that embraced the traditional American conception of human rights. The administration was ambiguous about whether the order of listing was intended to suggest an order of priority, but from then on this order was kept intact in almost all administration pronouncements. Deputy Assistant Secretary Mark Schneider says that when in a speech he varied the order, listing civil and political rights ahead of economic and social rights, he was told by superiors that they would prefer him to retain the order used in Vance's speech.[21]

There was probably more than a single reason behind the administration's decision to give this emphasis to a concept of "rights" that stands somewhat outside the American tradition. For some in the administration this step was merely tactical, a way of accommodating to sentiment in the Third World. As Carter speechwriter, Hendrik Hertzberg, described it:

> ...I think the main motivation behind it was a desire to get the Third World to buy a package, [as if] this was the toy inside the Cracker Jack box. [It] was supposed to pull them into the idea of human rights...and then they would find that there was this package that involved freedom of speech and stuff like that.[22]

Others in the administration seemed sincerely to share the Third World view. Patricia Derian said that "the dichotomy...between civil and political rights on the one hand, and economic and social rights on the other, is much overrated."[23] UN Ambassador Andrew Young took the view that the two kinds of rights are "inseparable."[24] And Jessica Tuchman, the human rights specialist of the National Security Council, was quoted as saying: "In much of the world the chief human right that people recognize is 800 Calories a day. We're beginning to recognize that fact."[25]

Sandra Vogelgesang, who served at the time on the State Department's Policy Planning Staff, says that the "emphasis on economic and social rights may have emerged more by accident than design. It was a belated addition to the draft text."[26] But whether it began by accident or design, the embrace of the category, "economic and social" rights, became a salient feature of the Carter human rights program. It came to serve both some of the administration's more "progressive" as well as some of its more conservative impulses. In the former category was the administration's craving to be more attuned to the Third World. In Andrew Young's approach to the UN, which administration spokesmen contrasted with the approach of Daniel Moynihan under the preceding administration, in its identification with the "frontline states" in southern Africa, and in other ways, the administration sought, by embracing at least in part the views of the Third World, to redeem Jimmy Carter's campaign pledge to improve America's standing in international forums. Embracing the concept, "economic and social rights," was an act of humility, a way of demonstrating America's willingness to defer to the ideas of others when they conflicted with our own. As one State Department publication explained: "First popularized by socialist thinkers, these [economic and social rights] eventually won universal acceptance."[27]

The same attitude was reflected in the way the administration chose to define economic and social rights. Warren Christopher explained to a congressional committee that the second category listed in Vance's Law Day speech "includes the various economic freedoms."[28] This perhaps infelicitous phrase served only to point up the irony that what was missing from the administration's formulation of economic rights was precisely those economic freedoms honored in the American human rights tradition: the right to own property, the right to engage in commerce, the right to bargain collectively, the right to shop wherever one can afford, all of which happen also to be rights to which the main proponents of "economic rights" on the international stage are indifferent or hostile.[29]

The term "social" in the phrase "economic and social

rights" seems never to have been defined or to have contained any precise meaning at all, but the American tradition also honors various rights that might well fit under that term: the right to choose a mate of one's choice at the time of one's choice and to determine the size of one's own family; the right not only to worship freely but also to build places of worship and other religious institutions and to educate one's children in one's chosen faith; the right to travel within and outside one's country and to choose one's place of residence. All of these rights are widely denied in the world, yet they were rarely, if ever, incorporated in the administration's discussions of economic and social rights.

National Security Adviser Brzezinski said that the human rights issue was a means of drawing the United States closer to the developing world, but given the records of most Third World governments on such central human rights matters as free expression, due process, or popular sovereignty, this issue should have been a source more of friction than of understanding with the U.S. By embracing the idea of "economic and social rights" and by acquiescing in the meanings attached to that term by spokesmen for the Third and Communist worlds, the Carter administration was able to some extent to elide the dismal record of the the Third World in terms of other rights and to find a common tongue in which to communicate.

In this manner, the category, "economic and social rights," also served one of the State Department's most conservative instincts, "clientitus." "Clientitus" refers to the inclination, attributed especially to professional foreign service officers, of treating the foreign nations with which they work as their "clients." As William Turpin put it, a foreign office "represents other nations inside and to our government; it is concerned less with the substance than the existence of foreign relations."[30] It is easy to see that a policy, such as the human rights policy, that focuses on the faults of other governments, would bring little joy to those afflicted with "clientitus." But their pain was eased by the inclusion of "economic and social rights," which provided a vast area for finding things to approve in the "human rights" records of undemocratic governments.

Thus when Senator S.I. Hayakawa asked what justified the administration's request for aid to Mozambique "given previous Congressional prohibitions on aid to Mozambique" that were based largely on human rights grounds, Under Secretary of State Lucy Benson replied: "Mozambique's government has an excellent record in developing programs to meet the basic needs of the population for food, health care, and education."[31]

Mozambique has a left-wing government, but the same argument was applied to right-wing governments as well. Jessica Tuchman explained it this way:

> A lot of third world countries, particularly those with right-wing governments, insisted that "human rights begins at breakfast, and you cannot expect us to worry about frills like civil and political liberties until we can feed our people" and there was a lot of sensitivity to that in the State Department.[32]

A good example of what Tuchman is describing was provided by Fereydoun Hoveyda, the Shah of Iran's ambassador to the United Nations, who argued that economic and social rights are the "most urgent" ones "because without carrying out the basic needs of human beings, all other rights are mere illusions." Thus, wrote Hoveyda, Iran could be seen to have "a very good record" in the realm of human rights in view of the fact that its "rate of economic growth has been over 14 percent since the early 1960s."[33] The State Department's receptivity to this line of argument was reinforced by provisions within U.S. human rights legislation, notably, for example, Section 116 of the Foreign Assistance Act, that exempted from restrictions on foreign aid, based on human rights, all programs which "directly benefit the needy people."[34]

The way that the embrace of "economic and social rights" worked both to appease the Third World and to gratify the State Department's tendency toward "clientitus" was perhaps best captured in one volume of Country

Reports. Rather than say simply that the Third World was mostly run by tyrants, the department came up with this nonjudgmental formulation: "Economic rights continued to rank higher than political and civil liberties on the agenda of many countries, especially in the Third World."[35]

One argument advanced by some Carter administration officials, including Andrew Young and Mark Schneider, for embracing the concept of "economic and social rights" was that, as Young put it, "where there is poverty...there cannot be full political participation and freedom."[36] There is surely some truth in this, but it is a platitude. "Full" political participation and freedom, if one could define such a state, might well require the absence of poverty just as it would require that all citizens be well educated and fully informed. But this is a truly utopian notion whose only effect can be to cloud distinctions vital to this world and to generate excuses for the denial of freedom. Freedom and political participation were established as norms in the United States more than two centuries ago when all but a few of its citizens lived at an economic level that would today be called poverty even by international standards.

Even if these arguments in favor of recognizing the concept, "economic and social rights," are weak, is there any reason to resist adopting it? Does it do any harm? There are reasons to believe that it does. Of the many desirable things in the world, there are only a few that we call "rights." By calling something a right, rather than a goal or a desideratum, we mean that a person's entitlement to it cannot be abridged except for extraordinary reasons. We mean that government is under an obligation to respect and defend that entitlement. Economic and social rights, it can quickly be seen, do not just pertain to a different subject matter from that of civil and political rights, they are "rights" of a different character.

Louis Henkin, the noted international human rights lawyer, cites two differences. One is that economic and social rights, unlike civil and political rights, depend on available resources. The second is that the former category cannot be enforced by the same means as the latter. But he adds that "I do not think any of these differences critical."[37] Patricia Derian said that she found only "one important" difference between the two kinds of rights. "A government can immediately stop torturing or censoring. It cannot immediately assure adequate nutrition, housing, or health facilities," she said.[38] Thus in the views of both Henkin and Derian the crucial issue is one of time or "resources." If a nation lacks the wealth to fulfill every citizen's economic and social rights today, it remains obliged to fulfill them as soon as it can.

Derian and Henkin assume that we know how to assure these rights and that all that is lacking is the political will or, in some short-run cases, the readily available resources. But even in so wealthy a country as the United States, not all people—indeed, not nearly all—enjoy the full range of "economic and social rights" as defined in the UN covenants. Some argue that this is because our political system has failed to enact those far-reaching measures of social welfare that would finally bring an end to poverty. But others believe that the vast additional taxes required for such programs would stultify economic growth and thus prove self-defeating.

The existence of such disagreement about how to achieve the "economic and social rights" compels us to choose one of two views. Either we take the view that we do not know which policies will lead to the realization of these rights; or we take the view that these rights require a particular set of policies. Either position has important and troubling implications.

To the extent that we take the view that we do not know which policies will serve to achieve these rights, they convey no correlative obligation. How can anyone or any government be obligated to achieve ends the means to which are unknown? In this sense social and economic rights can be viewed as desirable things, like, say, universal longevity, and as things to be pursued, as we pursue universal longevity through encouraging the medical sciences, but they do not convey the kind of instructions to governments that civil and political rights convey about what they may and may not do. The problem with calling such goals "rights" has been pointed out by Maurice Cranston in discussing the Universal Declaration:

> To put secondary and hypothetical rights in such a list is not only illogical; it is also likely to bring the whole concept of human rights into disrepute. People may recognize—and it is not difficult to recognize—that the right to holidays with pay is neither paramount nor categorical, and then go on to suppose that none of the other rights named in the Universal Declaration is a categorical or paramount right either.[39]

The point is that calling more and more things "rights" may have the effect not of making more things obligatory, but of making nothing obligatory. In a world in which the struggle to make most governments respect any rights is still uphill, this seems an imprudent path to follow.

An argument that is often made in response to Cranston's denies that calling certain economic and social goals, "rights," will weaken the concept of rights. This argument, which usually arises, as did Cranston's, in respect to the UN treaties, holds that the two covenants express a clear and logical distinction between the two kinds of rights. Each signatory to the covenant on civil and political rights "undertakes to respect and to ensure to all individuals within its territory and subject to its jurisdiction the rights recognized in the present Covenant."[40] In contrast, it is pointed out, each signatory to the economic and social covenant only "undertakes to take steps...to the maximum of its available resources with a view to achieving progressively the full realization of the rights recognized in the present Covenant."[41] It can be seen that the two covenants convey different kinds of obligations. There is no reason, the argument goes, why one of these categories of rights should dilute the other, why people should have difficulty keeping in mind the distinction. But, ironically, the distinction was confused by Jimmy Carter himself. In signing the two covenants, President Carter declared that they "can play a similar role in the advancement and the ultimate realization of human rights in the world at large" as that played by the "Declaration of Independence and Bill of Rights [which] expressed a lofty standard of liberty and equality."[42] If President Carter could not keep clear the difference in nature between the obligations conveyed by the International Covenant on Economic, Social and Cultural Rights, and those conveyed by the U.S. Bill of Rights, then the distinction, no matter how logically sound, is sure to be lost on many other people.

These problems may to a large extent be avoided if instead of taking the view that the "economic and social rights" are only general statements of desiderata which we are not sure how to achieve, we take instead the view that they compel a specific set of policies. For example, Henkin takes the view that these rights "imply a government that is activist, intervening, and committed to economic-social planning" and that they "advance a few small, important steps" away from capitalism "toward an equality of enjoyment."[43] But this view raises other problems.

At best we may infer, with Henkin, that "economic and social rights" compel some form of democratic welfare state. Such states have gone farther than any others toward realizing these rights. But many economists and citizens of these states believe that there are limits to the welfare state beyond which the burden of taxation and government intervention in the economy may begin to choke off the very prosperity that underwrites the welfare. These limits may be reached well before all of the "economic and social rights" have been realized. But even if no such limits exist, this view raises a more profound problem. Ernst Haas has put it this way:

> Those who exercise their political and civil rights may refuse, compromise, or delay the enactment of legislation protecting the right to social security, employment, decent housing, or full health. If, on the other hand, one wishes to give priority to economic and social rights that may themselves be controversial in any given country, the state must curtail the free exercise of political and civil rights. To do otherwise would leave the door open to democratically enacted legislation impairing economic

and social rights.[44]

This points up a basic tension in the idea of rights. All rights are limitations on the authority of governments or on the choices available to governments. Perhaps the most basic right is that of self-rule. Without it, other rights have never flourished. But if it is the people who rule, then all other rights constitute limitations on their rule.

To some extent these infringements are inescapable. If democracy is to survive, such basic rights as free speech and due process must be protected even against the will of the majority. But if too many rights, and rights that are too broad, are similarly insulated against popular will, then self-rule itself will be vitiated. Welfare programs of sufficient scope to guarantee to each citizen the "economic and social rights" defined in the covenant would reverberate into almost every area of domestic policy. If all of this were put beyond the bounds of majority will, then democracy will have been significantly truncated.

We have seen that if we take the view that "economic and social rights" compel no particular policies, their effect is to weaken respect for other rights. Now we see that if we take the view that they do compel certain policies, their effect is to narrow the scope of other rights. No matter which position we take, we find that the idea of economic and social rights is to some degree the enemy of civil and political rights.

This may not be as ironic as it first sounds. It is worth recalling that the idea of "social and economic rights" was embraced by the United Nations at the behest of those states which stood to be most embarrassed by international sanctification of human rights as they were traditionally defined. As Arthur Schlesinger put it: "the Universal Declaration....included both 'civil and political rights' and 'economic, social and cultural rights,' the second category designed to please states that denied their subjects the first."[45] And we have seen earlier that in the experience of the Carter administration, the recognition of "economic and social rights" had the effect of diluting or diverting criticisms of violations of other human rights. Taken together these facts lend strength to Walter Laqueur's argument that "giving priority to economic and social rights does not reflect a different political outlook, but is usually merely an alibi for states that practice oppression at home, and whose record even in the economic and social field is any thing but brilliant."[46]

CATEGORIES AND PRIORITIES

Inclusion of the category, "economic and social rights," was not the only noteworthy feature of the definition of human rights presented in Secretary Vance's Law Day speech. The other was his decision to divide human rights into three categories. The UN covenants divided human rights into two categories, social and economic, on one side, and civil and political on the other. Vance took what in UN terms would be the single category, civil and political rights, and divided it into two.

In one category he put:

the right to be free from governmental violation of the integrity of the person. Such violations include torture; cruel, inhuman, or degrading treatment or punishment; and arbitrary arrest or imprisonment. And they include denial of fair public trial and invasion of the home.[47]

In the other category he put:

the right to enjoy civil and political liberties—freedom of thought, of religion, of assembly; freedom of speech; freedom of the press; freedom of movement both within and outside one's own country; freedom to take part in government.[48]

There were several related reasons for this division. One was pessimism about the prospects for advancing civil and political rights. As Samuel P. Huntington, who served on

Carter's National Security Council Staff, later described it:

> In the early 1960's in Latin America...the goal of the United
> States was democratic competition and free elections. By the
> mid-1970's, that goal had been lowered from the fostering of
> democratic government to attempting to induce authoritarian
> governments not to infringe too blatantly the rights of their
> citizens.[49]

This revolution of declining expectations may have been
best represented by the father of the congressional human
rights movement, Donald Fraser, who, after having left the
Congress, appeared as a witness before the subcommittee
that he had once chaired to share the accumulated wisdom
of his years as a pioneer in the human rights field. Fraser
said: "it becomes quite clear that most governments are in-
capable of fulfilling the expectations that [the UN] covenants
generate....Where I am most militant is in the core rights
or basic rights....even an authoritarian regime can introduce
due process, and it doesn't have to torture people."[50]

A second reason for the division was the desire to identify an area of human rights that would be insusceptible,
not only in legal but also in cultural terms, to the accusation
that it reflected only "parochial American values." As Jessica
Tuchman put it: "I think that the attempt was to draw a
rather small category that we felt transcended political systems and were of universal human concern."[51]

The most compelling reason, however, for separating
violations of the integrity of the person from other denials
of civil and political rights was rarely articulated, perhaps
because it is so obvious. Murder, torture, kidnapping, and
other acts of physical brutality are more horrifying than other
human rights violations.

There is no evidence that Vance's decision to divide
human rights into three categories was controversial within
the administration, but apparently a controversy did develop
about how much emphasis to give each category. Jessica
Tuchman, the senior official within the National Security
Council staff with responsibility for human rights issues,

reports that this question of emphasis became one of the most controverted issues in the formulation of "PD-30," the administration's internal guidelines for its human rights policy.[52] In his Law Day speech, Vance elided this issue. "Our policy is to promote all these rights," he said. "There may be disagreement on the priorities these rights deserve, but I believe that, with work, all of these rights can become complementary and mutually reinforcing."[53]

The order in which Vance listed the rights seemed to suggest an order of priority, but some argued that the sentence about promoting "all these rights" meant that they were of equal importance. The National Security Council staff, as well as those at the State Department of a traditionalist bent, wanted to give a strong emphasis to issues concerning the "integrity of the person." On the other side, those in the State Department's Bureau of Human Rights wanted to treat all three categories more equally. Their view, as it was described by the Congressional Research Service, was "that amelioration of the conditions of individuals is only a form of firefighting in a much broader battle for the fostering of more open and competitive political systems with judicial institutions that routinely protect the rights of individuals."[54] In her first days in office, before Vance's speech, Patricia Derian told a congressional committee: "We can't pick and choose among human rights. There is no 'top ten' of those which we must emphasize and bear down upon."[55] But a year later, after the bureaucratic dust had settled, the administration decided in favor of placing emphasis on Vance's first category.[56]

While it was those identified as belonging to the more "liberal" camp within the Carter administration who wanted more emphasis to be placed upon civil and political rights, the same position became a major theme of the Reagan administration's human rights policy and of its critique of Carter's policy. As Reagan's Assistant Secretary of State Elliott Abrams put it, "Other human rights goals such as an end to physical brutality by the police, or an end to torture, or the right to form free trade unions, can sometimes be gained for a moment without a system of free elections. But without free elections these gains are ephemeral: They can disappear as quickly as they appeared, for they come only as the gift of the rulers to the ruled."[57]

Though hanging someone by his thumbs is surely a worse offense than denying him the chance to run for office, the most reliable way to assure that people are not hung by the thumbs is to assure that they do have the chance to run for office. It might be added that our ability to know about and prevent people from being hung by the thumbs depends on the ability to discover and publicize and protest against abuses. Violations of free expression or of political rights do not chill us to the bone the way torture does, but that does not make these rights less important.

The Carter administration's emphasis on violations of the "integrity of the person" helped to create the impression that, as Jeane Kirkpatrick charged, it favored America's totalitarian enemies over our authoritarian friends.[58] The citizens of the Soviet Union and of most other Communist countries enjoy far fewer rights than do those of any of the rightist dictatorships of Latin America which bore the brunt of Carter's human rights sanctions. In all of the latter, some independent institutions—opposition parties, labor unions newspapers, magazines, universities, churches, human rights organizations—survive, albeit often under pressure and harassment. The survival of these institutions is abetted by the fact that the economy is for the most part not owned by the government, a fact which also makes it easier for individuals who are out of favor with the authorities to survive.[59]

In Communist countries, such independent institutions, except in some cases for churches, have been able to exist at best for brief moments with little more than symbolic effect. Moreover, the "space" in which the average individual can live his life free from government interference is appreciably greater under rightist dictatorships than under Communism. In Communist states, individuals' decisions about religion, place of residence, child-rearing, education, and employment are affected by or subject to political considerations to a degree that is unknown under rightist regimes since Hitler. And while other dictatorships are content if the citizen remains apolitical, Communist states use a combination of coercion and incentives to elicit affirmative assertions of loyalty and to enlist each citizen to play his role in the repression of his fellows.

Nonetheless, because they have been in power so long, because they are so thorough in their repression, because they have so many levers of repression available, and perhaps for other reasons, the Soviet government and other European Communist governments have had less resort, in the years since Stalin, to the use of widespread, naked violence than have several rightist regimes. The latter, notably several in Latin America, clinging to power with an uncertain grip, lacking well-developed institutions of control like the Communist party or the KGB, and faced with violent revolutionary opposition, have made more wanton use of murder and torture than is the current practice among ruling European Communists.[60]

At first, "left-liberals" in the activist "human rights movement" complained little about the administration's emphasis on "integrity of the person," perhaps because this led to a focus on rightist authoritarian regimes which corresponded with the movement's own priorities.[61] This changed in 1979 when, due at least in part to the pressures brought by the Carter administration, there began to be a dramatic decrease in "disappearances" in Argentina.[62] Soon American human rights activists began warning that mere decreases of this kind were of little fundamental importance. A spokesman for the Lawyers Committee for International Human Rights said that "until the Argentine Government provides information on past cases and develops effective procedures to prevent new abductions from taking place, the diminished rate of new disappearances should not be interpreted as a significant improvement."[63] A spokesman for Amnesty International stressed that despite "a lessening of the number of disappearances," there had been "no substantial change in the institutional structures that permitted the disappearances to continue."[64] And a spokesman for the Washington Office on Latin America declared that "even a drastic reduction of integrity of the person violations is fundamentally meaningless without the simultaneous introduction of some procedural guarantees for the protection of those rights."[65]

The administration's best response to these criticisms aimed at its chosen emphasis on "integrity of the person" was expressed by Mark Schneider, who, ironically, is one of those reported to have opposed this emphasis when the issue was debated within the administration. Schneider argued that:

> it is easier to move repressive regimes on violations of the integrity of the person first. Once you begin to remove that sense of fear of the use of torture, or immediately being thrown in jail without any possibility of due process, at that point it becomes more difficult, hopefully, for them to maintain the denial of [other] freedoms.[66]

Schneider's argument is a good one, and it has been strengthened since by developments in Argentina. It is plausible that the administration's successful efforts to bring about a reduction in violations of the integrity of the person was one stepping stone on the path to the restoration of Argentine democracy. But it does not answer the question of whether violations of the integrity of the person ought to be regarded as violations of a special category of rights.

Treating this as a category of rights reflects a deep pessimism about the prospects for democracy in the Third World, a pessimism born of watching one after another of the states newly emancipated from colonialism after World War II degenerate into dictatorships after having begun life as democracies. But even if democracy must be written off in the Third World for the foreseeable future, how many other rights must be written off with it? Freedom House, for example, distinguishes between "political rights" and "civil liberties." Political rights include voting and other means by which people may participate in or have control over government. Civil liberties designate the freedom of the individual to think and say and do what he wants. Political rights presuppose civil liberties—the right to vote has little meaning in the absence of free debate—but the inverse is not true. It is possible to have a significant degree of liberty short of the right to change the government. Democracy requires that those in government acquire habits of mind that induce them to relinquish power at the end of their term of office. If this is too much to expect in the non-Western world, even a dictatorship can allow some freedom of expression.

And if even this is too much to expect, it is possible to think of some other rights that deserve to be considered "core rights," because they are so manifestly just, because they affect the happiness of so many people, and because a country need not be a democracy to allow them to be exercised. Such a list might include freedom of worship, freedom to emigrate, freedom of residence within one's country, freedom to make personal decisions about marriage and family. What excuse can there be for denying these? By formulating categories and drawing distinctions the way it did, the Carter administration made it seem that these very elemental rights belonged together with free elections off at the far end of some utopian horizon.

This problem was aggravated by the administration's very mistaken decision to place rights of "integrity of the person" at the top of its tri partite list, and "civil and political rights" at the bottom, with "economic and social rights" coming in between. This peculiar ordering seemed intended to signal that civil and political rights warranted very low concern.

It is hard to see what is gained by creating a special category of "rights" called "integrity of the person." Once it had determined to recognize the category, "economic and social rights," the administration might have defined human rights in terms of the two categories of the UN covenants, civil and political on the one hand and economic and social on the other, and have added the caveat that obvious humanitarian considerations compelled special concern for such egregious abuses as murder and torture.

"Integrity of the person" is really not a category of rights at all, but a category of violations. There is a clear logical distinction between the degree of latitude a government allows its subjects in exercising their rights, and the degree of viciousness with which it molests those who it feels have exceeded the bounds. The idea of human rights draws vibrance from certain philosophical premises about the nature of man. The idea that viciousness is wrong entails a much narrower philosophical premise; it is easy to believe, for example, that it is wrong to be cruel to animals without believing that animals have "rights." By creating the category, "integrity of the person," and emphasizing it above all others, the Carter administration helped to weaken or obscure the very ideas that it should have endeavored to strengthen and clarify—those of the Western human rights tradition.

NOTES

1. U.S., Congress, House, Committee on International Relations, *Arms Trade in the Western Hemisphere, Hearings before the Subcommittee on Inter-American Affairs*, 95th Cong., 2nd sess., 1978, p. 170.
2. "United Nations," *Weekly Compilation of Presidential Documents*, March 21, 1977, p. 401.
3. "The State of the Union," ibid., Jan. 20, 1981, p. 2995.
4. These mechanisms pertain only to the Covenant on Civil and Political Rights. The Covenant on Economic, Social, and Cultural Rights contains, for all practical purposes, no complaint procedure at all.
5. See, for example, Louis Henkin, "Human Rights as 'Rights'," in *Human Rights*, eds., J.R. Pennock and J.W. Chapman, Nomos XXIII, Yearbook of the American Society for Political and Legal Philosophy (New York, N.Y.U. Press, 1981), p. 272f.
6. U.S. Mission to the United Nations, Press Release, Dec. 9, 1948, reprinted in *The Dynamics of World Power: A Documentary History of United States Foreign Policy 1945-1973*, gen'l ed., Arthur M. Schlesinger, Jr., Vol. 5 (New York: Chelsea House Publishers,

1973), p. 463.

7. "The State of the Union," *Weekly Compilation of Presidential Documents*, Jan. 28, 1980 pp. 177-178.

8. In the Case of Missouri v. Holland (252 U.S. 416 (1920)), the Supreme Court ruled that the authority of treaties could extend even into areas beyond the ordinary authority of Congress. Justice Holmes stated for the court: "Acts of Congress are the supreme law of the land only when made in pursuance of the Constitution, while treaties are declared to be so when made under the authority of the United States." Holmes granted that he was not prepared to spell out all of the implications of this nuance of difference, but argued that the essential point was that there were some things that the federal government could do by virtue of a treaty which otherwise the Constitution would forbid it to do. In Cook v. United States (The Mazel Tov) (288 U.S. 102 (1933)) the Supreme Court ruled that even where legislation is more recent than a conflicting treaty, the legislation shall not prevail unless it is shown that that was the explicit will of Congress. Justice Brandeis ruled: "A treaty will not be deemed to have been abrogated or modified by a later statute unless such purpose on the part of Congress has been clearly expressed."

9. U.S., Congress, Senate, *Four Treaties Partaining to Human Rights*, Message from the President of the United States, 95th Cong., 2nd sess., Feb. 23, 1978, pp. iii-xv.

10. See Advisory Opinion: Reservations to the Convention on Genocide (1951) I.C.J. Rep. 15, and the Vienna Convention on the Law of Treaties, May 23, 1969, Article 20.

11. Paul C. Szasz, "The International Legal Aspects of the Human Rights Program of the United States," *Cornell International-Law Journal*, Vol. 12, No. 2 (Summer 1979), p. 173. Szasz holds the title of Principal Officer, U.N. Office of Legal Affairs.

12. Mark Schneider, "Tenets of Official Policy on Human Rights," *Rights and Responsibilities: International, Social, and Individual Dimensions*, Proceedings of a Conference Sponsored by the Center for the Study of the American Experience, Annenberg School of Communications, Univ. of Southern California, November 1978 (New Brunswick: Transaction Books, 1980), p. 195.

13. Jimmy Carter, "Bill of Rights Day, Human Rights Day and Week, 1980," *Department of State Bulletin*, Vol. 81, No. 2047 (February 1981), p. 54.

14. U.S., Congress, House Committee on Foreign Affairs and Senate Committee on Foreign Relations, *Country Reports on Human Rights Practices for 1979*, Report submitted by the Department of State, 96th Cong. 2nd sess., Feb. 4, 1980, p. 1.
15. "Human Rights and International Law," *Department of State Bulletin*, January 1981, p. 23.
16. John P. Humphrey, "The Implementation of International Human Rights Law," *New York Law School Review*, Vol. 24, No. 1 (1978), p. 33.
17. J.S. Watson, "Legal Theory, Efficacy and Validity in the Development of Human Rights Norms in International Law," *University of Illinois Law Forum*, Vol. 1979, No. 3 (1979), pp. 539-540.
18. Jimmy Carter, *Keeping Faith* (New York: Bantam Books, 1982), p. 144.
19. See, for example, the testimony of Deputy Secretary of State Warren Christopher in U.S., Congress, Senate, Committee on Foreign Relations, *Human Rights, Hearings before the Subcommittee on Foreign Assistance*, 95th Cong., 1st sess., 1977, pp. 63-64.
20. U.S., Department of State, *American Foreign Policy Basic Documents 1977-1980*, Department of State Pub. 9330, 1983, Document 160, p. 409.
21. Interview with Mark Schneider, held in Washington, D.C., Nov. 3, 1983.
22. Interview with Hendrik Hertzberg, held in Washington D.C., Nov. 2, 1983.
23. Patricia M. Derian, "Human Rights in American Foreign Policy," *The Notre Dame Lawyer*, Vol. 55 (December 1979) p. 270.
24. Andrew Young, "The Challenge of the Economic and Social Council: Advancing the Quality of Life in All Its Aspects, *Department of State Bulletin*, May 16, 1977, p. 496.
25. "The Push for Human Rights," *Newsweek*, June 20, 1977, p. 53.
26. Sandra Vogelgesang, *American Dream; Global Nightmare* (New York: W.W. Norton, 1980), p. 184.
27. U.S., Department of State, *Human Rights and U.S. Foreign Policy*, Pub. 8959, December 1978, p. 5.
28. U.S., Congress, House, Committee on Foreign Affairs, *Foreign Assistance Legislation for FY1980-81, Part 4, Hearings before the Subcommittee on Asian and Pacific Affairs*, 96th Cong., 1st sess., 1979, p. 183.
29. Amusingly, the Reagan administration, which has dropped "economic and social rights" from its definition of human

rights, and which is more execrated by organized labor than any administration at least since Hoover's, has made a point in compiling its Country Reports of placing "greater emphasis....on the right of labor unions to organize." (*Country Reports on Human Rights Practices*, February 1983, ibid., p. 3.)

30. William Turpin, "Foreign Relations, Yes; Foreign Policy, No," *Foreign Policy* No. 8 (Fall 1972), p. 33. Also on this subject, see John Krizay, "Clientitus, Corpulence, and Cloning at State— The Symptomatology of a Sick Department," *Policy Review*, No. 4 (Spring 1978).

31. U.S., Congress, Senate, Committee on Foreign Relations, Hearings on *FY1980 International Security Assistance Authorization*, 96th Cong., 1st sess., 1979, p. 79. Mrs. Benson offered no source for this evaluation, but it is likely that she drew it from the State Department's annual "Country Reports," the 1979 edition of which declared that: "The Mozambican government has dedicated itself to meeting the basic needs of its citizens for housing, health care, food and education." (U.S., Congress, Senate Committee on Foreign Relations and House Committee on Foreign Affairs, *Report on Human Rights Practices in Countries Receiving U.S. Aid*, Report by the Department of State, 96th Cong., 1st sess., Feb. 8, 1979, p. 128.) All Marxist governments claim such dedication. Whether the Department had any empirical basis for its endorsement of Mozambique's claims is unclear, but the endorsement grew fainter in each subsequent edition of the Country Reports, with the most recent stating merely that: "Because reliable statistics are unavailable, it is difficult to gauge how successful the country has been in its efforts to promote social welfare." (U.S., Congress, Senate Committee on Foreign Relations and House Committee on Foreign Affairs, *Country Reports on Human Rights Practices*, Report Submitted by the Department of State, 98th Cong., 1st sess., February 1983, p. 221.)

32. Interview with Jessica Tuchman, held in Washington, D.C., December 29, 1983.

33. Fereydoun Hoveyda, "Not All Clocks for Human Rights Are the Same," *New York Times*, May 18, 1977, p. A25.

34. 22 USC 2151n.

35. *Country Reports on Human Rights Practices*, Feb. 2, 1981, p. 3.

36. "A New Unity and a New Hope in the Western Hemisphere: Economic Growth With Social Justice," *Department of State Bulletin*, May 30, 1977, p. 571.

37. Henkin, "International Human Rights as 'Rights'," p. 266.
38. Derian, "Human Rights in American Foreign Policy," p. 269.
39. Maurice Cranston, *What Are Human Rights* (New York: Basic Books, 1962), p. 40.
40. Part II, Article 2[1].
41. Part II, Article 2[1]. Emphasis added.
42. "United Nations," *Weekly Compilation of Presidential Documents*, Oct. 10, 1977, p. 1489.
43. Louis Henkin, "Rights: American and Human," *Columbia Law Review*, Vol. 79, No. 3 (April 1979), pp. 410, 418.
44. Ernst B. Haas, "Human Rights," in Kenneth A. Oye, Donald Rothchild and Robert J. Lieber, eds., *Eagle Entangled* (New York: Longman, 1979), p. 175.
45. Arthur Schlesinger, Jr., "Human Rights and the American Tradition," *Foreign Affairs*, Vol. 57, No. 3, p. 511.
46. Walter Laqueur, "The Issue of Human Rights," Commentary, Vol. 63, No. 5 (May 1977), p. 30.
47. U.S. Department of State, *American Foreign Policy Basic Documents 1977-1980*, p. 409.
48. Ibid.
49. Samuel P. Huntington, "Human Rights and American Power," Commentary, Vol. 72, No. 3 (September 1981), p. 40.
50. U.S., Congress, House, Committee on Foreign Affairs, *Human Rights and U.S. Foreign Policy, Hearings before the Subcommittee on International Organizations*, 96th Cong., 1st sess., 1979, p. 303.
51. Tuchman interview, ibid.
52. Ibid.
53. U.S. Department of State, *American Foreign Policy Basic Documents*, p. 409.
54. U.S., Congress, Senate, Committee on Foreign Relations, *Human Rights and U.S. Foreign Assistance*, Report prepared by the Foreign Affairs and National Defense Division, Congressional Research Service, Library of Congress, 96th Cong., 1st sess., November 1979, p. 59.
55. Senate Committee on Foreign Relations, *Human Rights*, p. 71.
56. Tuchman interview, ibid.
57. U.S., Department of State, "Promoting Free Elections," Current Policy # 433, Bureau of Public Affairs, November 1982, p. 4.
58. Jeane Kirkpatrick, "Dictatorships and Double Standards," Commentary, Vol. 68, No. 5 (November 1979), pp. 34-45.
59. There is an argument within the liberal tradition, between socialists and those who believe in free enterprise, over whether

a private economy is essential to freedom. This argument is usually framed in terms of the question of whether a free society can remain free if the economy is brought under government control. Respectable arguments can be brought on both sides of this question, but there is another aspect to the relationship between freedom and free enterprise, about which there is much less room for thoughtful disagreement. In societies which are not free but dictatorial to begin with, there is no doubt that the existence of a private economy tends to serve the interests of freedom or liberalization by acting as a counterpoise to the concentrated authority of government.

60. There are, however, some Communist regimes, notably all of those in Asia, which were engaged throughout the Carter years in widespread use of naked violence. Kirkpatrick's accusation gains force from the fact that the administration responded to these violations with little alacrity, if at all. There were various other reasons that contributed to this inaction (see Chap. 5), none of which imply a sympathy for Communism. The administration appeared no more indifferent to reports of widespread violations of the integrity of the person in China than it did to the Saudi practice of severing hands, a most literal violation of "the integrity of the person." But even if it is true that one reasonable criterion led it to deemphasize human rights in Eastern Europe, a second reasonable criterion led it to deemphasize them in Indochina, and a third led it to ignore them in the PRC, it is also true that the Carter administration had no ideological compass that would make it feel that it was straying off course when it found itself pursuing a human rights policy that downplayed the Communist world.

61. One exception was Bruce Cameron, the foreign affairs lobbyist for Americans for Democratic Action and a Co-Chairman of the Human Rights Working Group, who testified in 1977 that securing the release of political prisoners might have a "token effect," but would not change "the system of repression." (U.S., Congress, House, Committee on Appropriations, *Foreign Assistance and Related Agencies Appropriations for FY1978*, Pt. 3, 95th Cong., 1st sess., 1977, p. 335.)

62. U.S., Congress, House, Committee on Banking, Finance and Urban Affairs, *Human Rights and U.S. Policy in the Multilateral Development Banks, Hearings before the Subcommittee on International Development and Finance*, 97th Cong., 1st sess., 1981, pp 47, 75-78, 96-98 passim.

63. Ibid., p. 374.
64. Ibid., p. 338.
65. House Committee on Foreign Affairs, *Human Rights and U.S. Foreign Policy*, p. 138.
66. U.S., Congress, House, Committee on Foreign Affairs, *Foreign Assistance Legislation for FY1980-1981*, Pt. 7, 96th Cong., 1st sess., 1979, p. 19.

FIVE

The Problem of Consistency

Much of the controversy aroused by the Carter administration's human rights activities centered on the accusation that the administration responded more sharply to violations in some countries than to violations of equal or greater severity in others. These discrepancies, observed Stanley Hoffmann, "are particularly unbearable in a domain which seems to call for consistency, since moral principles are at stake."[1]

Different observers, however, complained of different inconsistencies. Some found the administration to be too soft on rightist governments. Jonathan Dimbleby of the British Broadcasting Corporation, for example, pressed the president on why he "concentrated so very much on Russia and human rights there, where you are not actually able to do very much, and haven't apparently done anything, for instance, in Iran, a country which you have very close links with and where you could presumably very much influence what in fact went on."[2] Congressman Don Fraser complained about the omission of South Korea and the Philippines from the initial list of countries for which the administration announced reductions, for human rights reasons, in military aid. "Our track record on consistency or even-handedness is off to a dubious start," said Fraser.[3]

More often, the administration was criticized for being harder on rightist governments than on leftist governments. Congressman Henry Hyde (R.-Ill.), for example, complained of a bias in the way that the administration directed U.S. representatives to cast their votes in the international financial institutions. Said Hyde:

> if we continue to direct our representatives on these multilateral governing boards to vote "no" or to abstain from supporting development loans to such countries as the Philippines, Argentina, Chile, and Korea and to vote "yes" on similar loans to Romania, Madagascar, and Yugoslavia, then whatever support these financial institutions have had—support such as my own—will vanish.

> We have been more than merely eccentric in our application of human rights standards in the IFIs; we have been hypocritical.[4]

Making the same point in a more sweeping way, Jeane Kirkpatrick wrote that "while the Carter administration was reluctant to criticize Communist states for their human-rights violations..., no similar reticence was displayed in criticizing authoritarian recipients of U.S. aid....The Carter administration made an operational (if inarticulate) distinction between authoritarianism and totalitarianism and preferred the latter."[5]

This line of criticism has been echoed, albeit less pointedly, by former officials of the Carter administration itself. In his memoirs, Zbigniew Brzezinski reveals that in mid-1978 he brought to the president his concern that "our human-rights policy was in danger of becoming one-sidedly anti-rightist," a problem Brzezinski attributed to "the way State was implementing" the policy.[6] Richard Holbrooke, who was Carter's assistant secretary of state for East Asian and Pacific Affairs, testified after leaving office that "in the name of human rights, a small but vocal group of people [within the administration] sought to carry out far-reaching changes in the world structure....their targets were almost without exception regimes of the right which happened to be anti-Soviet."[7]

Still a third group of critics complained of a bias whose vector was neither leftward nor rightward, but rather away from criticizing governments of strong or important countries and toward criticizing the weak or geopolitically unimportant. Stanley Hoffmann wrote: "The danger is not, as some have charged, that we shall hit only our 'friends,' but rather that we shall predominantly hit those expendable offenders who play no important role in the power contests."[8] Arthur Schlesinger made a similar analysis:

> Washington was fearless in denouncing human rights abuses in countries like Cambodia, Paraguay and Uganda, where the United States had negligible strategic and economic interests; a good deal less fearless toward South Korea, Saudi Arabia, Yugoslavia and most of black Africa; increasingly circumspect about the Soviet Union; totally silent about China.[9]

Jessica Tuchman, the National Security Council staff member in charge of human rights issues, agreed that the policy was plagued by inconsistency, but she saw the cause as based on bureaucratic politics rather than on bias toward one kind of country or another. She said:

> The Asian bureaus, both at State and the NSC, were skeptical, if not opposed, to the whole policy. Whereas the Latin American officers, both at State and the NSC, were very much in favor of it. That accounted for one of the policy's chief weaknesses: it was so unevenly applied. We applied it heavily in the Soviet Union, not at all in China, forcefully in Latin America, weakly in East Asia. That was its great Achilles heel, in my view.[10]

The administration's responses to these criticisms varied. When Bernard Kalb asked Patricia Derian on "Face the Nation," "Where is the consistency on human rights?", she replied:

There's a consistency in the mechanisms that are set up for decision-making and for full inquiry...think of it a little bit like the structure of the system of justice...Real human beings come in with real problems and discrete events have taken place. It's the same way in reaching decisions about steps that you will take in the countries....and we decide on a case-by-case basis.[11]

The problem with the analogy is that in the criminal justice system, the main issue is whether or not the accused is guilty, whereas in the Carter administration's human rights deliberations the accused government was already known to be "guilty" and the main issue was whether or not the United States could afford to antagonize it.

As the administration's own classified policy statement on human rights, PD-30, which was leaked to *Time*, put it: "The policy shall be applied globally, but with due consideration to the cultural, political and historical characteristics of each nation and to other fundamental U.S. interests with respect to the nation in question." This, said *Time*, with perhaps unintended humor, "displays Carter's determination to continue using U.S. economic aid, military assistance and diplomatic pressure to promote human rights in foreign countries, wherever and whenever other U.S. interests permit."[12]

National Security Advisor Brzezinski offered a more straightfoward defense than Derian's:

I'm sure you must have confronted this same issue in other walks of life...If you cannot punish all the criminals, is it fair to punish the one that you can punish? The same thing applies to the international community. If, in fact, you are in a position, without damaging your other relationships, to make progress in the case of country A but not make progress in the case of country B, should you therefore abstain from making progress in country A? I would say no.[13]

But the reason that not all criminals can be punished is that they cannot all be detected, apprehended and convicted. The main reason that not all human rights violators could be punished by the Carter administration was that it did not dare offend some governments. Pursuing Brzezinski's metaphor, it was as if known criminals repeatedly went unpunished because the judge and prosecutor refused to act against any defendant with whom they had personal business dealings. Such a situation would pose the question whether the benefit that the community would derive from the punishment of some criminals would be worth the price of accepting the rule of arbitrary and capricious authority.

Moreover, the problem in the international human rights arena was that the United States, unlike a criminal court, was acting in a strictly self-appointed capacity. By what authority, it was often asked, does the United States judge the behavior of other sovereign states? There is only one compelling answer to this question—by the authority of justice, or, if you prefer, of natural law. But the United States cannot claim to act by this authority and at the same time insist upon obeying the dictates of expediency and self-interest. Patricia Derian seemed to understand this when she told Congress that "the thing that would probably subvert our human rights initiatives more than anything is a grossly inconsistent pattern of application."[14]

Despite Derian's qualms, the administration received considerable outside support for its attitude on this issue. Jerome Shestack, president of the International League for Human Rights, argued that "we have got to recognize that in the application of foreign policy, there cannot be an entirely single standard, except perhaps in the utopian sense, and you sometimes have to act despite a double standard."[15] Abraham M. Sirkin, a former diplomat who has written a thoughtful essay on this subject, concluded: "Since each case differs, in some respects at least, from every other, an intelligent human rights policy, sensitive to the different combination of factors in each situation, requires a deliberate 'inconsistency' in its application."[16] And even Arthur Schlesinger in effect gave back with one hand what he had taken away with the other: following his trenchant description of the administration's inconsistencies he added this observation:

Of course the double standard was inherent in the situation. Not only were other nations in varying stages of maturity, but the promotion of human rights could not in any case be the supreme goal of foreign policy...A nation's fundamental interest must be self-preservation; and, when national security and the promotion of human rights came into genuine conflict, national security had to prevail.[17]

If Shestack and Sirkin and Schlesinger are right that there are sound reasons why a human rights policy must be inconsistent, it still may be asked whether these reasons account for the inconsistencies in the Carter policy.

In the discussions of the problem of consistency by those both within and without the Carter administration who have argued that inconsistency must be accepted in a human rights policy, five major reasons are mentioned most often as the ones that make inconsistency unavoidable. These five are: 1) we should have different *expectations* of different countries which take into account the unique history of each; 2) the United States has different amounts of *leverage* with different countries; 3) evaluations of the human rights performance of various governments will differ in accordance with different opinions about which kinds of human rights deserve *priority*; 4) various external and internal *conditions*, notably war or insurrection, may affect what it is reasonable to expect from a government in the realm of human rights; and 5) *other interests* of the United States may impede its ability to act on its principles with regard to specific countries. How did these five reasons affect the Carter policy?

Expectations. Abraham Sirkin points out that "one might reasonably look for free elections in Uruguay, Chile, and the Philippines, whose people have had the voting habit, before expecting them in Saudi Arabia, where the ballot box is virtually unknown."[18] The point pertains to more than just elections. Among the nations whose governments today engage in significant human rights violations there are wide variations in political histories and in other cultural traditions that have bearing on the likelihood of the emergence of democratic forms, or on the degree of tolerance of the expression of dissenting opinions, or on the readiness with which their governments or other groups will resort to the use of violence. This may affect, said Mark Schneider, Carter's deputy assistant secretary of state for Human Rights, not only what it is reasonable for the United States to expect in other countries, but what people in those countries themselves expect. "If you look at some countries that have had democratic institutions and democratic experience," he said, "within their own context they accept that as being legitimate standards that you can hold them to and press for."[19]

The idea that human rights policy should acknowledge different expectations for different countries has found echoes in the Reagan administration. In discussing Carter's human rights policy toward Iran, Reagan's assistant secretary of state for Human Rights, Elliott Abrams, said:

> There are countries which have a much stronger democratic tradition than Iran, which has essentially none. There are a number of countries, unlike Iran, which have long experience with democracy, Chile, for example. It is not sensible to believe that the only alternative to Pinochet is chaos. It may be true, but one should entertain the theory that a stable democracy is possible. It's a hard theory to believe in Iran.[20]

But easy as it is to see the logic of holding different expectations for different countries, it is not so easy to see the logic of being harsher on one country than another merely because we expect more of the first. Perhaps Saudi history and culture make it unreasonable to expect its sudden transformation into a democracy. Should we say too that the strength of Islamic custom makes it unreasonable to expect that the Saudis abandon the practice of severing the hands of thieves and of stoning fornicators? If so, can we not at least expect that they cease maintaining their country *Judenrein*? Nothing in the Islamic tradition prevents Jews from living among Moslems or at least traveling among them, as they have done since the birth of Islam. The point is that although we may expect less from some countries than from others, we can, and if we are committed to advancing the cause of human rights we will, expect *something* from each one.

It is also far from clear that differential expectations were a genuine cause of the inconsistencies in Carter's policy. If it was Chile's democratic history that motivated the administration to place the emphasis it did on Chilean human rights violations, then what would one expect about its approach to, say, the German Democratic Republic, a country whose human rights violations are considerably more severe than Chile's? Germany, after all, had known democracy from 1918 to 1933, and for decades before that it had enjoyed a degree of pluralism including multiple flourishing political parties, powerful trade unions, a free press, and a functioning, albeit not very powerful, parliament. That German culture is capable of sustaining a democratic polity has been demonstrated beyond a reasonable doubt by the Federal Republic of Germany. Yet the GDR was almost never a focus of the administration's human rights attentions.

The Library of Congress looked at the Carter policy and issued a report implying that differences among countries may have been more an excuse than a cause for inconsistency. The study's author testified that:

> To the best of my knowledge, the Department of State has acknowledged the relevance of cultural and historical factors in determining the level of human rights protections one should expect from individual countries, but has not developed any more specific bases for establishing levels of expectation. Thus, the extent to which, and the ways in which, such factors shape human rights policy emphases is impossible for an outsider to determine. Our interviews suggest, however, that there is no systematic effort to use those factors in shaping levels of expectation of human rights performance.[21]

Leverage. The Congressional Research Service also concluded from its study that Carter administration human rights officials believed that "the leverage available to the United States with respect to specific countries should be a significant factor in determining the amount of human rights attention they receive."[22] Such an approach would flow from the dictum articulated by Deputy Assistant Secretary of State Mark Schneider that the goal of the human rights policy was to "do as much as we can wherever we can."[23] The concern for leverage could explain why the human rights mechanisms developed by the Carter administration were so heavily geared to the manipulation of foreign aid. Aid, it was believed, gave the United States its best leverage for the difficult task of influencing the domestic behavior of other governments.

This focus on the manipulation of aid had much to do with giving the Carter policy what the Congressional Research Service called its "pronounced focus on governments with which the United States has friendlier relations."[24] As Carter's Deputy Assistant Secretary of State for Human Rights Stephen Cohen put it: "The primary source of the 'double standard' charge had to do with cutting off security assistance and not providing security assistance to non-Communist right-wing governments." But, says Cohen, "I am absolutely convinced that the charge of inconsistency is wrong."[25] The explanation for the error, he says, "is that only non-communist countries are eligible for military aid...the one exception being Yugoslavia..." and therefore those were the only ones that got cut off.[26]

However, several Communist countries, and others with governments hostile to the United States, receive economic aid from the United States. The pattern of the Carter administration in using this kind of aid to apply human rights sanctions casts doubt on Cohen's explanation. Most of the unfriendly governments that receive bilateral aid from the United States do so under Public Law 480, the "Food for Peace" program. The law says that this aid may not be given to countries whose governments engage in a "consistent pattern of gross violations of internationally recognized human rights" unless the aid "will directly benefit the needy people in such country," and in such cases the aid agreement between the United States and the recipient country must "specify how the projects and programs will be used to benefit the needy people."[27] In FY1980, the last full year under the Carter administration, eighty countries received aid under PL480. Of these the Department of State decided that six qualified under the law as human rights violators requiring the special language about needy people in their aid agreements. The six were Guinea, Haiti, Indonesia, Liberia, Somalia, and Zaire. Among the seventy-four for whom the Department imposed no such requirement were Syria, Nicaragua, Panama, the People's Republic of China, Kampuchea, Angola, Benin, the People's Republic of the Congo, Ethiopia, Guinea-Bissau, Mali, Mozambique, and Tanzania—all of which had Communist or leftist governments. The record was quite similar in each of the previous Carter years.

And there is additional evidence that the charges of inconsistency cannot be laid to rest as easily as Cohen wishes. He and his colleagues recognized that the perception of inconsistency was damaging to the Carter policy. The notions that "we applied a double standard" and that "we were tough only on our non-Communist friends" are two premises "that have gained wide acceptance," wrote Cohen just after the Carter administration left office.[28] If the appearance that the Carter administration picked on friendly governments was merely an unintended consequence of the fact that these governments receive most U.S. aid, then it would seem natural that the administration would have sought, wherever the aid situation allowed, to find steps that it could take to counter the perception. Instead, it often took steps that reinforced it.

When the first set of annual "Country Reports" on human rights practices was published, early in the Carter years, it evoked a variety of criticism.[29] One of the criticisms was that the reports served to focus attention, inequitably, on governments friendly to the United States. Unfriendly governments, whose ranks comprised the world's worst human rights violators, received no aid from the United States, hence were ignored by the reports. To correct this anomaly the Congress eventually amended the law to require that the reports cover all countries belonging to the United

Nations. The rationale for making membership in the UN the basis for inclusion in the reports was the Carter administration's repeated assertions that U.S. human rights policy was based on international law, primarily the UN Charter. Yet, surprisingly, the State Department opposed, in congressional testimony, amending the law to increase the number of countries covered by the reports. The Department's reason was that "extending the report to all nations with whom the United States has some form of diplomatic relations....would add to the fairly heavy time and resource burden now involved in the preparation of the current list of countries."[30]

Perhaps an even more important area in which the administration missed the opportunity to compensate for the inconsistencies toward which it was impelled by its quest for "leverage" was in casting its votes within the multilateral development banks (also often referred to as the international financial institutions). A growing share of American foreign economic aid has come to be channeled through these banks out of the high-minded goal of not using our aid as an instrument of political pressure. Every loan or grant disbursed by these banks is voted on by the respective governing board, and U.S. representatives, who receive directions from the U.S. government, sit on all of these. Both the International Financial Institutions Act of 1977 and the Foreign Assistance and Related Programs Act of 1978 contain provisions directing U.S. representatives to oppose disbursements to governments engaged in a systematic "pattern of gross violations" of human rights, and the Carter administration did so on 116 separate votes. A broader range of countries receives aid from these institutions than receives direct bilateral aid from the United States, including countries with which the United States is on bad terms or has no diplomatic relations. Thus, in this setting, the United States did have leverage against some of the abusive governments who do not receive bilateral aid. The record in these institutions, say former Carter human rights officials, provides a unique opportunity to disprove the theory that the Carter administration was tougher on friendly or rightist governments than on hostile or leftist ones. Deputy Secretary Stephen Cohen said: "If you look at the votes in the IFIs, you will find no record of [the Carter administration] going easier on Communist countries than non-Communist ones."[31] In fact, said Cohen, "to the extent you don't find consistency between our actions, in the IFIs, on Communist and non-Communist countries, you'll find we were tougher on the Communists."[32]

The record does not sustain Cohen's assertion. The country that was the most frequent target of negative votes by the United States in these banks was Argentina. Twenty-eight times during the Carter years the U.S. voted "no" or abstained on projects for Argentina. (Abstentions, like "no" votes, are otherwise quite uncommon on these boards, and there was no practical difference in the degree of censure implied by one vote as opposed to the other. In the numerous reports to Congress, for example, "no" votes and abstentions were listed together as meaning in effect the same thing.) The second most frequent targets were Uruguay and the Philippines, each of which suffered thirteen negative votes. Then came the Communist government of Laos which received nine negatives, followed by South Korea, Chile, and Paraguay, with eight each. Several other leftist governments also were on this list. The People's Democratic Republic of Yemen received seven negatives; Vietnam, six; Afghanistan, four; Ethiopia, three; the "socialist" government of Benin, two; and the "socialist" government of Guinea, one. El Salvador, Guatemala, and the Central African Empire, each of which suffered two negatives during the Carter years, round out the list.

The votes against Vietnam and Laos were cast under especially intense congressional pressure. According to the Congressional Research Service:

The House voted to prohibit international financial institutions (IFI's) from using U.S. funds to assist these countries [Cuba, Uganda, Vietnam, Cambodia, Laos, Angola, and Mozambique] because of their poor human rights records, among other considerations. After World Bank President McNamara stated that the institution would not accept U.S. funds under the restrictions specified in the House-passed measure, the Senate deleted such provisions from the bill. When a House-Senate conference was unable to resolve the issue, President Carter promised to instruct U.S. representatives to the IFI's to oppose and vote against any loans to the seven named countries during fiscal year 1978.[33]

The president's pledge did not extend to the subsequent fiscal years, but the implicit congressional threat to renew the dispute did, and this no doubt had much to do with the administration's continuing toughness on Vietnam and Laos in the IFIs. So, too, did Vietnam's continuing imperial activities in Indochina and the fact that the government of Laos was regarded as little more than a puppet of Vietnam.

The two other established Communist governments that receive support from the multilateral banks, those of Romania and Yugoslavia, experienced very different treatment from the Carter administration. In eighteen votes on aid to Romania and twenty-one to Yugoslavia, the U.S. voted "yes" every time. There may be sound geopolitical logic to this, in terms of the West's interest in encouraging polycentrism in the Communist world, but there is little human rights logic to it. The governments of Yugoslavia and especially Romania are at least as repressive as those of Argentina, South Korea, Chile and the Philippines. And the laws under which the administration was working make no provision for geopolitical considerations. The law that applies human rights criteria to America's bilateral military aid programs does provide that certain national security considerations may override human rights matters, but there is no such "loophole" in the laws about the IFIs.

The only loophole in those laws provides that the U.S. may support IFI aid to governments that violate human rights if the aid goes directly to meet "basic human needs." This criterion proved insusceptible to precise definition, but the essential idea was that the aid should be aimed at directly alleviating poverty rather than for more general development goals. Deputy Secretary Stephen Cohen argues that when the U.S. voted in the IFIs for aid to Communist countries, it was for programs falling under this "basic human needs" rubric.[34] But neither Romania nor Yugoslavia is an especially poor country, the former having as of 1980 a GNP per capita of $1,900 and the latter, $2,620.[35] And the loans and grants voted to these countries by the IFIs were often for projects labeled "industry" or "transportation" or "power."[36] It is hard to imagine that all of these could have met the criterion of serving "basic human needs" except by a definition broad enough to have encompassed many of the projects in Argentina, Chile, Korea and the Philippines on which the United States voted negatively. These countries all have lower per capita GNP than Yugoslavia, and that of the Philippines, $ 720, is not much more than one-third of Romania's.[37]

Numerous other non-Communist but leftist dictatorships, with human rights records at least as bad as that of any of the rightist governments against whom the Carter administration voted in the IFIs, received support from the banks, with the United States voting "yes" every time. These included Syria, Togo, Tanzania, Somalia, Rwanda, Mali, Panama, Madagascar, Guinea-Bissau, Burma, and Algeria. No doubt some of these outlays went for programs that addressed "basic human needs," but to the extent that items such as a $ 14 million credit to Tanzania for the development of "tourism" did so, the "needs" may not have belonged to Tanzanians.[38]

To further complicate this picture, the administration announced that, on occasion, it had voted against loans for projects that in its judgment did indeed meet the "basic human needs" criterion. Arnold Nachmanoff, deputy assistant secretary of the Treasury for Developing Nations, testified in 1978: "The United States voted 'no' on 3 loans of the international development banks for human rights reasons even though the projects would directly meet basic human needs. In each instance, the Administration's objective was to indicate to the government the seriousness with which the United States viewed continuing violations of the human rights of the citizens of that country." [39] The three countries in question were the Central African Empire, the People's Democratic Republic of Yemen (South Yemen), and Chile.

This raises many questions. The People's Democratic Republic of Yemen was (and still is) surely one of the world's most repressive governments. In search for a comparison, Freedom House noted that year that it was "as free as Kampuchea."[40] South Yemen received no bilateral aid at all from the United States, so it is possible to imagine why U.S. officials searching for some kind of leverage might have felt impelled to take the exceptional step of opposing even a "basic human needs" project. All the more so because U.S. officials may have reasoned that the loan in question, intended for an irrigation project, might only free additional resources that the government of South Yemen could put to use in its campaigns of military support for guerrilla fighters seeking to conquer neighboring North Yemen and Oman. In light of the South Yemeni government's coercive efforts at settling the Bedouins and collectivizing agriculture, it may also have been wondered whether irrigation projects would ultimately serve the basic needs of the people or of their rulers.

The Central African Empire also rated as one of the world's most repressive governments. The United States did give some bilateral aid to the empire, but the amounts were so small—less than a million dollars during the year in question, excluding the Peace Corps—as to afford very little leverage. Perhaps the absence of any other leverage impelled a vote against even a "basic human needs" project in the Central African Empire. But what about Chile? The United States possessed and had used other leverage with Chile in the form of bilateral military and economic assistance. It also had the opportunity in the banks to oppose numerous loans for projects that did not qualify as directly aimed at basic human needs. The loan in question, for a rural health project, was hardly one whose purposes lent themselves to abuse. And the human rights record of the Chilean government, while bad, was not as bad as numerous other governments for which the United States never opposed a "basic human needs" project: Guinea, Somalia, or Mozambique, for example.

If "basic human needs" projects were not sacrosanct in a case such as Chile's then the explanation that it was differential leverage that led to inconsistencies in U.S. policy loses much of its persuasiveness. The list of countries that receive some form of *bilateral* assistance from the United States includes, as has already been noted, many unfriendly, repressive governments. The reason the United States lacks leverage with these governments, so it is argued, is that the only assistance that it gives them is for programs meeting "basic human needs" and such programs are not cut for human rights purposes. But, if they are cut in some cases, why not in others?

Finally, one other question arises about the issue of exempting programs falling in the "basic human needs" category. Of the more than 120 loans on which the United States has cast negative votes in the multilateral banks, not a single one has ever been voted down! Ours has usually been a lone dissent; we have always been in the minority. Thus it has been recognized that the only purpose of the negative U.S. votes is symbolic. It is a way of making a statement of American disapproval of human rights violations in the country in question. The only direct concrete effect has been in some instances in which countries have withdrawn or postponed loan applications to avoid the embarrassment of a negative vote from the United States.

Since the negative vote of the United States almost never has the effect of actually blocking a project, what difference does it make if the project serves human needs? The law does not require the United States to vote in favor of all "basic human needs" loans, it merely *allows* favorable votes for such loans to governments with bad records. If U.S. human rights policy was suffering, as it was, from the appearance of inconsistency caused in part by variations in available "leverage," why shouldn't the United States have voted against a batch of "basic human needs" loans to governments over which it otherwise had no leverage?

Another area in which the administration might have found "leverage" over countries that were not the recipients of bilateral military or development aid from the United States was in the activities of the Export-Import Bank. In October 1977, the Congress had adopted an amendment to the Export-Import Bank Act of 1945 that required the bank's directors to "take into account...the observance of and respect for human rights in the country to receive the exports supported by a loan or financial guarantee" from the bank. A year later, the Congress had second thoughts about using the Eximbank as a vehicle for human rights policy and passed a new amendment greatly diluting the human rights provisions. Nonetheless, as of mid-1983, the bank's president reported that "Eximbank continues as a policy matter to adhere to the human rights procedures previously established."[41] These procedures, he said, include the following: "Specific clearance on human rights issues is obtained from the State Department on every transaction involving a direct loan or guarantee." By the State Department, he explained, he meant "in particular, the Bureau of Human Rights and Humanitarian Affairs."[42]

The reason why the Eximbank might have provided leverage over countries over which the United States otherwise had little is that the bank does business with almost all of the countries in the world, far more than receive aid from the United States or from the multilateral development banks. Deputy Secretary of State Christopher testified that in 1978, the year that the more stringent human rights legislation was in effect, the Eximbank operated in 169 countries. Of these the Carter administration decided to take action on human rights grounds against only four, said Christopher.[43] One of the four was South Africa, toward which there existed longstanding statutory restrictions on Eximbank programs. Of the other three, none was a country over which the United States lacked other forms of leverage. The three were Argentina, Chile, and Uruguay.

A similar situation existed with the Overseas Private

Investment Corporation (OPIC). In 1978, Congress adopted an amendment, using language similar to its 1977 Eximbank amendment, that applied human rights criteria to the activities of OPIC which consist mostly in guaranteeing U.S. investments in developing countries. Throughout the rest of the Carter years, according to OPIC President Craig Nalen, only "one formal application for OPIC assistance...was rejected by OPIC on human rights grounds subsequent to a recommendation from State." The country in question, says Nalen, was El Salvador.[44] OPIC's activities do not range over as many countries as those of the Eximbank, but the list of countries in which OPIC advertised that it had programs available in FY1980 included, for example, Afghanistan, Benin, the People's Republic of the Congo, Ethiopia, Grenada, Guinea, Malawi, Mali, Nicaragua, Panama, Romania, Rwanda, Saudi Arabia, Somalia, Syria, Tanzania, Togo, and Yugoslavia—all countries whose records of respect for human rights run from bad to appalling. The fact that programs were "available" did not mean that programs were actually in effect, but OPIC's literature encouraged American businesses to apply for assistance in investing in these countries. The list of countries in which OPIC reported programs in effect during the Carter years included Syria, Saudi Arabia, the People's Republic of the Congo, Yugoslavia, Rwanda, Panama, Guyana, Malawi, and Benin.

In sum, there is reason to doubt that the variations among countries in the amount of leverage available to the United States for bringing to bear pressures with respect to human rights matters was an important cause of the inconsistencies in the Carter administration's actions. In some situations, as with the Food for Peace program or the Eximbank, there was inconsistency of applications even where essentially the same leverage was available for a large number of countries. In other situations, as in the multilateral banks, available leverage that might have been used to redress inconsistencies was left unused.

Priorities. In the Soviet Union, decades of totalitarianism have left a society in which only a courageous few dare to dissent openly, and the repression of these few puts little strain on the vast police apparatus. In several countries in Latin America, on the other hand, governments that tolerated the existence of independent parties, churches, newpapers and labor unions also tolerated widespread assassinations by "death squads" with varying degrees of connection to police and military services. This comparison illustrates the ironic fact that an older, better established, more thorough tyranny whose population has all but given up hope for effective dissent may have less "need" to engage in eye-catching domestic violence than a newer, less repressive government struggling to impose or preserve its authority.

When the Carter administration chose to distinguish three categories of human rights and to place the emphasis of its human rights policy on the category that it labeled "integrity of the person," it was naturally led to select for special attention those countries where the most egregious violations of the integrity of the person occurred. Those countries may not have had the most repressive governments or the worst human rights violations measured by other standards. El Salvador, for example, rated an average of 3.5 during the Carter years on Freedom House's scales of political rights and civil liberties, scales on which the best possible score is 1 and the worst 7.[45] Literally scores of countries scored worse. Freedom House does not distinguish the "integrity of the person" as a separate category of human rights. By its standards there is thus little justification for the special attention that the Carter human rights policy gave to El Salvador. The same can be said for the other Latin countries that bore the brunt of the Carter policy. During the Carter years Uruguay averaged a score of 6 on the Freedom House scales. Guatemala averaged 3.75 and Chile, Argentina and Paraguay all averaged between 5 and 6. All of these scores, Guatemala's somewhat less so, bespeak serious violations of human rights. But there were many other countries that averaged in the range of 6 to 7—some even a worst possible flat 7—that seemed to receive less attention from the U.S. administration.

The apparent reason for the discrepancy was that these Latin countries were the scenes of severe violations of the "integrity of the person." In this respect at least the Carter policy could be seen as exhibiting, to use a distinction formulated by the Congressional Research Service, "consistency as policy coherence," if not "consistency as commensurate response."[46] You might not agree with a human rights policy that responded more forcefully to, say, Guatemala than to Romania, but you could understand its rationale. But, alas, the Carter administration was not consistent in this sense either.

Probably no group of countries, neither in Latin America nor in the Warsaw Pact, was a more certain target of the Carter human rights policy than the white supremacist regimes of southern Africa. In the administration's first days, its human rights policy was launched with three actions: words aimed at Czechoslovakia, words aimed at the Soviet Union, and words and a trade embargo aimed at Rhodesia.[47] The administration successfully appealed to the Congress to repeal the "Byrd Amendment" which prohibited the United States from joining in a UN-sponsored boycott of Rhodesian chrome as long as the United States continued to import chrome from the Soviet Union. A few months later Vice President Mondale was dispatched to a meeting with South African Prime Minister Vorster to whom he presented an ultimatum. "I made it clear," announced Mondale, "that without evident progress that provides full political participation and an end to discrimination, the press of international events would require us to take actions based on our policy to the detriment of the constructive relations we would prefer with South Africa."[48] And the ultimatum was reinforced with this threat: "We hope that South Africans will not rely on any illusions that the United States will, in the end, intervene to save South Africa from the policies it is pursuing, for we will not do so."[49]

Elizabeth Drew, whose portrayal of the first six months of the human rights policy has been widely praised for its accuracy, wrote that "Mondale assured South African Prime

Minister John Vorster, who raised the question...that we would be tough on the black African regimes, but one administration official says that in fact our first priority in Africa is elimination of racism, and human rights deprivations are second."[50] Drew's report was corroborated by the Congressional Research Service which reported in late 1979 that the "bad...human rights records of socialist governments of Africa were rarely mentioned" by the administration.[51]

Some members of Congress expressed displeasure with the apparent double standard toward Africa. Representative Clarence Long, urging tougher U.S. action against Uganda's Idi Amin, had this exchange with Patricia Derian:

Mr. LONG. We are very free with our criticism of Rhodesia.

Ms. DERIAN. The situation in Rhodesia is equally serious.

Mr. LONG. Equally serious with Uganda?

Ms. DERIAN. Yes. [52]

If the administration found the two situations to be "equally serious," it did not treat them equally. It moved swiftly to overcome congressional reluctance to join the UN's economic boycott of Rhodesia, but it firmly resisted congressional pressure for a boycott of Ugandan coffee.[53] Secretary Vance said that:

the administration has expressed its strong views with respect to the situation in Uganda in terms of human rights and the failure to respect the dignity of individuals. We have, however, refused to go along with a proposal that there should be an economic boycott with respect to Uganda; and we believe that a distinction should be drawn between such activities as an economic boycott, on the one hand, and the expression of our strong views.[54]

Moreover, it was, as Congressman Long's reaction implied, far from obvious that the situation in Rhodesia was as serious as the mayhem and carnage that reigned in Uganda. One administration official who tried to articulate a justification for this discrepancy was Assistant Secretary of State for International Organization Affairs Charles William Maynes. He said:

> we must also attempt to comprehend why—from a human rights perspective—South Africa poses such a special problem. There are many lessons we might have derived from World War II but one lesson we clearly did derive: That in the wake of the holocaust, never again could the world permit millions of people to be judged legally by their fellow countrymen on the basis of the color of their skin or their ethnic origin, as opposed to their individual actions or political beliefs. It is in this respect, and this respect alone, that South Africa stands apart in the world and must be judged apart.[55]

Maynes' argument is cogent in its own terms, but two questions arise about its relation to the administration's policy. One is whether the administration was consistent in assailing state-sponsored ethnic persecution wherever it was to be found. Persecution, even violent persecution, of tribal groups or of Asians is tragically common in black Africa, yet little was made of this by the Carter administration. In Mozambique, for example, Amnesty International reported that: "Certain religious groups have also been targets for government disapproval, particularly the Jehovah's Witnesses, most of whom are now believed to be detained at re-education camps...Those held at re-education camps are reportedly made to do heavy labour but are poorly fed and are subject to random brutality by camp guards."[56] Far from campaigning against these religious persecutions, the administration sought closer ties with the government of Mozambique. In his memoirs Cyrus Vance quotes his own memo to the president outlining goals for the administration: "We must continue to shore up the 'front line countries' and move toward closer relations with Angola and Mozambique."[57] It was, presumably, toward the goal of such

THE PROBLEM OF CONSISTENCY

"shoring up" that the administration joined in the Maputo Declaration describing the government of Mozambique (and that of Angola) as having extended "the frontiers of freedom" in Africa.[58]

The more important question about Maynes' formulation is whether it is at all compatible with the Carter administration's chosen emphasis on "the integrity of the person." That emphasis focuses on the frequency or severity of acts of official brutality rather than on the overall degree of freedom or justice in a system. To the extent that we want to evaluate societies, that emphasis tells us to count the number of executions or beatings or arbitrary imprisonments, rather than as, say, the Freedom House approach would suggest, to count the numbers of independent newspapers or political parties or labor unions or churches or judicial acquittals. One approach focuses on measuring the cruelty; the other on measuring the freedom.

Violations of the integrity of the person did occur in South Africa and Rhodesia, but on this score many other governments, especially several black African governments, had worse records. In 1978, the year of Maynes' speech, for example, Amnesty International reported on brutalities and killings committed by South African and Rhodesian authorities, and Amnesty reported that it had "adopted" numerous "prisoners of conscience" in each of those countries.[59] At the same time Amnesty reported that it was not able to "adopt" prisoners in Uganda "because the number of prisoners who are not murdered in detention is small and information about them difficult to obtain."[60] In Guinea that year Amnesty reported that "instead of adopting individuals, Amnesty International groups adopted two entire prisons."[61] Meanwhile in nearby Equatorial Guinea the situation, as described by Amnesty, was as follows:

Prisoners in the country are divided into three categories: "Brigade A" consists of political opponents (or suspected opponents) of the President, and although they receive no trials, they are all considered to be under sentence of death. "Brigade B" prisoners have committed no major offenses against the

President, but are considered a threat and detained indefinitely. "Brigade C" prisoners are common-law criminals, many of whom are persuaded to help the prison guards beat and maltreat the Brigade A and B prisoners.... [62]

Also during that year, the government of Ethiopia was carrying out the campaign it called "Red Revolutionary Terror." According to Amnesty:

....This policy was implemented in an extreme and arbitrary manner, especially against children of both sexes, whose ages ranged from eight to twenty. Government officials constantly justified the campaign activities as necessary "to protect the Revolution", but their claim that emphasis was on "rehabilitation" rather than "liquidation" was not borne out by the constant reports of the "liquidation" of "counter-revolutionaries" and the constant unofficial reports of widespread political killings by government officials, which often amounted to massacres.[63]

Maynes' point was that the injustice inherent in the systems of South Africa and Rhodesia was more important than any mere body count or enumeration of the barbarities perpetrated by other African regimes, more important, in short, than any number of violations of the integrity of the person. This may be right, but it is not easy to see why the principle involved should apply only to racialist systems and not to the other inherently and appallingly unjust kinds of regimes that can be found in the world.

Conditions. The Congressional Research Service reported that another of the reasons cited in interviews by Carter administration officials for the apparent inconsistencies in human rights policy was the country to country variations in the degree of authentic domestic or external threat to the stability of the regime. The clearest example of this concerned Korea. Vance wrote:

the human rights situation [was] a subject that always arose when Korea was discussed. While the situation in the south fell far short of what most of us felt was desirable, we constantly had to weigh the fact that only thirty-five miles to the north of Seoul was a nation in which control of the population was absolute and freedom nonexistent. The contrast could not be ignored, and although some critics felt that we were not vigorous enough in advocacy of human rights in South Korea, I felt that a careful balance was essential, and made sure that it was maintained.[64]

Other than Korea, however, it is not easy to find instances in which the threats facing a government influenced the Carter administration in the application of its human rights policy, especially not domestic threats.

One paltry example in which the administration attenuated its human rights policy in consideration of the domestic threats facing a regime occurred when Zbigniew Brzezinski and William Sullivan, U.S. ambassador to Iran, persuaded Cyrus Vance to overrule Assistant Secretary Derian in order to allow shipment of tear gas to the government of the Shah.[65] However, considering that the ban was only lifted during the Shah's last hopeless weeks in power, after having been in effect throughout the period of burgeoning rebellion against his regime, and that, even then, Vance's order did not apply to other crowd control devices sought by Iran, it is debatable whether this example shows how much the Carter human rights policy took into account the domestic threats that regimes confronted, or how little.

A plausible case can be made that the effect on the Carter policy of such considerations was the inverse of what the Congressional Research Service inferred from the officials it interviewed. The presence of insurrectionary forces within a country often seems to have led the Carter administration to toughen its human rights policies aimed at that country. The Latin American countries that made up the bulk of the prime targets of the Carter policy were in most cases countries where violent revolutionary movements were at work.

There are several reasons that might account for this. The first is simply that the existence of such a situation serves to focus the attention of the American public and U.S. officials on a country; more journalists are dispatched, more congressional hearings held, often more U.S. aid is proposed, and human rights problems are brought into full glare.

A second reason was the influence of the human rights movement on administration policy. The Congressional Research Service found that "external political organizations become important sources of direct reports [to the State Department's Bureau of Human Rights] that serve to focus attention on specific countries."[66] Some of these activist human rights groups are distinctly sympathetic to revolutionary movements in places like Latin America, and are therefore likely to press hardest for U.S. sanctions against governments that are resisting such movements.

A third reason why the administration may have been toughest on governments that were in jeopardy may be inferred from a comment Secretary Vance made about Africa. "Our policy toward the region of Southern Africa proceeds from the unmistakable fact that change is coming," he said. "The great question is whether peace or violence will be the instrument of change."[67] Not only in southern Africa, but wherever else it found turmoil within the reach of its influence, the Carter administration sought to resolve conflicts, and it rarely if ever seemed to believe that repression or the status quo offered a basis for solution. The solutions on which it rested its hopes invariably entailed "change." The implication was that it was often necessary to bring more, not less, pressure to bear on governments under challenge.

A final reason is suggested by the comments of Mark Schneider in response to the accusation by Carter's Assistant Secretary of State for East Asian and Pacific Affairs Richard Holbrooke, that "in the name of human rights some people in the Carter administration really sought to use American leverage to undermine governments and change regimes."[68] Holbrooke's remark apparently referred to Schneider, Derian, and some of their colleagues. Asked if the charge was valid, Schneider said:

Phrased that way, the answer is no....If you phrase it another way, that we were pressing to try and see democratic govern-ments and respect for human rights become the norm in a given country, then he's absolutely right. At times that would only occur through a change in government. But we weren't going out to change the government. If that government determined to change, then we had no qualm with whoever happened to be the individual. It was a question of whether or not they were going to respect human rights and permit democratic processes to take place.[69]

Schneider's response shows that in the eyes of Carter's human rights bureau, the prospect of the overthrow of a government that was resistant to democratic change—as, for example, Schneider said Somoza was—was something seen less as a danger than as an opportunity. In this view, such situations would call for an increase in U.S. pressure on the government in question, not a decrease.

Other Interests. All four sources of inconsistency in human rights policy discussed thus far could be classified as considerations intrinsic to the policy. They are questions about how most effectively to pursue a human rights policy. The fifth source of inconsistency is extrinsic. As long as the advancement of human rights is not the *sole* goal of American foreign policy, the possibility exists that measures that will serve this goal will disserve some other goal, and that there-fore some of these measures will have to be foregone. Since conflicts of this kind are bound to arise more often in regard to some countries than to others, they will impel a degree of inconsistency in the application of human rights policy. While, as has been shown, there is considerable room for doubt about whether the four intrinsic factors most fre-quently mentioned as sources of inconsistency in the Carter administration's policy really were significant causes, there is no room for doubt that the conflict between human rights goals and other foreign policy goals was indeed a very major source of the visible inconsistencies in the Carter policy. The Congressional Research Service reported that its interviews with Carter administration officials "suggest that the most powerful and far-reaching basis for shaping and delimiting

U.S. human rights initiatives is potential conflicts between those initiatives and other foreign policy interests."[70]

In the first weeks of the Carter administration, when Secretary Vance brought to Capitol Hill proposals for a few symbolic cuts, on human rights grounds, in the Ford administration's security assistance budget, he explained that "In each case we must balance a political concern for human rights against economic or security goals."[71] A few weeks later in his "Law Day" speech, which the adminstration thereafter treated as the definitive statement of the guidelines for its human rights policy, Vance stated that "in each instance" of applying its human rights policy the administration would ask itself several questions, including: "Have we been sensitive to genuine security interests, realizing that outbreak of armed conflict or terrorism could in itself pose a serious threat to human rights?"[72] Time and again this theme was reiterated by administration representatives, perhaps most clearly by Deputy Secretary Christopher, who said:

> ....human rights is one element of our foreign policy, but it is not the sole element. In some situations, the security considerations are sufficiently important that they alter the direction that our policy would be driven if we were concerned solely with human rights matters.[73]

The rubric "security considerations" encompassed a host of situations. The most obvious was that of authoritarian regimes in countries deemed to be of geopolitical importance that were allied to the United States. In the eyes of the Carter administration, most of these, perhaps all of them, were located in Asia. Patricia Derian recited the list:

> We must maintain our bases at Subic and Clark Airfield; we must prevent the repressive regime in North Korea from conquering South Korea; we must try to keep ASEAN alive...Indonesia is the biggest country in ASEAN...and strategically located...Pakistan must be heavily armed so that it can withstand and discourage a Soviet invasion.[74]

Derian went on to say that, in her view, all of these considerations, except for the one about Pakistan, "seem to be sound," and had to be weighed against human rights considerations, but that they deserved less weight than the Reagan administration, as well as some of her colleagues in the Carter administration, wanted to give them.[75]

Had Derian's testimony occurred before the fall of the Shah, her list certainly would also have included Iran, whose centrality to world energy politics gave it great importance in the eyes of various Carter administration officials, less so in Derian's eyes. Her deputy, Stephen Cohen, has said: "the Shah was protected from U.S. human rights policy....we [i.e., the Bureau of Human Rights] would have liked to have applied some human rights pressures to the Shah, but we lost. All during 1977 and 1978 we argued for them and we always lost the argument. Iran was too important; there were too many national security considerations."[76] Cohen exaggerates. There were *some* human rights pressures brought against the Shah, but far fewer than had the world run on coal. Ledeen and Lewis argue that the Carter human rights policy contributed to the downfall of the Shah, but they also agree that the administration pulled its punches.[77]

Policy toward the Shah was in fact a bit schizophrenic, the administration one day signaling its disapproval and the next day rushing to reassure, the latter impulse best expressed in the president's own comments on his visit to Iran:

> Iran, because of the great leadership of the Shah, is an island of stability in one of the more troubled areas of the world.

> This is a great tribute to you, Your Majesty, and to your leadership and to the respect and admiration and love which your people give you.[78]

The politics of energy also affected U.S. human rights policy toward Saudi Arabia, which, observed the Congressional Research Service, "though it would likely be considered a significant violator of human rights, is clearly of major significance to the United States."[79] The first set of

Country Reports on Human Rights produced by the Carter administration described Saudi Arabia as a "basically egalitarian and individualistic" society, and it noted delicately that "Saudis have a finely drawn sense of justice." It conceded that the Saudis practice the severing of hands, but it added reassuringly that, "This punishment is not meted out to first or second offenders but only to clear recidivists."[80]

If "security considerations" worked to attenuate the vigor with which the Carter administration pursued its human rights policy in regard to strategically placed allies or key energy suppliers, these considerations had the same effect, even perhaps a stronger one, with respect to America's adversaries. This was true because peace-making was the centerpiece of the Carter administration's security policies. Carter was very conscious of being the first post-Vietnam president. As a candidate, Carter had said that "countries don't trust us and don't respect us at this moment, because we're considered to be warlike,"[81] and he promised that his first act in office would be to pardon Vietnam era draft evaders, a promise he kept. In his first major foreign policy speech in office, President Carter said that "Vietnam [was] the best example of [the] moral and intellectual poverty" that had led the United States to fight "fire with fire, never thinking that fire is better quenched with water."[82] Peace-making, to the Carter administration, was not merely another foreign policy goal against which human rights goals had to be balanced. Patricia Derian said: "World peace is and must be the overriding human rights objective of our government."[83] Seen this way, peace-making automatically overrode all "other" human rights goals.

Arms limitation was at the center of the administration's peace-making strategy. SALT II, said Secretary Vance, was the administration's answer to the question of "how best to assure our security in an era of nuclear weapons."[84] It followed that human rights issues should not be allowed to interfere with SALT. Even Brzezinski, noted as the most anti-Soviet voice in the administration, said that we must "ask whether a given government, which grossly violates human rights...is also involved in relationships that are of importance to us....[S]hould we refuse to negotiate arms-control agreements with the Soviets because they violate the human rights of dissidents or Jewish would-be emigres?"[85] Brzezinski's answer was no, but he was arguing against a straw man. The question was not whether these issues should lead the United States to withdraw from SALT, but whether the United States should avoid making too much of these issues for fear that overly antagonizing the Soviets would lead *them* to be less cooperative in SALT. As Brzezinski himself put it, the question was, "would such relationships be adversely affected...if we pressed the human rights issue beyond some reasonable point?"[86]

The Soviet Union was the target of some of the administration's very early human rights actions, but after these events had brought a sharp public and private reaction from Soviet officials, Carter was consistently on the defensive, sometimes almost apologetic, about his human rights stance toward the Soviet Union.[87] When, for example, Carter was questioned on this subject at a July 1977 press conference, he stressed that "we are not trying to punish anyone."[88] But when he addressed the Organization of American States about human rights in Latin America, the president struck a different note. There he declared manfully:

> My government will not be deterred from...promoting human rights...in whatever ways we can. We prefer to take actions that are positive, but where nations persist in serious violations of human rights, we will continue to demonstrate that there are costs to the flagrant disregard of international standards.[89]

The Congressional Research Service observed: "the President's early comments and gestures with respect to the Soviet Union were soon displaced...by a pronounced focus on governments with whom the United States had friendlier relations."[90]

If the Carter administration pulled its human rights punches both with key allies and with adversaries, the countries that may have gotten the freest ride were those that were in a sense both allies and adversaries, i.e., Communist countries that sought under U.S. aegis to maintain their independence of Moscow. Questions about the status of human rights in the People's Republic of China, for example, were virtually never raised by the Carter administration. And when the subject was raised by others, adminstration spokesmen resorted to tortured evasions. When asked on his 1977 visit to China whether he had raised "the subject of human rights," Secretary Vance replied, "Yes, I did." But when a skeptical reporter probed further, wanting to know if "human rights [was] discussed in relation to China" or just in the abstract, Vance replied: "I don't want to get into any further detail on that."[91] Back home, a few months later, the secretary had this exchange at a news conference:

> Q. There have been political executions in China. I wonder if the United States is still concerned about the situation—the human rights situation—in mainland China.
>
> A. Yes, the United States is concerned about the human rights situation in any part of the world where there are executions. The information which we have with respect to that particular situation is limited, and that is all I can say at this point on it.[92]

Derian has testified since leaving office that her "Efforts to extend the work for human rights improvement to the Communist Government of the People's Republic of China and the right-wing Government of Taiwan were stymied time and again" within the State Department.[93]

The same treatment applied to Yugoslavia. Yugoslavia was the one Communist country over which the Carter administration possessed an abundance of its chosen form of "leverage." Yugoslavia receives both economic and military aid from the United States, receives loans from the multilateral development banks, and benefits from the activities of both OPIC and the Export-Import Bank. Yet Yugoslavia never was subjected to punitive measures in any of these areas, as were numerous other countries. South Korea and the Philippines, for example, were exempted from cuts in military aid in deference to their strategically sensitive locations, but neither was exempted from the embarrassment of negative U.S. votes in the multilateral banks. Yugoslavia, in contrast, was exempt not only from aid cuts but also from negative votes.

Yugoslavia's special treatment extended to the realm of rhetoric, as well. In its first *Country Reports*, the Carter State Department explained that in Yugoslavia "freedom of thought is generally upheld, but there are strong restrictions on the public expression of thoughts,"[94] rather a fine distinction this side of Winston Smith's Oceania. While the State Department treated Yugoslavia delicately, President Carter himself treated it sycophantishly. During President Tito's 1978 visit to the United States, President Carter, at various moments, declared him "a great and courageous leader" who "has led his people and protected their freedom almost for the last forty years," and "a man who believes in human rights" and who "as much as any other person...exemplifies...the eagerness for freedom, independence, and liberty that exists throughout Eastern Europe and indeed throughout the world."[95] Carter might have added to his list of Tito's virtues that he was no flatterer, for he reciprocated none of this rhapsody.

Another Communist country in whose independence, or partial independence, from Moscow the United States has long felt itself to have a stake is Romania. Like Yugoslavia, Romania was exempt from the punishments that the Carter administration applied to various U.S. allies. And like Yugoslavia, Romania's president came in for lavish praise when he visited the United States. Carter said of Ceaucescu:

> Our goals are the same, to have a just system of economics and politics, to let the people of the world share in growth, in peace, in personal freedom, and in the benefits to be derived from the proper utilization of natural resources.
>
> We believe in enhancing human rights. We believe that we should enhance, as independent nations, the freedom of our own people.[96]

Nor was it necessary that an Eastern European country be outside the Warsaw Pact, as is Yugoslavia, or that it pursue an independent foreign policy, as does Romania, for it to receive this kind of treatment from President Carter. In Poland, President Carter drank a toast to "the freedom of the Polish people [and] to your enlightened leaders— particularly First Secretary Gierek and his wife."[97] Earlier, Carter had observed that "our concept of human rights is preserved in Poland...much better than other European nations with which I'm familiar," and that "Poland shares with us a commitment...to have our own faults publicized evocatively at conferences like the one in Belgrade."[98] Later, the word "some" was inserted before the word "other" in the first of these remarks when the official White House Press Office transcript was released.[99] Carter's comments in Poland and while hosting Tito and Ceaucescu seemed to reflect a strong psychological need within the president, "an eagerness to please," suggests his former speechwriter, Hendrik Hertzberg.[100] They also no doubt reflected a view shared by all postwar administrations that the United States has an interest in strengthening its own ties, independent of Moscow, with the nations of Eastern Europe. And they seemed to demonstrate the impulse of Carter and his administration to be peace-makers, to bring about a reconciliation with all those nations that had been our adversaries, an impulse that was expressed in the administration's efforts to restore normal relations with Cuba, Vietnam, the People's Republic of China, Angola, and Mozambique, and in other acts.

This peace-making impulse militated against the firm application of the human rights policy to those countries with which reconciliation was sought. This factor may even have muted the administration's response to Pol Pot's reign of terror in Cambodia. Although the fact that Cambodia was in the grip of a rampage that had no equal for sheer barbarity since Hitler's holocaust was common knowledge for a year or two before Carter took office, he himself did not remark on it until April of 1978. When, in December of 1977 Patricia Derian was asked why the administration wasn't "speaking out more" about Cambodia, she replied: "I'm not sure what you can say beyond saying that it's awful, that people are dying, that there is serious trouble there."[101] When thinking about El Salvador, on the other hand, she did think of something more to say. "No description of hell touches the bestiality of what is happening to the people of El Salvador," she said.[102] Sandra Vogelgesang, who was in charge of human rights issues in the State Department's Policy Planning Staff during the early part of the Carter administration, offers a different explanation of why more was not said about Cambodia. "Many officials inside the executive branch and the Congress believed that speaking out too strongly would jeopardize prospects for future contacts with the Cambodia government," wrote Vogelgesang.[103]

While making peace with our adversaries, preserving alliances with certain friends, and staying on the good side of petroleum exporters were the major "other interests" that conflicted with Carter's human rights policy, there were several minor ones. For example the administration made much of the fact that, thanks to Andrew Young, as Vance said, "the U.S. is beginning to establish relations with the Africans where they believe we really do care about their future." This, he said, "is going to be very important to us in the future."[104] Apparently for this reason the administration said rather little about human rights in black Africa despite the fact that the governments of that region have, on the average, probably worse records for respecting human rights than those of any other region.

Though the administration came to acknowledge and defend inconsistency as inevitable and necessary in human rights policy, it apparently could not abide the embarrassment of inconsistencies that it thought were especially obvious. The results were expressed by the Congressional Research Service after conducting confidential interviews with human rights officials this way:

> restraint with respect to [human rights] initiatives must also be shown when a country is a logical parallel or analogue to one that has been exempted for other reasons. Thus, for

example, cultures and regimes of North Korea and Vietnam bear many resemblances to those of the People's Republic of China, so to publicly raise human rights issues with respect to those countries would open the administration to highly plausible charges that it was being inconsistent in not calling attention to comparable violations in the People's Republic of China. Similarly, extensive public comment on Eastern European Communist countries would open the administration to arguments that it should be further emphasizing human rights violations in the Soviet Union. This line of argument has apparently been applied equally successfully to Arab states other than Egypt with the result that they too have been exempt for the most part from human rights pressures.[105]

This shows that, despite its protestations to the contrary, the administration knew that inconsistency could seriously compromise its human rights policy. But it seemed more concerned with imagery than substance. Thus, in the hope of avoiding the *appearance* of inconsistency the administration introduced a new source of inconsistency. Now, not only did one group of countries receive special treatment in terms of human rights policy because of some other interest which the United States wished to pursue with them, but a second group also received special treatment merely because they resembled countries in the first group.

In sum, of the five reason for inconsistency that are most often cited in discussions of human rights policy, the one whose effect was by far the most powerful on the Carter administration was the conflict between human rights and its other foreign policy goals. The reality of what did or did not contribute to the inconsistency was masked by what the administration called its "case-by-case" or "country-by-country" approach,[106] and by the fact that not only security concerns but a wide variety of other foreign policy interests clashed with the human rights policy.

Stanley Hoffmann observed that "a case-by-case approach tends to give precedence in almost every instance to a conflicting concern, a more urgent interest or a special circumstance."[107] Perhaps in "almost every instance," but not in every one. The practical consequence of the administration's country-by-country approach was that the countries of Latin America became the principal targets, outside of southern Africa, of the Carter human rights policy. As Lars Schoultz has put it:

> Once the Carter administration recognized that a universal, absolute standard of human rights would conflict with other foreign policy values to an intolerable extent—once the administration adopted a case-by-case approach to human rights abuses—attention shifted to the nations of Latin America. By the end of 1977, it was clear that the United States' efforts to protect human rights were to be concentrated upon Latin America's repressive governments.[108]

Because we were trying to make new friends in black Africa, because we needed oil from the nations of the Near East, because we wanted detente with the Russians and the rest of the Warsaw Pact and also to encourage polycentrism within it, and because in Asia we were trying to build new relationships with some Communist governments while continuing to protect non-Communist countries against possible Communist aggression, practically the only place left to which the Carter administration felt it could apply its human rights policy was Latin America.

It inevitably seemed that it was the weakness of the Latin countries and the friendliness of their governments toward the United States that led the U.S. government to single them out for punishment. More than one observer was reminded of the traditional Yanqui propensity for bossing southern neighbors. This awkward situation was not unavoidable. It came about as the result of the conflict between the Carter administration's human rights policy and its other chosen foreign policy goals. But the United States has, or ought to have, other goals with respect to Latin America, too. Why should it be more important to make new friends in Africa than to keep old ones in Latin America? Of course being friendly toward a dictatorial government is not necessarily the same as being friendly toward the people over whom it rules, but this is not more true on one continent than on another. The question of where to draw the line, of which other interests to subordinate to human rights goals and which to superordinate was a matter of judgment. The judgments that the Carter administration made, often in a rather ad hoc way, sapped the moral authority of its policy.

To point to the errors of the Carter policy is not, however, to answer the more general question—is there something inherently wrong with inconsistency in a human rights policy? This question, it should be stressed, has to do with standards, not necessarily with performance. As long as human beings are fallible, it may be impossible to achieve perfect consistency any more than perfect objectivity. Our legal system, however, works on the premise of the objectivity of judges and juries. We know that human frailty will cause a certain derogation from perfect objectivity in our courts, but objectivity remains the goal and the standard by which we measure the performances of judges and jurors. Analogously, the issue here is not whether it is possible to achieve perfect consistency, but whether this ought to be the goal.

A human rights policy that does not set itself the goal of consistency is on a slippery slope, as the Carter experience illustrated. Perhaps a few exceptions are unavoidable: perhaps China must be exempted from human rights pressure because of its strategic importance, or Saudi Arabia because of its oil, or the USSR because of SALT, or South Korea because of North Korea, but where does this end? To abjure the goal of consistency is to invite the fate of the Carter human rights policy in which the big majority of countries were for one reason or another exempted and only a select few ended up bearing the full brunt of the policy.

Of course no policy will achieve perfect consistency, but a policy that fails to strive for consistency is likely to yield to capricious inconsistency. It will be endlessly susceptible to the temptations of political expedience, to the distorting influence of outside pressure groups, and to the wrath or blackmail of recalcitrant governments. The Congressional

Research Service found that during the Carter years, "the level of public interest seems to have played a significant role in determining that some countries would receive disproportionate attention. The initiatives of interest groups concerned with conditions in specific countries or regions have stimulated government action."[109] Some of these groups had approaches to "human rights" that were so tortured that they could find little to criticize in Communist countries. Why were they so influential? Part of the reason was that the Carter administration was open to the Left; but part of it, too, was that a policy that is not steered by the goal of consistency and goes instead by a case-by-case approach will always be hard put to resist whatever political pressures are applied to it.

Another one of the pitfalls of inconsistency is exemplified in President Carter's memoirs. He writes:

> Since I had made our nation's commitment to human rights a central tenet of our foreign policy, it was impossible for me to ignore the very serious problems on the West Bank [and the] continued deprivation of Palestinian rights....In my opinion it was imperative that the United States work to obtain for these people the right to vote, the right to assemble and debate issues that affected their lives, the right to own property without fear of its being confiscated, and the right to be free of military rule....I had promised to do my best to seek resolution of problems like these, *no matter where they might be found.*[110]

Despite his last pietistic phrase, Carter did not work to secure the right to vote or to assemble and debate issues for the people of Algeria, Bahrain, Egypt, Iraq, Jordan, Kuwait, Libya, Morocco, Oman, Qatar, the Sudan, Syria, Tunisia, the United Arab Emirates, Yemen, and especially not Saudi Arabia, just to mention Arab peoples, although obviously the same could be said for scores of other nations. Nor did Carter, or anyone working under him, ever breathe a word about the right to own property to Deng Xiao Ping or Gierek or Tito or Ceaucescu or to any other official of any Communist country.

Moreover, it is likely that the human rights of the Arabs of the West Bank will be better protected under Israeli rule than under rule by Jordan or the PLO. The only Arabs in the world, other than those who have emigrated abroad, who enjoy the right to vote and to assemble and debate issues are Israeli Arabs. Israeli rule would be especially preferable in terms of the category of human rights chosen for emphasis by the Carter administration, those involving the integrity of the person. Israel, for example, has no death penalty, while the PLO, which would become the rulers of the West Bank state that Carter wished to create, routinely executes those who offend it, not to mention the sanguinary fashion in which it resolves its own leadership contests.

None of this is to deny that the West Bank Arabs give every indication that they yearn to be free of Israeli rule, nor even to argue that they ought not to be granted their wish. It is, however, to deny that self-determination is likely to lead to enhancement of the protection of the human rights of the West Bank Arabs, and especially to deny that it was considerations of human rights that brought Carter to this issue or shaped his views on it. The reason that Carter was concerned about the West Bank Arabs was that he was convinced that they were the key to peace in the region, surely a worthy concern. Another reason is that their case was pled to him by Saudi Arabia and other suppliers of petroleum, an important if less-elevated consideration. The reason that he introduced the rhetoric of human rights into this discussion was probably that he felt the need to marshall strong and morally compelling arguments to counter the political and polemical strength of pro-Israeli sentiment. This kind of exploitation of the cause of human rights, which cheapens and ultimately weakens it, is made possible by the absence of the standard of consistency.

These are some of the many pitfalls of inconsistency, but there is a still more profound reason why consistency is important in human rights policy. The struggle for human rights is a struggle for the hearts and minds of people, to use an abused phrase. The extent to which human rights will be protected in the world depends more than anything else on the extent to which people believe in the idea of human rights: on the numbers of people who believe in it; on the strength of their belief; on their willingness to take risks and make sacrifices to secure rights for themselves and their willingness to discipline themselves not to impede the rights of others. The idea of human rights is in essence the idea that relations among people ought to be governed by principle rather than unbridled self-interest.

The triumph of human rights in a society entails the concordance among its members to live by certain rules. This concordance needn't be unanimous, but it must embrace a majority large enough to restrain those who wish not to live by the rules. It entails convincing people not only that the rule of principle is desirable, but also that it is possible—that my self-restraint will be matched by the self-restraint of others and not merely lead to my exploitation.

The advocate of the rule of principle, to be persuasive, must be regarded as principled himself. It is logically true that the force of an argument has nothing to do with the sincerity of the speaker, but it is not psychologically true. All the more so on issues of ethical behavior, such as human rights. U.S. human rights policy, to be effective, must be seen as a principled policy. If it is not consistent it is more likely to seem hypocritical.

It must be recalled that the world has much experience with hypocritical human rights advocacy. Indeed it has more experience with that than with the principled kind. This experience comes not only from Communist governments and other dictators, real and aspiring, but even from the august halls of the United Nations. When he was U.S. ambassador to the UN, Daniel P. Moynihan said in one speech:

> the selective morality of the United Nations in matters of human rights threatens the integrity not merely of the United Nations, but of human rights themselves. There is no mystery in this matter. Unless standards of human rights are seen to be applied uniformly and neutrally to all nations, regardless of the nature of their regimes or the size of their armaments, unless this

is done, it will quickly be seen that it is not human rights at all which are invoked when selective applications are called for, but simply arbitrary political standards dressed up in the guise of human rights. From this perception it is no great distance to the conclusion that in truth there are no human rights recognized by the international community.[111]

It is of course logically possible that the inconsistencies in the human rights actions of the UN flow from sheer hypocrisy, while the inconsistencies in those of the United States flow from something else, but how many people are likely to believe that? And will they be wrong not to? We have seen that the main source of inconsistency in U.S. policy is conflict with other U.S. interests. Is it hypocrisy for others to put what they see as their interests ahead of human rights, but not hypocrisy for us when we do so? A human rights policy that does not accept the principle of consistency may achieve some marginal benefits, but it will contribute little in the long run to advancing the idea of human rights.

NOTES

1. Stanley Hoffman, "A View from at Home: The Perils of Incoherence," *Foreign Affairs*, Vol. 57, No. 3, p. 476.
2. "Interview with Foreign Broadcast Correspondents," *Weekly Compilation of Presidential Documents*, May 9, 1977, p. 634.
3. Donald M. Fraser, "Human Rights and United States Foreign Policy—The Congressional Perspective," in *International Human Rights Law and Practice*, ed., James C. Tuttle, rev. ed. (Philadelphia: International Printing Co., 1978), pp. 174-175.
4. U.S., Congress, Senate, Committee on Foreign Relations, *Nomination of Ernest W. Lefever*, 97th Cong., 1st sess., 1981, p. 188.
5. "Human Rights and American Foreign Policy: A Symposium," *Commentary*, Vol. 72, No. 5 (November 1981), pp. 43-44.
6. Zbigniew Brzezinski, *Power and Principle* (New York: Farrar, Straus, Giroux, 1983), p. 128.
7. U.S., Congress, House, Committee on Foreign Affairs, *Reconciling Human Rights and U.S. Security Interests in Asia*,

Hearings before the Subcommittees on Asian and Pacific Affairs and on Human Rights and International Organizations, 97th Cong., 2nd sess. (1982), p. 9.

8. Hoffman, "The Perils of Incoherence," p. 479.
9. Arthur Schlesinger, Jr., "Human Rights and the American Tradition," *Foreign Affairs*, Vol. 57, No. 3, p. 515.
10. Interview with Jessica Tuchman held in Washington, D.C., Dec. 29, 1983.
11. CBS, "Face the Nation," Dec. 25, 1977.
12. "A Crusade That Isn't Going to Die," *Time*, Feb. 27, 1978, p. 22.
13. "What's Right with our Foreign Policy?", *U.S. News and World Report*, Feb. 13, 1978, p. 32.
14. U.S., Congress, House, Committee on Appropriations, *Foreign Assistance and Related Agencies Appropriations for FY1978, Part 3*, 95th Cong., 1st sess., p. 353.
15. Ibid., p. 354.
16. Abraham M. Sirkin, "Can a Human Rights Policy Be Consistent?", in *Human Rights and U.S. Foreign Policy*, eds., Peter G. Brown and Douglas MacLean (Lexington, Mass: Heath, 1979), p. 209.
17. Schlesinger, "Human Rights and the American Tradition," p. 519.
18. Sirkin, "Can a Human Rights Policy Be Consistent?", p. 206.
19. U.S., Congress, House, Committee on Banking, Finance and Urban Affairs, *U.S. Participation in Multilateral Development Institutions, Hearings before the Subcommittee on International Development Institutions and Finance*, 95th Cong., 2nd sess., 1978, p. 330.
20. Interview with Elliott Abrams held at Department of State, Sept. 30, 1983.
21. U.S., Congress, House, Committee on Foreign Affairs, *Human Rights and U.S. Foreign Policy, Hearings before Subcommittee on International Organizations*, 96th Cong., 1st sess., 1979, p. 357.
22. U.S., Congress, Senate, Committee on Foreign Relations, *Human Rights and U.S. Foreign Assistance: Experiences and Issues in Policy Implementation (1977-1978)*, Report by the Foreign Affairs and National Defense Division, C.R.S., Library of Congress, November 1979, p. 4.
23. Interview with Mark Schneider held in Washington, D.C., July 21, 1983.
24. Senate Committee on Foreign Relations, *Human Rights and U.S.*

Foreign Assistance, p. 52.

25. Interview with Stephen Cohen held in Washington, D.C., November 14, 1983.

26. Stephen Cohen, "Wrong on Human Rights," *The New Republic,* March 28, 1981, p. 13.

27. *Agricultural Trade and Development Assistance Act of 1954, as amended,* (Public Law 480), Sec. 112(a), (7 USC 1712).

28. Cohen, "Wrong on Human Rights," p. 13.

29. See, for example, *Christian Science Monitor,* Feb. 13, 1978, p. 28, col. 1; *New York Times,* Feb. 19, 1978, p. 4, col. 1; *Atlanta Constitution,* Feb. 23, 1978, p. 5, col. 1.

30. U.S., Congress, House, Committee on Foreign Affairs, *Foreign Assistance Legislation for FY1980-1981,* Part 7, 96th Cong., 1st sess., 1979, p. 160.

31. Cohen interview, Nov. 14, 1983.

32. Ibid.

33. Senate Committee on Foreign Relations, *Human Rights and U.S. Foreign Assistance,* pp. 106-107.

34. Cohen interview, Nov. 14, 1983.

35. Roger D. Hansen and contributors, *U.S. Foreign Policy and the Third World: Agenda 1982* (New York: Praeger, 1982), p. 166.

36. National Advisory Council on International Monetary and Fiscal Policies, *International Finance,* Annual Report to the President and to the Congress for Fiscal Year 1978, pp. 351-354; and identically titled volumes: for FY1979, p. 326; for FY1980, p. 341; for FY1981, pp. 361-363.

37. Hansen, et al, *U.S. Foreign Policy,* p. 162.

38. National Advisory Council, *International Finance,* FY1979, p. 333.

39. House Committee on Banking, *U.S. Participation in Multilateral Development Institutions,* pp. 324-325.

40. Raymond D. Gastil, *Freedom in the World: Political Rights and Civil Liberties 1978* (G.K. Hall & Co.: Boston, 1978). p. 323.

41. William H. Draper III, President, Export-Import Bank of the United States, to Congressman Martin O. Sabo, June 15, 1983, Files of Congressman Sabo.

42. Ibid.

43. House Committee on Foreign Affairs, *Human Rights and U.S. Foreign Policy,* p. 321.

44. Craig A. Nalen to Congressman Martin O. Sabo, June 15, 1983, Files of Congressman Sabo.

45. Gastil, *Freedom in the World: 1982,* p. 41.

46. Senate Committee on Foreign Relations, *Human Rights and U.S.*

Foreign Assistance, p. 3.
47. *Washington Post*, Jan. 27, 1977, p. 2; *New York Times*, Feb. 1, 1977, p. 1.
48. "Vice President Mondale Visits Europe and Meets With South African Prime Minister Vorster," *Department of State Bulletin*, June 20, 1977, p. 662.
49. Ibid. p. 663. The most sensible meaning of this threat was an implicit green light to the Soviet Union to intervene militarily in a future South African civil war, for what other imaginable danger is there about which South Africans might have illusions of American salvation?
50. Elizabeth Drew, "A Reporter at Large: Human Rights," *The New Yorker*, July 18, 1977, p. 58.
51. Senate Committee on Foreign Relations, *Human Rights and U.S. Foreign Assistance*, p. 3.
52. U.S., Congress, House, Committee on Appropriations, *Foreign Assistance cnd Related Agencies Appropriations for FY1979, Part 2*, 95th Cong., 2nd sess., 1978, p. 449.
53. For a detailed account of the wrangle between Congress and the Executive over the issue of a boycott of Uganda, see Ralph D. Nurnberger, "The United States and Idi Amin: Congress to the Rescue," *African Studies Review*, Vol. XXV, No. 1, pp. 49-65.
54. "The Secretary: U.S. Relations with Africa," *Department of State Bulletin*, August 1978, p. 14.
55. "United Nations: What's Wrong With the UN and What's Right?", ‹Department of State Bulletin›, Jan., 1979, p. 48.
56. *Amnesty International Report 1978* (London: Amnesty International Publications, 1979), p. 61.
57. Cyrus Vance, *Hard Choices* (New York: Simon and Schuster, 1983), p. 451.
58. "United States Reiterates Support for the Independence of Namibia and Zimbabwe at Maputo Conference," *Department of State Bulletin*, July 11, 1977, p. 60.
59. *Amnesty International Report 1978*, pp. 68-72, 76-83.
60. Ibid., p. 91.
61. Ibid., p. 55.
62. Ibid., pp. 46-47.
63. Ibid., p. 49.
64. Vance, *Hard Choices*, pp. 127-128.
65. Michael Ledeen and William Lewis, *Debacle: The American Failure in Iran* (New York: Alfred A. Knopt, 1981), pp. 146-147; and Interviews with Stephen Cohen, Nov. 7 and Nov. 14, 1983.

66. Senate Committee on Foreign Relations, *Human Rights and U.S. Foreign Assistance*, p. 66.
67. "The Secretary: U.S. Relations with Africa," *Department of State Bulletin*, August 1978, p. 11.
68. U.S., Congress, House, Committee on Foreign Affairs, *Reconciling Human Rights and U.S. Security Interests in Asia, Hearings before the Subcommittees on Asian and Pacific Affairs and on Human Rights and International Organizations*, 97th Cong., 2nd sess., 1982, p. 4.
69. Interview with Mark Schneider, Washington, D.C., Nov. 3, 1983.
70. Senate Committee on Foreign Relations, *Human Rights and U.S. Foreign Assistance*, p. 63.
71. U.S., Congress, Senate, Committee on Appropriations, *Foreign Assistance and Related Programs Appropriations for FY1978*, 95th Cong., 1st sess., 1977, p. 186.
72. U.S., Department of State, *American Foreign Policy: Basic Documents 1977-1980* (Washington, D.C.: G.P.O., 1983), p. 410.
73. U.S., Congress, House, Committee on Foreign Affairs, *Foreign Assistance Legislation for FY1980-1981, Part 4, Hearings before the Subcommittee on Asian and Pacific Affairs*, 96th Cong., 1st sess., 1979, p. 179.
74. House Committee on Foreign Affairs, *Reconciling Human Rights and U. S. Security Interests in Asia*, p. 477.
75. Ibid.
76. Cohen interview, Nov. 14, 1983.
77. Ledeen and Lewis, *Debacle*, p. 234.
78. "Tehran, Iran," *Weekly Compilation of Presidential Documents*, Jan. 2, 1978, p. 1975.
79. Senate Committee on Foreign Relations, *Human Rights and U.S. Foreign Assistance*, p. 63.
80. U.S., Congress, House, Committee on International Relations, and Senate, Committee on Foreign Affairs, *Country Reports on Human Rights Practices*, Report submitted by the Department of State, 95th Cong., 2nd sess., Feb. 3, 1978, p. 402.
81. U.S., Congress, House, Committee on House Administration, *The Presidential Campaign 1976*, Vol. 1, Pt. 1, p. 80.
82. "University of Notre Dame," *Weekly Compilation of Presidential Documents*, May 30, 1977, p. 774.
83. U.S., Congress, Senate, Committee on Appropriations, *Foreign Assistance and Related Programs Appropriations for FY1980, Pt. 1, Hearings before the Subcommittee on Foreign Operations*

Appropriations, 96th Cong., 1st sess., 1979, p. 731.

84. U.S., Congress, Senate, Committee on Armed Services, *Military Implications of the Treaty on the Limitation of Strategic Offensive Arms and Protocol Thereto (SALT II Treaty,* Part 2), 96th Cong., 1st sess., 1979, p. 438.

85. Zbigniew Brzezinski, "Human Rights and American Foreign Policy: A Symposium," *Commentary,* Vol. 72, No. 5 (November 1981), pp. 29-30.

86. Ibid.

87. See Chap. 2.

88. "Interview With the President," *Weekly Compilation of Presidential Documents,* July 25, 1977, p. 1028.

89. "Western Hemisphere: OAS General Assembly Convenes," *Department of State Bulletin,* September 1978, p. 55.

90. Senate Committee on Foreign Relations, *Human Rights and U.S. Foreign Assistance,* p. 52.

91. "News Conference, Peking, August 25, 1977," *Department of State Bulletin,* Sept. 19, 1977, p. 371.

92. "The Secretary: News Conference of December 6," *Department of State Bulletin,* January 1978, p. 20.

93. House Committee on Foreign Affairs, *Reconciling Human Rights and U.S. Security Interests in Asia,* p. 480.

94. *Country Reports on Human Rights Practices,* Feb. 3, 1978, p. 324.

95. "Visit of President Josip Broz Tito of Yugoslavia," *Weekly Compilation of Presidential Documents,* March 13, 1978, pp. 473-476 passim.

96. "Visit of President Nicolae Ceausescu of Romania," *Weekly Compilation of Presidential Documents,* April 17, 1978, p. 735.

97. "Warsaw, Poland," *Weekly Compilation of Presidential Documents,* Jan. 2, 1978, p. 1970.

98. "The President's News Conference of December 30, 1977," ibid., p. 1962.

99. Ibid.

100. Interview with Hendrik Hertzberg held in Washington, D.C., Nov. 2, 1983.

101. CBS, "Face the Nation," Dec. 25, 1977.

102. *Washington Post,* Feb. 6, 1983, p. B7.

103. Sandra Vogelgesang, *American Dream: Global Nightmare* (New York: W.W. Norton, 1977), p. 38.

104. " 'People Want to See Coonskins'," *Time,* April 24, 1978, p. 21.

105. Senate Committee on Foreign Relations, *Human Rights and U.S. Foreign Assistance,* p. 64.

106. U.S., Congress, House, Committee on International Relations, *Foreign Assistance Legislation for FY1978*, *Pt. 1* 95th Cong., 1st sess., 1977, p. 5.
107. Hoffman, "The Perils of Incoherence," p. 479.
108. Lars Schoultz, *Human Rights and United States Policy toward Latin America* (Princeton, N.J.: Princeton U. Press, 1981), pp. 118-119.
109. Senate Committee on Foreign Relations, *Human Rights and U.S. Foreign Assistance*, p. 5.
110. Carter, *Keeping Faith*, p. 277. Emphasis added.
111. Cited in Daniel P. Moynihan, "The Politics of Human Rights," *Commentary*. Vol. 64, No. 2 (August 1977), p. 19.]

SIX
Punitive Measures: Origins and Impact

The heart and soul of the Carter human rights policy was the application of punishments to governments found to be violating human rights. According to a Department of State description of the policy: "Finding positive and creative ways to encourage governments to respect human rights is far better than penalizing them for poor performance. But when improvements do not ensue, governments must understand that there are costs to continued repression."[1] In nine cases during the Carter years, the Agency for International Development (AID) reported that it was increasing its programs in individual countries as a reward for good human rights behavior.[2] The administration was, however, able to find few other "positive and creative" measures, so it gave greater emphasis to punitive ones. Something of the flavor of this approach was captured in a remark one official made to Elizabeth Drew about the experience of the first few months of the human rights policy: "I think that the mulish world has noticed the two-by-four."[3] But once it had gotten the mule's attention, the administration just kept flailing away at it for four solid years. A fifteen-page "transition" memo prepared to acquaint the incoming Reagan administration with the workings of the "Christopher Group," the main coordinating body for the Carter administration's human rights policy, devoted a single sentence to "positive" inducements, while dealing exhaustively with the meting out of punishments.[4]

THE ROLE OF CONGRESS

One reason why the Carter administration may have found it so difficult to shift from a punitive to a positive approach was that its human rights policy did not begin from scratch. As Under Secretary of State David Newsom put it:

> the first thing to keep in mind about the Carter human rights policy is that it was essentially...a congressional policy. What seems so infrequently to be recognized is that by the time Carter took office there was already a considerable body of legislation on the books requiring a consideration of human rights...[5]

Patricia Derian has said much the same thing. "Actually, the whole base of what we do springs from the initiative that the Congress took in '75, '76 and 1977," she testified.[6]

The legislation consisted almost entirely of punitive measures. Congress adopted measures designed to withhold military aid and others to withhold economic aid from governments that violated human rights. Another measure compelled the American representatives on the boards of directors of international financial institutions to vote against loans to human rights violators. Still others restricted the activities of the Overseas Private Investment Corporation (OPIC) and the Export-Import Bank, according to similar criteria. In contrast, a positive measure, a bill introduced by Rep. Dante Fascell(D.-Fla.) to create an Institute for Human Rights and Freedom which would have provided funds to support foreign human rights groups, to publish suppressed materials, to aid the families of victims of political repression and for other such purposes, withered on the congressional vine.[7]

Hans Morgenthau argued that in the fifties U.S. policy proceeded from the "unexamined assumption" that the infusion into developing countries of U.S. aid would lead to the growth of democratic institutions.[8] When this hope was disappointed, Congress in the seventies began to act from the equally unexamined and intuitively less-plausible assumption that the same goal could be achieved by withdrawing U.S. aid. This attitude was exemplified by Representative Clarence Long, chairman of the House Subcommittee on Foreign Operations Appropriations, who, in one hearing, asked Secretary Vance, "how will the reduction of assistance solve the problem [of human rights violations]?", and then asked, "won't it take a complete termination of assistance?"[9] Similarly, in 1976, Congressman Ed Koch, after helping to lead a successful effort to cut off military aid to Uruguay, declared that if Latin American governments that violated human rights "don't get the message, then next year [we'll cut aid] to Nicaragua."[10]

What was faintly ridiculous about this was that neither Long nor Koch nor anyone else in Congress ever adduced the least bit of evidence that either reducing or terminating aid ever had the effect of engendering increased respect for human rights, and rarely if ever did any of them even formulate an argument stating why such actions might have that effect. The question is not whether the government of the United States is capable of "imposing" human rights on another country. That, it surely is, if it is willing to involve itself deeply enough, as the experience of Japan and West Germany proves. The question is whether similar results can be achieved by reducing, rather than increasing, American involvement.

Why did Congress seem so indifferent to the question of whether the course it was setting would lead to its ostensible goals? The reason is that much of the motivation behind the human rights legislation had to do with concerns other than the promotion of human rights. The legislation's support in the Congress, according to Bruce Cameron, the foremost lobbyist of the "human rights movement," consisted at critical moments of a "coalition of new and younger liberals greatly influenced by the anti-war movement and Watergate, and conservative Republicans and Democrats."[11] The liberal group was motivated, among other things, by the wish to assert congressional control over foreign policy. As one history published by the State Department put it: "burgeoning public opposition to the war in Vietnam during the 1960s caused Congress to question executive behavior and even to sponsor international activities on its own. The most significant initiative of Congress has been in the field of international human rights."[12] It was also motivated by the wish to reduce the American role in the world. As the Congressional Research Service observed, congressional human rights initiatives "originated during...a period of growing popular disenchantment with an activist U.S. role abroad."[13]

The conservative part of the coalition, on the other hand, was motivated by an eagerness to cut foreign aid on whatever pretext. The coalition's effectiveness reached its high point in 1977 with the passage of an amendment requiring that human rights criteria guide U.S. votes in the multilateral development banks. On that issue, Representatives Tom Harkin and Herman Badillo(D.-N.Y.) and Senators James Abourezk and Mark Hatfield worked in league with Representative John Rousselot(R.-Cal.), a former member of the John Birch Society, to overcome the opposition of a broad band of moderates including the House and Senate leadership. [14]

Of course, the coalition also had its limits. The liberal human rights militants[15] were eager to extend human rights criteria to cover the actions of such agencies as the Export-Import Bank and the Overseas Private Investment Corporation, but there was less conservative support for this. These agencies are not primarily in the business of giving aid to foreigners, but of underwriting American business ventures. This activity, unlike foreign aid, was in good favor with most conservative legislators.

The congressional human rights militants, on the other hand, were not entirely dependent on their coalition with the Right. That coalition was effective for placing restrictions on economic aid. In enacting restrictions on military aid they lost the support of the Right, but gained that of a broad spectrum of liberals who are uncomfortable with military aid even where they acknowledge its necessity. In attaching human rights criteria to OPIC, they worked with organized labor which is hostile to OPIC in principle, believing that it encourages the export of American jobs. The varying coalitions succeeded in attaching human rights restrictions to most U.S. aid and trade programs.

THE HUMAN RIGHTS MOVEMENT

The congressional human rights militants were supported by an active lobbying network, referred to often as the human rights movement, or "community," as it was called from within. Its activities were coordinated by the Human Rights Working Group of the Coalition for a New Foreign and Military Policy. The traditional human rights organizations, like Amnesty International, Freedom House, the International Commission of Jurists, and the International League for Human Rights, do not engage in lobbying and participated not at all or only tangentially in the Working Group. Rather, the human rights movement was an outgrowth of the anti-Vietnam War movement, and drew upon the experience and contacts that had been developed in the drives to force a withdrawal of U.S. forces from Vietnam and an end to U.S. aid to the government of South Vietnam.

John Salzberg, chief aide to Congressman Fraser in his groundbreaking hearings on human rights, describes the human rights movement as having had a "very important role" in bringing "knowledge of situations in other countries to counterbalance what we might be hearing from the State Department."[16] Congressman Harkin, the leader of the congressional human rights militants has said: "From the year

I came into office, I saw that the human rights community was very influential in initiating and developing legislation and supporting it with grass roots activity."[17] Lars Schoultz, a scholar sympathetic to this group, points out that "every piece of human rights legislation that passed the Ninety-fourth and Ninety-fifth Congresses (1975-1978) did so with the active support of human rights interest groups."[18] Oddly enough, this "human rights movement," that contributed so importantly to the growth of human rights legislation, is not really in favor of human rights, at least not as that term is understood by most Americans. To put it more carefully, the movement sees "human rights" flourishing in societies where, in the eyes of most Americans, those rights are brutally trampled by Communist dictatorships. This vast discrepancy may bespeak a difference in values, or a difference in perceptions, or both. But whatever its sources, its practical consequence is that when the movement uses the term, "human rights," it often has in mind a set of institutions quite different from those the term connotes to most Americans.

The Human Rights Working Group was founded by Jacqui Chagnon, a member of the staff of a group called Clergy and Laity Concerned. Although its name evokes images of moderate gentility, CALC was not merely antiwar, but dogmatically pro-Hanoi. After Hanoi's victory in 1975, CALC worked to secure American aid for Vietnam and to rebut allegations that the Communist victors were engaged in any human rights violations. (CALC leaders also worked to rebut charges that the victorious Khmer Rouge were committing human rights violations in Cambodia, but they abandoned this argument after the Vietnamese invasion of Cambodia when they were assured by Vietnamese authorities that the Khmer Rouge were indeed guilty.) When, for example, Joan Baez gathered the signatures of other antiwar veterans in an "open letter" to Hanoi charging that "thousands of Vietnamese, many of whose only 'crimes' are those of conscience, are being arrested, detained and tortured in prisons and re-education camps," CALC's co-director, Don Luce, was one of a small group of pro-

Hanoi diehards organized by Corliss Lamont, the old stalwart of the National Council on American-Soviet Friendship, to rebut Baez and defend Hanoi's good name. In their response, Luce, Lamont and their co-thinkers argued that although "some Saigon collaborationists have been detained in re-education centers....On balance....[t]he present government of Vietnam should be hailed for its moderation and for its extraordinary effort to achieve reconciliation among all of its people."[19]

For three years after its founding, Jacqui Chagnon served as co-leader of the Human Rights Working Group, leaving that post in 1978 to move to Laos where she and her husband served for three years as field directors for the American Friends Service Committee. Today she is back in Washington where, together with her husband and her old colleague Don Luce, she serves on the staff of the Southeast Asia Resource Center (formerly the Indochina Resource Center), another of the old "antiwar" groups that was and remains militantly pro-Hanoi. There she is spearheading the drive to debunk reports by Laotian refugees of being attacked with chemical weapons known as "yellow rain."[20]

Chagnon's views, about which she is quite open, are startling, given her pivotal role in the genesis of U.S. human rights policy. In the eyes of most Americans, the Communist governments of Laos and Vietnam rank among the world's worst violators of human rights. Assistant Secretary of State Abrams went so far in releasing the 1982 edition of the Department's annual "Country Reports" to venture the conjecture that Vietnam might be the world's "worst country to live in."[21] Yet, these same governments have always been viewed by Mrs. Chagnon with a sympathy bordering on admiration. She also believes that "the stereotype that the American press has put on Laos that it's colonized by Vietnam is a stereotype that's incorrect...I think that they influence Vietnam as well as Vietnam influences Laos."[22] Laos has few if any newspapers, she says, "because they can't afford it; they only have one printing press in the whole country."[23] Although she complains about the absence of any constitution in Laos, she says that "village seminars give people a voice....it's a town meeting...which I wish we had more of [in the U.S.] today....This is one way to effectively democratize the system...getting people involved in their system and encouraging them to speak up. "[24] Also on the question of democracy in the Lao People's Democratic Republic, "What I found," says Chagnon, "is that most of the rich people, not all, didn't like the current government and most of the poor people did. But the majority are poor; therefore the majority do like the current government."[25] As for Laotian "re-education camps," Chagnon says: "They simply just took the heavy-duty 'baddies' and put them in remote areas essentially and said 'take care of yourselves.'....I think there was some injustice in [it], I think there was some justice in [it], frankly....Their life is no different from other villages surrounding."[26] According to the State Department, 300,000 people, nearly 8 percent of the population, have fled Laos since the Communist victory.[27] But according to Chagnon, refugees seeking to come to America are motivated not by the desire to escape repression, but by the desire to escape paying taxes. "They have this conception that we don't pay taxes. In some way the word 'freedom' and the word 'free' got mixed up. So therefore they were blaming their government for making them pay a tax that we would consider wonderful by our standards," she says.[28]

Chagnon also defends the government of Vietnam for its role in the episode of the flight of the "boat people." The reason for the suicidal exodus, she says, was that Western governments refused to cooperate with the government of Vietnam in organizing an "orderly departures" program. "The problem here is what government was going to accept them; it is not what government was going to let them out," she says.[29]

In sum, Chagnon looks upon Communist regimes, at least those of Indochina, with an attitude of benevolence, while she views rightist regimes in Asia—those of Indonesia, South Korea, the Philippines—with bitter hostility. Startling as these views are, they are not disconsonant with those of most of her colleagues in the core group of the "human rights movement," at least in its hey-day in the 1970s. This is confirmed by the person who shared with her the leadership of the Human Rights Working Group, Bruce Cameron. Cameron reports that during the main period of the activity of the HRWG, he, too, felt a general sympathy for Communist forces in the Third World. Cameron's attitude on this subject has changed markedly, although he continues to play a leading role in the liberal wing of the Democratic party as a lobbyist on human rights and other issues. Cameron describes the political philosophy of the activist human rights movement this way:

> Among the leadership and among the core, it was predominantly, including myself at that time, people who viewed themselves as anti-imperialist. That is, that they saw the world divided between those forces who were struggling to maintain the hegemony of the U.S./free world market economy, with all the relationships that that entailed with the Third World which involved subjugation through various types of mechanisms—that's one side. On the other side were the Third World peoples attempting to become free....

> I can remember in that time that one of my lines used to be that I find 80 percent of Soviet foreign policy acceptable and basically on the side that I was on. I don't remember other people saying anything like that, but I remember no dissent....There was this very strong anti-imperialist view.

> The core group clearly thought of the world divided between the evil U.S., the questionable Soviet Union, and the good Third World people....

> [The group] had no trouble at all justifying the presence of the Soviet Union in Angola....[30]

Given views such as these, the inconsistencies in the public posture of the movement are hardly surprising. It was critical of the Carter administration, says Chagnon, for being insufficiently tough on rightist regimes. "We wanted more aid cut," she says.[31] On the other hand, as Cameron wrote in 1978, "aid to left-wing governments, particularly Vietnam and Laos is almost uniformly supported by members of the HRWG."[32] The aid sought was not merely to meet "basic human needs," but rather, in the words of CALC, "reconstruction aid."[33]

These inconsistencies reflected not merely an unconscious outgrowth of the group's attitudes, but an explicit policy decision. Cameron reports that "the agreements made at the beginning of the Human Rights Working Group [were] that Human Rights Working Group would not touch either the Soviet bloc or the Middle East, the Soviet bloc because they were regarded as on the side of the 'good guys' and the Middle East because various groups for one reason or another didn't want to go after the Middle East. It was a way of preserving the coalition."[34]

The most important implication of Chagnon's views and Cameron's statement is that they show that in promoting, lobbying for, and indeed in initiating and writing much of the human rights legislation, the movement was after something quite different from what most of the public and the Congress thought was the purpose of the legislation. To the latter groups, the purpose was to bring to bear greater American pressure in order to induce other countries to adopt what were essentially American values. But "human rights," as the term was understood by the movement, was antithetical to American values, and American influence was seen as the chief *obstacle* to achieving human rights. In the eyes of the movement, the purpose of legislating cuts in U.S. aid was not to bring greater American pressure to bear, but rather to sever the bonds of U.S. influence so as to improve the prospects for victory by the forces of liberation. "The motive was that if you cut the link...then you create more space for the revolutionary Third World people to assert their right to self-determination," says Cameron; the purpose was not, he says, to force existing governments to liberalize.[35]

It would of course be mistaken to assume a perfect correspondence between the objectives of the movement and the effects of the legislation it generated or supported. What motivated the representatives and senators who voted for the human rights amendments was not in most cases identical to what motivated the activists, and although the movement achieved impressive victories, the legislation often fell short of the movement's goals. Bruce Cameron, though disavowing his own previous goals, still believes that the legislation is valuable and constructive, albeit in part because it is not enforced with the rigidity that he once favored. There is little doubt, however, that the movement's influence was substantial.

In sum, the human rights legislation of the 1970s was the product of many factors that had little to do with human rights. Among them were the desire of some conservatives for another tool with which to chip away at foreign aid, the desire of the "movement" to reduce U.S. interference with the process of Third World "liberation," and, above all, a yearning, evident both in Congress and in public opinion, for a reduction in America's involvement in the world in the wake of our debacle in Vietnam. Indeed the very first "human rights" amendments were designed to cut off U.S. aid to South Vietnam for human rights abuses by its government. There was little if any pretense that the purpose of these amendments was to enhance respect for human rights; the purpose was to end U.S. participation in the war. If there was any uncertainty on this score, it has been cleared up by the fact that although Hanoi's victory has resulted in a reign of tyranny in South Vietnam far more brutal than anything that preceded it,[36] this has stimulated very little response from the Congress.

THE ADMINISTRATION AND CONGRESS

Because of these origins, the human rights legislation focused primarily on cutting U.S. aid, with little consideration given to whether this would in fact serve to enhance respect for human rights. Some of this legislation was already on the books when Carter took office; more was passed while he was in office. It was a major factor in guiding the administration's human rights policy toward heavy reliance on punitive measures. As Deputy Assistant Secretary Mark Schneider put it when asked about this reliance: "There's a law. You have to obey the law. The law requires you to make certain judgments."[37]

But Schneider's response is too facile. "The Ford Administration," said a report by the Congressional Research Service, "took the position that any cut in aid made on the grounds of human rights would be counterproductive,"[38] and it found ways to circumvent and resist congressional pressure for such cuts. Carter, on the other hand, was far more than a passive executor of congressional mandates. As one State Department publication put it: "With the inauguration of President Carter, the full power of presidential leadership was thrown into the struggle for human rights worldwide, and an era of renewed and heightened emphasis on human rights in American foreign policy began."[39] And much of the same impulse that had underlain congressional actions now guided the administration's human rights policy. Not only was the impulse the same, but so were many of the key actors, as is best exemplified by Schneider, himself, who came to the State Department's human rights bureau after having worked on the issue for Senator Kennedy, a leader in the passage of human rights legislation.

The administration's attitude toward the human rights legislation was ambivalent. Deputy Secretary Warren Christopher said that he found the "broad range of statutes which restrict the flow of economic and military assistance to countries with serious human rights problems" to be "very helpful in administering the human rights policy of the administration."[40] But Jessica Tuchman, the person who was in charge of human rights issues on the National Security Council staff, says that the administration would have preferred to have more maneuvering room than it felt the legislation gave it. She says:

> Congress had gotten into the mode vis-à-vis the previous ad-
> ministration...of feeling that...without pushing and forcing,
> the administration would do nothing....We were saying to
> Congress: "Hey, you're dealing with a different administration
> now. We want to take the initiative. You don't have to force us
> and lock us in with these amendments." But it takes a long time
> in a collective body like that for the view to get reversed....It
> was very hard to both have what was a tough and aggressive
> policy that was flexible and sophisticated, on the one hand, and
> also have these inflexible legal requirements.[41]

The key word here is "flexible." The administration
rarely if ever disagreed with the approach embodied in the
legislation or with the kinds of sanctions imposed, but it
wanted the freedom to exercise its own discretion in applying the sanctions. This on one occasion led Congressman
Long to complain: "I think you want to keep the leverage in
your own hands....You crack down on Nicaragua after you
lobbied Congress not to do anything about Nicaragua."[42]
The instance to which Long referred was only one
of several in which the administration opposed moves in
Congress to add further layers of human rights legislation.
This allowed Carter to respond to those questioning the judi-
ciousness of his policy by claiming that "my own attitude on
the human rights question has been fairly moderate....some
members of Congress would go much further than I."[43]
There was some truth to this, but the issue was not really one
of "moderation"; it was one of flexibility and prerogatives.
The Congress wanted to assert its authority over foreign
policy, while the administration wanted to remain free to
conduct its diplomacy on a day-by-day basis, hampered as
little as possible by congressional restrictions.

Patricia Derian, speaking about the restrictions the administration imposed for human rights reasons on foreign
aid, said: "We have also gone beyond the strict requirements of this legislation. Some countries with serious human
rights problems might not technically fall within the language

'consistent pattern of gross violations.' Nevertheless, we have tried to make sure that our assistance levels reflect their human rights performance."[44]

Thus, the Carter administration and the Congress, while wrestling with one another over turf, were working in tandem in carrying out the idea that cutting aid to governments that violate human rights is in itself a beneficial policy. The president declared in his first foreign aid message to the Congress: "We are now reforming the policies which have, on occasion, awarded liberal grants and loans to repressive regimes which violate human rights."[45] Yet the administration no more than the Congress seems to have paused to ask itself or to examine whether such an approach actually serves the cause of human rights. That it does is far from self-evident. Arguably the greatest victory for human rights in this century, perhaps in all history, was the defeat of Hitler. This victory was in significant measure attributable to the copious amounts of aid given by the United States to the government of Stalin, the one other tyrant in modern history who deserves to be ranked alongside Hitler in the annals of butchery. Had we in 1941 reformed our policies so as to prohibit aid to repressive regimes, we might today be living in the fourth decade of the "thousand-year Reich."

Of course the circumstances of 1941 were extraordinary, but the example suffices to prove that the value of cutting aid to violators must be examined, not assumed.

EFFECTIVENESS

The first question to ask is whether such measures appear to have achieved their goal. Have they brought about improvements in observance of human rights in those countries to which they have been applied?

Most close observers believe that they have not. The Congressional Research Service studied the effects of U.S. human rights policy on fifteen countries and reached this conclusion:

the record on direct and explicit use of foreign assistance as leverage to bring about specific improvements in human rights conditions is hardly encouraging. In only five or six instances did we find evidence that actual or explicitly threatened reductions in aid played a significant role in bringing about changes in human rights conditions.[46]

The conclusions of the CRS have been echoed in the observations of several human rights activists. Former Representative Don Fraser had, by the time he left the Congress, grown ambivalent about the use of punitive measures in which he had been a pioneer. He testified:

The longer I worked in the human rights area, the more conservative I became in assessing our capacity to enforce change in other parts of the world. The U.S. has foregone the role of acting as policeman of the world....

We should not now make the mistake of replacing that lost role of policeman with a new one, that of being the world's judge.

Just as we did not fully understand the nature of the forces at work in other parts of the world when we came to apply our military might, equally we must be cautious in assuming that we fully appreciate all the circumstances and antecedents which cause governments to act differently than we think they should.[47]

Jo Marie Griesgraber, a key human rights activist, found in her study of the effects of human rights legislation that by the end of the period of the greatest congressional activity in this field, "there was little to show for congressional human rights efforts."[48]

There are surely some situations where U.S. sanctions have helped to bring about improvements, for example, Argentina. When measured against the hopes of human rights activists like Fraser and Griesgraber, these improvements may seem very small, but measured against less ambitious standards they might seem more noteworthy.

However, the critical question about the use of punitive measures is not whether they *ever* do any good, but whether they *often* do any good, as well as whether they do any harm, and whether the good they do could be achieved by other means.

In order to attempt a crude measure of whether punitive actions often help to improve the human rights situations in the countries to which they are applied, I have compiled a list of all countries to which concrete punitive measures were applied by the Carter administration. I have tried to see whether any measurable change in the human rights situation occurred in these countries during the course of the Carter administration. For this purpose I have relied on the annual "Survey of Freedom" published by Freedom House which constitutes the only extant attempt to measure the human rights performance of countries on a standard scale. Freedom House rates each country in the world on two scales, one for political rights, the other for civil liberties. On each scale, a country receives a numerical rating ranging from a best of 1 to a worst of 7. For the purpose of this exercise I have combined the two scales so that a country's best possible total rating would be 2, and its worst possible rating 14.[49]

The Carter administration took punitive measures against 28 countries. In the beginning of 1977, when the Carter administration took office, these 28 countries had an average score of 11.7 on the combined Freedom House scales. In the beginning of 1981, when the Carter administration left office, these 28 had an average score of 11.9, slightly worse than when Carter began.

The other 136 countries rated by Freedom House had an average combined score at the beginning of 1977 of 8.1. At the beginning of 1981 their average was 7.9, a slight improvement. To make one other comparison, I found that there were 30 countries, among the 136 that had received no sanctions, each of which had a score of 11 or 12 at the outset of the Carter administration. The averge score of these 30 was 11.7, exactly equal to the average of the 28 countries that had received sanctions. In 1981 these 30 unpunished countries had an average score of 11.0, a small improvement, that contrasts with the deteriorating average score of the punished countries.

In sum, the countries that received punitive measures from the Carter administration were slightly worse off in terms of human rights at the end of Carter's term than they had been end at the beginning, while other countries were slightly better off. Of course, it may have been the worsening situations in these countries that led to their punishment. In fact, there is often no reliable way to determine which came first, the deterioration or the punishment. That is because the deterioration never consisted of a single discreet event, but was always a long chain of events. It is impossible to pinpoint when a certain number of these events registered a certain impression on Freedom House or on officials in the administration. Less obviously, it is also very difficult to pinpoint "when" a punitive measure occurred: did it happen at the moment the decreased aid allocation was announced, or during the span of time during which those withheld dollars would have been spent?

But this uncertainty is not large enough to bring into question the basic inference that the use of punishments had no measurable positive effect. Even if we assume that in almost all cases the deterioration preceded the punishment, there is no pattern evident in these 28 cases of improvement in the Freedom House ratings after the application of the punishments.

Two important caveats need to be added. The first is that although the Freedom House scale is a rather sensitive one—a combined scale of 2 to 14 leaves a lot of opportunity for registering gradations—any such scale still has its limitations. It may not be sensitive enough to reflect events that may be of consummate importance to individuals or even hundreds of individuals. Thus it is quite possible that pressures from the Carter administration saved many individuals from undeserved imprisonment or from torture or even murder, without Freedom House registering a change in the overall level of freedom in their countries. This appears to have been the case in Argentina, for example. Whether or not the punitive measures constituted an indispensable part of that pressure is a separate question, but every human life is sacred, and the saving of some number of lives is an estimable achievement even if the overall level of freedom in a country is not measurably changed.

The second caveat is that although the punitive measures may have no beneficial effects on the countries to which they are applied, they may have a deterrent effect on other countries or on future governments. Thus David Newsom has written about the sanctions contained in human rights legislation: "The laws are more effective in abeyance than in application....It is difficult to find cases where the actual application of the law has led to changes in another country's human rights practices. Knowledge of the law, however, can sometimes help a faction within a foreign government seeking more liberal practices to prevail."[50] In the same vein, Robert Pastor, the chief Latin American specialist on Carter's National Security Council staff, argues that punitive measures

> were essential to establish credibility. If you never take such steps then your public statements and private demarches have no credibility. If you are unwilling to follow up occasionally with something that is costly....then you don't have any credibility for the broader policy. [And] if you ask if the broader policy had any impact on human rights, there is just no question in my mind, it had a tremendous positive impact on the human rights of individuals and on developing an international consciousness.[51]

HARMFUL EFFECTS

If the punitive measures had some benefits, they also had some harmful effects. The most obvious of these was the strain put on relations with the governments that were subjected to our punishments. The principal author of several Congressional Research Service studies reported that: "Direct pressures seem often to provoke counterproductive reactions. Chile, Argentina, Ethiopia and the Philippines represent cases in which such pressures clearly contributed to significant deterioration of bilateral relations."[52] A strain in relations may not only be detrimental to the diplomatic interests of the United States, it also may impair our ability to have a beneficial influence in terms of human rights, as was suggested by Secretary Vance's reply to critics of the Panama Canal treaties who pointed out that the Panamanian government violated human rights. "The closer relations between our two countries that will grow out of the new treaties will provide a more positive context in which to express such concerns," he argued.[53]

Almost all observers agree that at best foreign aid is an unwieldy instrument to use for human rights leverage. For example, David Newsom reports: "In some countries, the U.S. actions on bank loans were resented by the very officials who might, otherwise, have had an understanding and sympathy for a sound human rights policy, the managers and technocrats. They were frequently the initiators of the projects" that got cut off.[54]

For this reason it often seems preferable to withhold military aid, rather than economic aid, for human rights leverage. But to withhold security assistance where it is genuinely needed is to play a dangerous game. The human rights situation within the country is likely to be aggravated, not improved, if the country falls victim to foreign aggression, and U.S. security interests and the cause of world peace may suffer, as well. To threaten to withhold security assistance in such circumstances is to apply to the realm of human rights policy the logic that underlies the strategic nuclear policy known acronymically as MAD, Mutual Assured Destruction. In this case, if the government receiving U.S. security assistance fails to stop violating human rights, then we threaten to retaliate by destroying it and our own interests as well. This may be true even if the military threat that a government is facing is primarily internal.

The experience of Nicaragua is a good case in point. There was ample reason to want to punish or pressure dictator Anastasio Somoza. But the cut-off of U.S. aid contributed directly to his overthrow by the Sandinista National Liberation Front. The Sandinista government may prove in time to be even more abusive of human rights than was Somoza and it poses a far greater threat to the peace of the region.

The other harm that is done by the use of punitive measures in human rights policy is that they vastly complicate the problem of maintaining even a modicum of consistency in the policy. That is because the United States tends to give more aid to countries that are friendly to it than to those which are hostile to it, but countries friendly to the United States tend to have better human rights records than those hostile to it. The result is that where aid is used as a lever, there tend to be more levers available for use against lesser violators than against greater violators. The fact that we don't have the leverage to bash all dictators equally does not make it immoral to bash those we can. But such inconsistencies rob a human rights policy of its clarity and moral force.[55] This problem is exacerbated if, as was the case with the Carter policy, the press of other foreign policy objectives makes the United States reluctant to use levers against some governments where it has no shortage of leverage, with the result that the bulk of its punitive measures fall on a small number of easy targets.

The Carter administration itself seems to have experienced growing doubts about the utility of punitive measures, but rather than abandon them, it developed a new justification for their use.

Lars Schoultz, who sympathized with the administration's approach, described the transition this way:

....At first HA [the Human Rights Bureau] viewed the threat of aid reductions as a tool to force decreases in recipients' levels of political repression....By 1978, this goal had proven to be unrealistic—aid or no aid, most of Latin America's most repressive governments refused to alter their policies....At that point, HA began to speak of aid reductions as a tool not to reduce repression but to dissociate the United States from repressive regimes. By 1978, in fact, the word "dissociate" had become the most frequently used verb in the lexicon of human rights officials.[56]

Early in her tenure, Derian had said: "I think anything we do, we ought to see what the results are beyond our own feeling good about it."[57] But a year later she was saying: "What we must do is see to it that we don't contribute to the violations."[58]

There are various degrees to which the United States can "dissociate" itself from a repressive government. The most elementary is to avoid direct complicity in acts of repression. As Bruce Cameron puts it: "we should never, ever sell instruments that can be directly used in the violation of the integrity of the person to a government with human rights problems."[59] That this is not a merely abstract question is proven by the experience of Soviet dissident, Vladimir Bukovsky, who relates in his autobiography: "what the guards always did when they were going to beat you [was] put American handcuffs on you, which tightened automatically at the least movement of the wrists."[60] The argument for dissociation at this level is virtually incontrovertible. It is true that KGB guards will beat prisoners with or without American handcuffs, but if they find that American handcuffs help them to make a good job of it, then that in itself is a powerful argument for withholding these devices. And what possible considerations could weigh on the other side? The profits of handcuff manufacturers seem an insufficient consideration.

A second level of dissociation involves things that the United States can give or sell to an unelected government that aren't used to brutalize people, but may be used to help it stay in power. Thus, the Carter administration withheld riot control equipment, such as tear gas, from the Shah of Iran, even while supplying the Shah's army with advanced warplanes and missilery.[61] The thought seemed to be that as long as he kept his throne he could be our surrogate in the gulf, but keeping his throne was his own problem. The flaw here, as the Iran experience demonstrates, is that undemocratic governments are often replaced by other undemocratic governments. All undemocratic governments may be in some fundamental sense illegitimate, but some are much crueler than others. Is it ever legitimate for the United States to help an unelected government to stay in power in the face of domestic opposition? To answer "no" convincingly requires a cogent reprise to former Secretary Haig's argument that the United States should "examine the credentials and program of the opposition as well as the government [to] see clearly what change portends for human rights..."[62]

A further degree of dissociation involves economic aid and those forms of military aid that may help a country to defend itself against foreign foes but are ordinarily of little practical value against internal enemies, say, air defense systems. Aid of this kind is not used against a population, but presumably for its benefit, either, in the case of economic aid, by improving the standard of living, or, in the case of military aid, by protecting the independence of the country. Nonetheless, it is argued, as Jo Marie Griesgraber, former deputy director of the Washington Office on Latin America, has put it, "*any* aid to a human rights violator (even BHN aid) has symbolic and political impact that bolsters the position of the recipient government."[63] In this view, "dissociation" requires that the United States give no aid at all to repressive governments.

This approach was the one adopted by Derian and her colleagues, except that for the most part the administration's policy was to exempt aid designed to meet "basic human needs." Even this exemption was not always enforced. The State Department informed Congress that "if a regime engages in egregious abuses of human rights, we may oppose assistance projects even if they meet basic human needs in order to dissociate the United States from the regime..."[64] The regimes the State Department found that fell in this category were those of Pinochet in Chile, Somoza in Nicaragua, Bokassa in the Central African Empire, and that of South Yemen.[65]

Patricia Derian argues that failure to dissociate creates the danger that a "revolution might...bring to power groups resenting and blaming the U.S. Government for having supported the previous government."[66] There is a little grain of truth in this and a big dollop of foolishness. The likelihood that revolutionary movements will succeed in seizing power vastly increases if U.S. aid is withheld from existing governments. Many of these movements are hostile to the United States for ideological reasons, and not merely, if at all, because the United States supports the incumbent government. Indeed, people do not become revolutionaries merely, as Derian implies, because they have grievances; they become revolutionaries only once their imaginations have been gripped by an ideology. Democracy, too, may be an ideology, but people who embrace democracy as their ideology are much less likely to take the path of revolution than those who embrace some variant of Marxism or another millenarian philosophy. The reason is that the very habits of mind that lead one to embrace the democratic creed, especially the acceptance of one's own fallibility, militate against the single-minded determination, the discipline, the ruthlessness that are so essential to the enterprise of revolution.

Moreover, if a revolution brings about a democratic government, this inherently favors the interests of the United States, even if, in the circumstances Derian suggests, the new government or the populace harbors resentment against the United States. Some democratic polities, say, India or France, have sometimes shown resentment toward the United States, but none has ever been our enemy. On the other hand, if a revolution brings about a new dictatorship, then its friendliness or hostility to the United States would be immaterial, because, according to Derian's formula, the United States would have to dissociate itself from that new government in anticipation of *its* overthrow.

The main argument for "distancing," however, is not instrumental, but ethical. It is exemplified by this flat assertion made by Derian in 1981 in criticizing the Reagan administration for giving aid to Guatemala: "Guatemala's government is a gross violator of human rights, and we have no business having a security relationship with it."[67] This emphasis on keeping our hands clean reflects what Max Weber called the "ethic of ultimate ends."[68] Those guided by this ethic demand to be judged by the purity of their intentions rather than the consequences of their acts. Weber made clear that he preferred the opposite approach, which he called the "ethic of responsibility," but he was not able to prove its superiority because such basic moral choices are not susceptible to "proof."

For the same reason it is not possible to prove "wrong" those who would make it an ethical absolute that no aid be given to autocrats. Nonetheless, it is instructive to consider what the consequences of such a policy would be.

Such a policy would leave the United States free to pursue friendly relations with only a few handfuls of countries outside of Western Europe, that is, turning its back on almost the entire Third World, thus giving meaning to Henry Kissinger's warning that "the issue of human rights if not handled with great wisdom could unleash new forces of American isolationism."[69]

In addition, there is a contradiction between Derian's penchant for "dissociation" and the Carter administration's chosen emphasis on violations of "the integrity of the person." The key motivations for this emphasis were that such violations are amenable to diplomatic intercession and that they merit priority because of the sheer intensity of suffering that they entail. But a policy based on a moral absolute has little grounds for interest in something so prosaic as the intensity of suffering. A violation, after all, is a violation.

And if it is hard to reconcile the penchant for "clean hands" with a stated emphasis on violations of the integrity of the person, it is impossible to reconcile it with the pragmatic approach that the Carter administration put forward as the justification for the admitted inconsistencies in the way it applied its human rights policy to differing countries. Mark Schneider, the administration's best defender on the issue of consistency, coined the phrase that the administration's goal was "to do the most we can, wherever we can."[70] How is it possible to believe that and also believe that in principle the United States should dissociate itself from all dictators?

In sum, the case for dissociation is far from compelling, with the exception of Cameron's incontrovertible dictum that the United States should never be in the business of supplying the instruments of cruelty.

ALTERNATIVES TO PUNITIVE MEASURES

If the argument for dissociation is weak and if the value of punitive measures is mitigated by their harmful effects, what alternatives are there? The most obvious alternative is *words*. In their book about Iran, Michael Ledeen and William Lewis write:

> From the beginning there were only two real possibilities: either the administration was serious, in which case some form of "linkage" would have to be adopted, which meant in practical terms that the United States would have to punish governments of which it did not approve by withholding trade benefits or aid packages; or there would be no linkage, in which case the human rights campaign would shortly be regarded as mere rhetoric with no concrete payoff.[71]

This argument ignores the fact that "mere rhetoric" has been one of the most potent forces shaping the history of our time, indeed of all time. It is necessary to go no further than the tale Ledeen and Lewis themselves were telling, that of the fall of the Shah, to be forcefully reminded of this truth. Only a few years earlier, when Khomeini was in exile and Reza Pahlavi was upon his throne and commanding a prodigiously equipped army, one might have asked: "how many divisions has the Ayatollah?" The answer, as all soon the justification for the admitted inconsistencies in the way it applied its human rights policy to differing countries. Mark Schneider, the administration's best defender on the issue of consistency, coined the phrase that the administration's goal was "to do the most we can, wherever we can."[70] How is it possible to believe that and also believe that in principle the United States should dissociate itself from all dictators?

In sum, the case for dissociation is far from compelling, with the exception of Cameron's incontrovertible dictum that the United States should never be in the business of supplying the instruments of cruelty.

ALTERNATIVES TO PUNITIVE MEASURES

If the argument for dissociation is weak and if the value of punitive measures is mitigated by their harmful effects, what alternatives are there? The most obvious alternative is *words*. In their book about Iran, Michael Ledeen and William Lewis write:

> From the beginning there were only two real possibilities: either the administration was serious, in which case some form of "linkage" would have to be adopted, which meant in practical terms that the United States would have to punish governments of which it did not approve by withholding trade benefits or aid packages; or there would be no linkage, in which case the human rights campaign would shortly be regarded as mere rhetoric with no concrete payoff.[71]

This argument ignores the fact that "mere rhetoric" has been one of the most potent forces shaping the history of our time, indeed of all time. It is necessary to go no further than the tale Ledeen and Lewis themselves were telling, that of the fall of the Shah, to be forcefully reminded of this truth. Only a few years earlier, when Khomeini was in exile and Reza Pahlavi was upon his throne and commanding a prodigiously equipped army, one might have asked: "how many divisions has the Ayatollah?" The answer, as all soon

Communist or other unfriendly governments may be able to slough off inquiries or public criticisms voiced by the United States about human rights issues as so much "bourgeois propaganda." But for most friendly Third World governments, their ties with the United States bolster their legitimacy and add to their standing in the eyes of their own people and of at least part of the international community. Frequently, these governments are under challenge or criticism from forces allied with one of the world's other power centers (the Soviet Union or China or, these days, Iran). Under these circumstances, the threat of expressions of American disfavor, albeit of a strictly rhetorical kind, can be a potent one.

Indeed, as it turned out, the concrete punitive measures most often applied by the Carter administration were essentially rhetorical. The United States voted negatively, on human rights grounds, on more than 120 loan applications considered by the multilateral development banks, a number greater than the combined total of all other punitive acts taken by the Carter administration in the name of human rights. And yet not once did the United States win a majority of any bank's board of directors to its side! Not once was a loan voted down! Each one of these votes was nothing more than a lonely symbolic gesture of American displeasure with the government in question. It is true that in some cases governments withdrew loan requests for fear of a negative vote by the United States, but here, too, what was feared was the public expression of American disfavor, not that the loan would be voted down. Thus, Mark Schneider, one of the more militant advocates of punitive measures within the Carter administration, acknowledges:

> My view has always been that any of the individual items is not the relevant issue. What is relevant is the political relationship to the United States. All of these things are symbolic of that. In only very rare instances does a single loan, grant, [or] project...of itself provide a significant pressure point. Rather it is the reflection of the U.S. relationship. That is ultimately what you are asserting is going to be affected by the country's action

or lack of action...on human rights objectives.[74]

There probably are some instances in which concrete measures—aid cuts or negative votes—are more effective as punishments or threats than "mere words." And "mere words" can have some of the harmful effects that material punishments have; they, too, can evoke undesired reactions. But a greater reliance on "mere words" rather than material measures is likely to reduce the harmful more than the beneficial effects.

For one thing, it would immediately eliminate the tendency of punitive measures to push the United States toward an inconsistent policy because we can only punish those who are receiving our aid. (Former Congressman Edward Derwinski [R.-Ill.] once inquired whether we could extend military aid to the People's Republic of China for just one year, so that we could then cut it off to punish their human rights violations.[75]) If we rely instead on verbal spankings, we can dish those out even-handedly to all miscreants. For another, the use of "mere words" eliminates the suspicion that the ulterior motive for our aid cuts is mere niggardliness, a suspicion that turns out to have some merit, given the central part played by Congressman Rousselot and his co-thinkers in the adoption of the human rights legislation. Above all, cutting aid in order to send symbolic messages allows for no nuance nor precision to the message. It constitutes a broad-brush condemnation, oblivious to consequences. The use of "mere words" allows the United States to send a message that says precisely what we may wish to say in a given situation, for example, to encourage democratic dissidents while condemning antidemocratic forces, or to criticize a government while recognizing genuine threats it faces or progress it has made.

Another alternative to punitive measures is positive inducements. Early in its term, the Carter administration had stressed its desire to move in this direction, but aside from several increases in AID allocations, it found few ways to do so.[76] The Congressional Research Service wrote:

Offering rewards for good behavior rather than punishment for misconduct provides a way to maintain satisfactory bilateral relations. This, too, was recognized by the administration from the start, but punitive measures were more readily available, became more pronounced and attracted more attention. Working level officials on several occasions voiced frustrations that the procedures for generating an increase in foreign assistance were often too slow and cumbersome to be useful in rewarding human rights advances.[77]

In addition to its cumbersomeness, it is easy to see that the use of material incentives could create even more wicked dilemmas regarding consistency than the use of material punishments. If a government that held ten thousand political prisoners released half of them, does it deserve a reward for its progress? What about the government that never held any? To take a real life example, when the rate of "disappearances" in Argentina fell from hundreds or thousands in a year to several handfuls, did its government deserve a reward?

Moreover, the use of "carrots" has one critical limitation in common with the use of "sticks." Both are actions aimed at governments, as if tyrannical governments can be induced simply to bestow human rights upon their subjects.

Experience teaches that systemic change of the kind that secures human rights is not something bestowed by rulers, but something won by peoples. That it is not easy to foster such change from the outside is obvious, for it is not easy to foster it from the inside, either. But surely this must be the goal of U.S. human rights policy, even though it requires the kind of long-term interest that Americans have historically been so poor at sustaining in any foreign policy goal.

If systemic change is not the goal, if the goal is nothing more than saving some lives and freeing some people from jail, then our human rights policy is nothing more than what Moynihan has called "a special kind of international social work."[78] There is much to be said for such social work. Each life saved is precious. But if this is all our human rights policy is after, then we might well want to reassure ourselves that the resources wouldn't touch more lives if used to feed hungry children or in the search for a cure for cancer.

We don't know much about how to encourage the development of democracy in other countries in the absence of U.S. military occupation, but we do know some general truths. One is that the development of democracy must depend to some significant extent on the acceptance of the *idea* of democracy. People must be willing to fight for democracy and to subject themselves and their political leaders to the rules of democratic behavior—compromise, self-restraint, relinquishment of office, tolerance of opposing views, and more. The second is that the development of democracy depends to some extent on the development of participatory private organizations, which serve both as training grounds in democratic behavior and as independent centers of power able to constrain and counterbalance the power of government. A human rights policy that aims to achieve systemic change might well begin by seeking better ways to broadcast the idea of democracy, to teach the rules and encourage the habits of democratic behavior, and to aid the growth of participatory private organizations that can form the infrastructure of democracy.

Neither the Carter administration nor the Congress during the Carter years showed much interest in this problem. From fiscal year 1978 on, certain funds were disbursed each year under section 116(e) of the Foreign Assistance Act for "programs and activities which will encourage or promote increased adherence to civil and political rights." But the sums were quite small, and both Congress and the executive treated this as an inconsequential addendum to the main human rights policy of administering punishments. The Reagan administration, to its credit, has moved to address more seriously the problem of how to encourage the growth of democracy. In 1982, it initiated a study which resulted in the creation of the National Endowment for Democracy. The Democrats, too, can claim some credit for this, not merely because the endowment was created with bi-partisan support in Congress, but also because the Endowment is reminiscent of an earlier proposal of Congressman Dante Fascell's to create an "Institute for Human Rights and Freedom." It will be a long time before any informed judgment can be made about the effectiveness of the endowment, but certainly it is a step in the right direction. Whether or not punitive measures ought to be a part of U.S. human rights policy, there is a strong case to be made that the central focus of that policy ought to be on helping peoples to build democracy, not on punishing, or for that matter, rewarding the actions of governments.

NOTES

1. U.S., Department of State, *Human Rights and U.S. Foreign Policy*, Pub. 8959, December 1978, p. 8.
2. U.S., Agency for International Development, "Section 116(d)(2) Report," February 1978, and identically titled reports dated January 1979, January 1980, and January 1981. The nine were Gambia, Costa Rica, Peru, India, Ecuador, Kenya, Sri Lanka, Upper Volta, Equatorial Guinea.
3. Elizabeth Drew, "A Reporter at Large: Human Rights," *New Yorker*, July 18, 1977, p. 62.
4. "Memorandum, To: Members of the Working Group on Human Rights and Foreign Assistance, From: HA/HR - G. Michael Bache and EB/OFD/IDF - David Pierce, Subject: Historical Reports, Feb. 3, 1981" Copy in author's files.
5. Interview with David Newsom held in Washington, D.C., June 22, 1982.
6. U.S., Congress, House, Committtee on Appropriations, *Foreign Assistance and Related Agencies Appropriations for 1979*, Pt. 2, 95th Cong., 2nd sess., 1978, p. 434.
7. U.S., Congress, House, Committee on International Relations, *Institute for Human Rights and Freedom, Hearings and Markup before the Subcommittees on International Operations and on International Organizations*, 95th Cong., 2nd sess., 1978.
8. Hans J. Morgenthau, "A Political Theory of Foreign Aid," *The American Political Science Review*, Vol. 56 (1962), pp. 301-309.
9. U.S., Congress, House, Committee on Appropriations, *Foreign Assistance and Related Agencies Appropriations for FY1978, Pt. 1, Hearings before the Subcommittee on Foreign Operations*

Appropriations, 95th Cong., 1st sess., 1977, p. 583.

10. House Report 94-1228, p. 49. Quoted in Lars Schoultz, *Human Rights and United States Policy toward Latin America* (Princeton: Princeton U. Press, 1981), p. 60n.

11. Bruce Cameron, unpublished paper on the history of the Human Rights Working Group, copy in author's files, p. 31.

12. David Trask, "A Short History of the U.S. Department of State 1781-1981," *Department of State Bulletin*, Vol. 81, No. 2046, p. S37.

13. U.S., Congress, Senate, Committee on Foreign Relations, *Human Rights and U.S. Foreign Assistance*, Report Prepared by the Foreign Affairs and National Defense Division, C.R.S., Library of Congress, November 1979, p. 84.

14. Ibid., pp. 12-15.

15. The term "militants" is used here with no pejorative connotation, but simply to designate a group of legislators who pushed the human rights issue with great intensity. All were liberals, but many prominent liberals were not among them.

16. Interview with John Salzberg held by telephone, Jan. 24, 1984.

17. Statement conveyed by telephone by Rep. Harkin's Press Secretary, Feb. 6, 1984.

18. Shoultz, *Human Rights and United States Policy*, p. 105.

19. "Vietnam: A Time for Healing and Compassion," *New York Times* (paid advertisement), Jan. 30, 1977, Sect. 4, p. 5.

20. See Jacqui Chagnon and Roger Rumpf, "Search for 'Yellow Rain,'" *Southeast Asia Chronicle*, No. 90, June 1983 pp. 3-17; "Relief Workers in Laos Debunk Yellow Rain Claims," *New Scientist*, Vol. 99, No. 1373 (1 Sept. 1983), p. 604.

21. U.S., Department of State, "On the Record Briefing," Feb. 8, 1983.

22. Interview with Jacqui Chagnon held in Washington, D.C., Dec. 16, 1983.

23. Ibid.

24. Ibid.

25. Ibid.

26. Ibid.

27. U.S., Congress, Senate Committee on Foreign Relations and House Committee on Foreign Affairs, *Country Reports on Human Rights Practices for 1982*, Report by the Department of State, February 1983, p. 752.

28. Chagnon interview.

29. Ibid.

30. Interview with Bruce Cameron, held in Washington, D.C., Jan. 21, 1984.
31. Ibid.
32. Cameron paper, p. 15.
33. CALC Membership application form, copy in author's files.
34. Cameron interview, Jan. 21, 1984.
35. Ibid.
36. See Stephen J. Morris, "Human Rights in Vietnam Under Two Regimes," in Raymond D. Gastil, *Freedom in the World: Political Rights and Civil Liberties 1982* (Westport, Conn.: Greenwood Press, 1983), pp. 219-253.
37. Interview with Mark Schneider held in Washington, D.C., Nov. 3, 1983.
38. Vite Bita, *Human Rights and U.S. Foreign Policy*, Issue Brief No. IB77056, Library of Congress, Congressional Research Service, Archived 2/23/81, p. 3.
39. Department of State, *Human Rights and U.S. Foreign Policy*, p. 7.
40. U.S., Congress, House, Committee on Foreign Affairs, *Human Rights and U.S. Foreign Policy, Hearings before the Subcommittee on International Organizations*, 96th Cong., 1st sess., 1979, p. 8.
41. Interview with Jessica Tuchman held in Washington, D.C., Dec. 29, 1983.
42. House Committee on Appropriations, *Foreign Assistance and Related Agencies Appropriations for FY1979, Part 2*, p. 468.
43. "Interview With the President," *Weekly Compilation of Presidential Documents*, July 25, 1977, p. 1029.
44. Patricia M. Derian, "Human Rights in America Foreign Policy," *The Notre Dame Lawyer*, Vol. 55 (December 1979), pp. 273-274.
45. "Foreign Assistance Programs," *Weekly Compilation of Presidential Documents*, March 21, 1977, p. 405.
46. Testimony of Stanley J. Heginbotham in U.S., Congress, Senate, Committee on Foreign Relations, *FY1980 International Security Assistance Authorization*, 96th Cong., 1st sess., 1979, p. 75.
47. House Committee on Foreign Affairs, *Human Rights and U.S. Foreign Policy*, p. 298-299.
48. Jo Marie Griesgraber, "Implementation by the Carter Administration of Human Rights Legislation Affecting Latin America" (Doctoral dissertation, Georgetown U., 1984), p. 65.
49. For various methodological notes and explanations see Appendix.
50. David Newsom, "Human Rights and Foreign Policy: The Real

Issue," unpublished manuscript, 1982, p. 24.

51. Interview with Robert Pastor held in College Park, Md., Nov. 10, 1983.

52. Stanley J. Heginbotham testimony in Senate Committee on Foreign Relations, *FY1980 International Security Assistance Authorization*, p. 75.

53. "Secretary Vance and Other Administration Officials Urge Ratificaion of Panama Canal Treaties," *Department of State Bulletin*, Nov. 7, 1977, p. 618.

54. Newsom, "Human Rights and Foreign Policy," pp. 25-26.

55. See supra, Chap. 5.

56. Schoultz, ibid., p. 205. For the quote of Derian, Schoultz cites: "Speech to the American Bar Association's National Institute on International Human Rights Law, Washington, D.C., April 26, 1978."

57. U.S., Congress, House, Committee on Appropriations, *Foreign Assistance and Related Agencies Appropriations for FY1978, Part 3*, 95th Cong., 1st sess., 1977, p. 349.

58. Cited in Schoultz, *Human Rights and United States Policy*, p. 205.

59. Interview with Bruce Cameron held in Washington, D.C., Nov. 4, 1983.

60. Vladimir Bukovsky, *To Build a Castle—My Life as a Dissenter* (New York: Viking Press, 1979), p. 432.

61. Michael Ledeen and William Lewis, *Debacle: The American Failure in Iran* (New York: Alfred A. Knopf, 1981), pp. 146-7. Their account of this issue is confirmed by former Deputy Assistant Secretary Stephen Cohen in interviews held in Washington, D.C., on Nov. 7 and 14, 1983.

62. Speech to Trilateral Commission, Washington, D.C., March 31, 1981, quoted in Vite Bite, "Human Rights and U.S. Foreign Policy," Issue Brief No. IB81125, Congressional Research Service, Library of Congress, updated May 26, 1982, p. 2.

63. Griesgraber, "Implementation of Human Rights Legislation," p. 189. Emphasis as given. "BHN" stands for aid designed to meet "basic human needs."

64. U.S., Department of State, *Report Submitted to Congress in Response to Title VII, Public Law 95-118* printed in U.S., Congress, House, Committee on Foreign Affairs, *Foreign Assistance Legislation for FY1980-1981, Part 1*, p. 72.

65. U.S., Department of State, "Section 116(d)(2) Report," February 1978, p. 3; and supra, Chap. 5, note 39.

66. House Committee on Foreign Affairs, *Reconciling Human Rights*

and U.S. Security Interests, p. 480.

67. U.S., Congress, House, Committee on Foreign Affairs, *Implementation of Congressionally Mandated Human Rights Provisions (Vol. I*, Hearings before the Subcommittee on Human Rights and International Organizations), 97th Cong., 1st sess., 1981, p. 75.

68. Max Weber, *Politics as a Vocation*, trans. by H.H. Gerth and C. Wright Mills (Phila.: Fortress Press, 1965), pp. 46-55.

69. Henry A. Kissinger, "Continuity and Change in American Foreign Policy," *Society*, Vol. 15 (November-December 1977), p. 102.

70. Interview with Mark Schneider held in Washington, D.C., July 23, 1983.

71. Ledeen and Lewis, *Debacle*, op. cit., pp. 68-69.

72. House Committee on Foreign Affairs, *Reconciling Human Rights and U.S. Security Interests in Asia*, p. 71.

73. Griesgraber, "Implementation of Human Rights Legislation," p. 203.

74. Schneider interview, op. cit., Nov. 3, 1983.

75. U.S. Congress, House Committee on International Relations, *Foreign Assistance Legislation for FY1979, Part 4, Hearings before the Subcommittees on International Organizations and on Inter-American Affairs*, 95th Cong., 2nd sess., 1978, p. 9.

76. See supra, Chap. 6, note 2.

77. Senate Committee on Foreign Relations, *Human Rights and U.S. Foreign Assistance*, p. 82.

78. Daniel P. Moynihan, "the Politics of Human Rights," *Commentary*, Vol. 64, No. 2 (August 1977), p. 23.

SEVEN
Evaluating the Carter Policy

It is not easy to reach a comprehensive evaluation of the Carter human rights program. How much did it succeed? How much did it fail? Is the world a better place for it? The answers to such questions are difficult to formulate, and even more difficult to defend. There are various criteria that ought to be applied in reaching such a judgment, but none of them involves "variables" that can be measured with any rigor, and the ones that may be the most important are the least concrete. Any evaluation, then, is necessarily impressionistic.

The first question is: did the Carter policy raise the level of observance of human rights in the world? The annual Survey of Freedom issued by Freedom House registered very slight gains for freedom in the world during the Carter years, except during Carter's first year in office when Freedom House reported that the percentage of the world's population living in free countries jumped from 19.6 percent to 35.7 percent, a truly startling improvement.[1] But more than 99 percent of that gain was attributable to the restoration of democracy in India and Spain, neither of which was a particular focus of the administration's policy, nor was even mentioned among the couple of dozen countries for whose progress administration spokesmen did on occasion claim credit.

Aside from India and Spain, the gains registered by Freedom House were of little statistical significance and of unknown cause. In all, it is probably fair to conclude that the administration's human rights emphasis had some small overall beneficial impact on the international atmosphere.

Whatever the uncertainty about its effects on the state of human rights in the world as a whole, there is strong reason to believe that U.S. human rights policy had an important beneficial impact on certain countries. In the Dominican Republic, the evidence seems overwhelming that only direct American pressure dissuaded military officials from aborting the election of 1978. Indonesia made good on the release of thirty thousand political prisoners held since the unsuccessful Communist putsch of 1965. David Newsom, the U.S. ambassador to Indonesia who handled the pertinent discussions with the Indonesian government, reports that they "really pre-dated the Carter administration."[2] Nevertheless, the Carter administration deserves much credit for bringing them to a successful conclusion.

In Argentina, pressures brought by the Carter administration helped to bring about an end to "disappearances." It is hard to say whether American policy deserves any credit for the return to democracy in that country. The Reagan administration maintained some of the pressures against Argentina that had been begun under Carter, and discarded others. Can the reemergence of democracy in Argentina be attributed to the pressures that Reagan maintained? Or to his easing of pressures? Was it a delayed benefit of Carter's actions? Most likely, the answer is none of the above. Their catastrophic misadventure in the Falklands/Malvinas was probably the undoing of the generals—the single most important factor leading to restoration of civilian rule. Nonetheless, President Alfonsin's statement that the Carter administration's campaign against "disappearances" saved thousands of lives is testimony to an impressive accomplishment.

Some countries moved from dictatorial to democratic rule during the Carter years—Bangladesh, Ecuador, Ghana, Nigeria, and Peru—but there is no way to judge how much credit for this, if any, should be given to the Carter policy. Once again, it seems fair to guess that the atmosphere created by the Carter policy added some unquantifiable weight to the scales on the side of restoration of democracy. Three of those five, all but Peru and Ecuador, have since lapsed back to dictatorship. Is this because Reagan has not pressed the human rights issue as hard as Carter, or does it merely show that the changes were ephemeral in the first place? There is no good way to judge.

In some countries where there was no overall movement toward a freer or more democratic system, the administration was nonetheless able to secure the release of various individual prisoners. This was the case with the Soviet Union, as is well-known, and Brzezinski, in his memoirs, cites some less well known cases, about which there is no reason to doubt—Guinea, Niger, Rwanda, Swaziland.[3] There were surely many other such cases. Similar things are being done by the Reagan administration,[4] and were even done, although perhaps less often, under Carter's predecessors, as Kissinger claims.[5]

"What can we conclude from this record?" asked Ernst Haas. His answer:

> There has been some marginal improvement in behavior on the part of a few countries. Nobody can tell how permanent that change may be, but past experience with similar waves of relaxation in repression strongly suggests that, unless the regime changes basically, people released from prison can always be rearrested. The skills of the torturer, though perhaps not used for a while, are never forgotten. No fundamental change in the global human rights picture can be discovered.[6]

There is nothing in Haas's judgment that is untrue, but it is too cynical. Some number of lives were saved or spared from grievous suffering. Even where this was unaccompanied by any change in the political system, it is a benefit of inestimable value. Some countries were moved toward democratic process, and here the gain is all the greater. And even where moves toward democracy were soon reversed, it is not necessarily the case that these were for naught. If nations that have not known democracy are going to achieve it, might it not take several attempts? And might not each attempt strengthen the next one?

As for Carter's other goals, there is more reason to doubt that they were achieved. The first of these was, as Carter put it, to "restore...to our people a pride again."[7] Carter was probably right to think that articulating America's idealism would be a good tonic for post-Vietnam self-doubt, but in the end there is little reason to believe that Carter's policy made Americans feel proud again. Had it done so, it is hard to imagine that he would have been beaten so badly for reelection. This is not to suggest that Carter's defeat in 1980 was the result of his human rights policy or even of his foreign policy as a whole, but surely he would have done better in the election had he succeeded in making Americans feel proud.

In preelection surveys by CBS News and the *New York Times* voters were asked: "If [Carter or Reagan] is elected, do you think he will see to it that the United States is respected by other nations?" When the question was asked about Reagan, 77 percent responded "yes." When it was asked about Carter only 55 percent responded "yes."[8] Of course, many of those who answered yes, especially in regard to Reagan, may have had in mind the criteria of diplomatic and military toughness. But there are many ways to win respect: you can win respect for your strength or for your ideals. It is reasonable to assume that if Carter had succeeded in restoring Americans' pride in their foreign policy, he would not have compared so unfavorably in their estimation of his ability to make others respect us.

Another of the indirect goals of the human rights policy

was to achieve, as Carter put it, "a resurgence of admiration for our country" in the Third World.[9] It would be hard to argue that this goal was achieved. To be sure there were individual democrats, dissidents, lovers of freedom, in various countries around the world who appreciated deeply the new U.S. emphasis on human rights, but the Carter years were rife with evidence of Third World contempt and hostility toward the United States. The Ayatollah Khomeini swept to power in Iran on a platform of rabid anti-Americanism. He quickly won a following throughout the Near East, signified by such grassroots activities as the burning of the American embassy in Pakistan. Also in the Near East, the administration was unable to induce a single Arab state to stand by Egypt in the face of its ostracism for having made peace with Israel.

In Latin America, the Sandinistas took over Nicaragua and gave it a new national anthem declaring the Yanqui "the enemy of mankind." A month before the Sandinista triumph, the United States had proposed that an OAS peacekeeping force be used to ensure a transition to democracy in Nicaragua without further bloodletting, but this proposal was rejected overwhelmingly, marking the nadir of U.S. influence in the regional body. Moreover, during the Carter years, the conference of "nonaligned" nations became more blatantly aligned—against the United States—than ever before, creating the absurd situation in which the leadership of those who wished to resist total obeisance to the USSR fell by default to an obviously somewhat nonplussed Marshall Tito.

Also during the Carter years, the United States found itself with so little support in its efforts to resist the politicization of the International Labor Organization that it felt compelled to withdraw from that venerable institution in 1978. True, the United States rejoined the ILO two years later, after the withdrawal of American participation and financial contributions had a sobering effect on the remaining members, but the whole episode hardly bespoke a "resurgence" of Third World "admiration" for the United States.

A third goal of the human rights policy, articulated by several of the leading figures in the administration, was to capture the ideological initiative. There is little doubt that in its first weeks—with the Sakharov letter and the Bukovsky visit—the administration did have the Soviets on the defensive. And the feeling, in those weeks, that the United States had seized the initiative extended beyond U.S.-Soviet issues. When the president was speaking loudly about human rights, he to some extent altered the international agenda. But the administration was of no mind to pursue an ideological offensive against the Soviets: when it discovered that this made the Russians angry, it quickly backed off.

As its human rights policy came to focus on the abuses of rightist governments in Latin America, southern Africa, and a few in Asia, the administration often was in the position of playing into the ideological offensives of America's adversaries. After all, "human rights" as a slogan is not anathema to them. Moynihan has pointed out that, "as defined by the totalitarian nations...the issue of human rights has long been at the center of international politics."[10] In the name of human rights, the Communists conduct worldwide campaigns against the governments of Pinochet, Somoza, Muzorewa, and Begin, not to mention in behalf of such as the "Wilmington ten." To be sure, in some of these cases—Pinochet and Somoza are clear examples—egregious abuses exist and the United States must address them, but when these come to dominate, as they did under Carter, U.S. human rights policy, then, far from holding the ideological initiative, the United States finds itself following someone else's agenda.

It is hard to see how, under the Carter administration, the United States could have held the ideological initiative. Carter's foreign policy team was made up of what Carl Gershman has called "the new foreign policy establishment,"[11] one of whose central tenets in the wake of Vietnam was that the United States needed to accept gracefully a diminution of its influence in the world. As Thomas Hughes, president of the Carnegie Endowment for

International Peace, put it, the task of the Carter administration was to forge "a constructive new American accommodation with mankind."[12] Such attitudes on the part of its leaders leave a nation ill-suited to seize initiatives, ideological or otherwise. Charles Fairbanks has pointed out that Britain's campaign in the last century to abolish the slave trade owed its success to the connection that was perceived, both by the British themselves and by those they were trying to influence, between "Britain's success in the world" and "its principles." Fairbanks goes on to argue:

> ....A nation's insistence on human rights cannot have a powerful effect if that nation does not provide an example of the success of those principles. A weak, poor, and despised nation cannot provide an attractive example. In recent years the United States sometimes seemed to base its human rights policy on the opposite assumption. In his Notre Dame speech defining his administration's new human rights emphasis, President Carter declared that "through failure, we have now found our way back to our own principles and values."[13]

In its first weeks in office the Carter administration succeeded in demonstrating the potential that human rights policy held for enabling the United States to take the ideological initiative, but it was a potential that the administration left unfulfilled.

The fifth goal of the Carter human rights policy was the ulterior one—to give the administration "running room on the Right" that would help it win ratification of a SALT treaty. That it never got its SALT treaty ratified was of course not the fault of its human rights policy. That failure was due to the Soviet invasion of Afghanistan, to the discovery of the Soviet combat brigade in Cuba, to the disastrous selection of Paul Warnke as SALT negotiator, to the loss of American intelligence installations in Iran—all told, to the feeling in the country and in the Senate that the Carter administration was weak. It was surely not the human rights policy that gave rise to this perception of weakness, but the handling of it toward the Soviets did nothing to counteract that perception.

The two top officials who guided Carter's foreign policy had conflicting approaches to the Soviet Union. Brzezinski had some inclination to confront the Soviets, while Vance's inclination was to placate them. Rather than choose between the paths offered by Vance and Brzezinski, Carter chose instead to be guided a little by each. On the issue of human rights, Carter first confronted the Soviets rather boldly, thus provoking them, and then, feeling their wrath, he sought to placate them. This may have been the worst course of all. It elicited only contempt from the Russians, and helped to make Carter appear weak in the eyes of Americans. If this didn't contribute to Carter's problems with SALT, it certainly didn't contribute to solving them either.

In sum, the Carter human rights policy achieved little in the realm of its indirect goals—restoring American pride, winning the admiration of the Third World, capturing the ideological initiative, boosting SALT—although it does seem to have achieved some benefits in the realm of its most direct and central goal—raising the level of respect for human rights in some countries. Against this gain must be balanced any losses. Are there any countries in which the Carter human rights policy caused a deterioration in the human rights situation? This question presents itself most urgently with respect to Nicaragua and Iran where Carter's human rights policy has been blamed for contributing to the overthrow of existing governments.

The replacement of governments friendly to the United States in those two countries with governments hostile to the United States is a clear setback for U.S. geopolitical interests. Because America is the world's most important democracy and the protector of all other democracies, a setback for American interests is, all other things being equal, *ipso facto* a setback for the cause of human rights. Of course, all other things are not often equal, but in this case the pros and cons are not hard to sort out. The changes in government in Nicaragua and Iran were not only inimical to U.S. interests, they also brought no gain for human rights in any other significant respect.

This is easiest to see in Iran where the rule of Ayatollah Khomeini and his cohorts has eclipsed that of the Shah in terms of many different kinds of human rights violations, notably the frequency of executions on political or religious grounds, the absence of due process, the persecution of Jews, Bahais and other minorities, the denial of rights to women, the persecution of dissenting views, and the censorship of expression and of the arts according to rigid clerical precepts, not to mention such additional peccadilloes as the use of human wave attacks and of human mine detectors by the Iranian armed forces in their war with Iraq.

In Nicaragua, it is not so clear that the present Sandinista government is worse than Somoza's was in terms of human rights. The present government is clearly worse in terms of censorship of the press and restrictions on the churches. It has abused the Miskitos and smaller Indian populations far more viciously than ever before. It has created a system of neighborhood organizations that stretches the tentacles of government control and surveillance down into the daily lives of every citizen in a way that was unknown under Somoza. It is argued on the other side that such gross abuses as executions, torture and "disappearances" are fewer under the Sandinistas than under Somoza. Whether or not the human rights situation in Nicaragua is yet as bad or worse than it was under Somoza, there is little room for doubt that the intention of the ruling Sandinistas is to turn Nicaragua into a full-fledged Communist state, and if they succeed in this endeavor there is no doubt that the abuse of human rights will be far worse than it was under Somoza.

The human rights effects of the Iranian and Nicaraguan revolutions are felt not just in Iran and Nicaragua. Both are having powerful deleterious repercussions on the human rights of neighboring peoples. The success of Khomeini's revolution has kindled a wave of fanatical Islamic fundamentalism throughout the Near East. It may not be for us to say whether or not this movement is pleasing to God, but it clearly is inimical to the cause of human rights on this Earth. It is inciting bloodshed and instability throughout the region, and in whatever countries or areas it succeeds in establishing its authority it can be relied upon to impose a regime of narrow intolerance and repression. The victory of the Nicaraguan revolution has strengthened Communist guerrillas in other Central American countries both through the power of its example and through direct material support.

These Communist revolutions entail vast losses of life and treasure—"treasure," that is, often in the form of the meager possessions or crops of impoverished people. This is not to say that the loss of life that revolutions entail is never justified. Only a strict pacifist would deny that the blessings that could be brought by a genuine democratic revolution could ever outweigh, in the scales of human rights, the toll exacted by the revolution. But the special tragedy of Communist revolutions is that they bring no blessings.

If, then, the Iranian and Nicaraguan revolutions were clear defeats for the cause of international human rights, the question remains whether the Carter human rights policy bears any responsibility for the victory of these revolutions. The answer is surely yes, it bears *some* responsibility, but it is harder to say how much. William Bundy, someone not unsympathetic to the Carter administration, asked himself these questions in the immediate aftermath of the two revolutions and concluded that the Carter policy bore a great deal of responsibility for the overthrow of Somoza and at most only a little for the overthrow of the Shah.[14]

Jeane Kirkpatrick has been most forceful in placing responsibility for Somoza's overthrow on the Carter policy. The Carter administration didn't merely tolerate Somoza's fall, she says, "*it brought down the Somoza regime.*"[15] To this Robert Pastor, chief Latin American specialist on Carter's National Security Council, has replied: "Somoza fell of his own corrupt and repressive weight."[16]

In 1977, when the Carter administration took office, a state of siege had been in effect in Nicaragua since a celebrated guerrilla raid in Managua in 1974. During the administration's first weeks in office, Under Secretary of State for Security Assistance Lucy Benson encouraged Congress to cut off aid to Somoza. Testifying before the House Subcommittee on Foreign Operations Appropriations, Mrs. Benson was asked by Subcommittee Chairman Clarence Long: "...if this committee were to suspend all aid to Nicaragua....What would be lost to the United States ...?" She replied: "I cannot think of a single thing."[17] In addition to congressional aid cuts that were enacted against Somoza, the administration exacted sanctions of its own, withholding authorized military aid and blocking licenses for the private sale of military goods.

In September 1977, Somoza, responding to U.S. pressure, lifted the state of siege, and, according to leftist academic Richard R. Fagen: "There was an immediate response: labor unrest, student demonstrations, a wave of disclosures in the local press, and armed attacks by the FSLN against several provincial towns."[18]

In January 1978, Nicaragua was convulsed when Somoza's most prominent political opponent, Pedro Joaquin Chamorro, editor of *La Prensa*, was assassinated. Suspicion (still unconfirmed) that Somoza was behind the assassination sparked massive protests. *Time* magazine reported in February:

> Last month opposition elements mounted a two-week nation-wide general strike to protest the assassination of an anti-Somoza newspaper editor. Ambassador Solaun cautioned Somoza that Washington would not support him unless he responded to the strike with reform rather than repression. "If it were not for Carter's concern for human rights," an opposition leader told TIME, "this general strike would not have been possible."[19]

Also during February, Miguel D'Escoto, now the foreign minister in the Sandinista government, in testimony before a congressional committee, expressed his gratification that "during the Carter administration...much progress has been made" in getting "the United States to cease the interventionist policy of giving military and economic aid to the Somoza regime."[20]

In July 1978, the *Washington Post*'s Karen DeYoung reported that a source in the Carter administration had told her that it had threatened Somoza with the withdrawal of the U.S. ambassador and even a severing of diplomatic relations should he respond to the growing challenge to his regime with repression. "We are not intriguing against any opposition faction. The fact is, we're against Somoza," DeYoung quoted her source as saying.[21]

In the fall of 1978, a U.S.-led OAS mediation effort foundered. The mediators had taken up a proposal by Somoza that his rule be put to a national plebiscite. But when Somoza and the mediators could not come to agreement on the conditions for the plebiscite, the administration came down hard on him. It withdrew the U.S. military assistance group from Nicaragua and "terminated" the military assistance program, which had been in a state of "suspension." It announced that it would consider no further economic aid programs and would not implement two loan projects which had been signed but not yet begun. It withdrew all Peace Corps volunteers and reduced the number of U.S. diplomatic personnel in Nicaragua.[22] At the same time, according to transcripts of secret tape recordings made public by Somoza in his memoirs, the authenticity of which has not been challenged, a series of special diplomatic messengers traveled from Washington to Managua to urge Somoza to leave office.[23]

Somoza refused to leave, and in a few months U.S. spokesmen began to call publicly for his ouster. In June the United States joined in an OAS resolution making the position formal.[24] The administration reinforced its boycott on military aid to Somoza by bringing pressure to bear on its allies, notably Israel, to cease selling arms to him. These acts paved the way for the success of the Sandinistas' well-armed "final offensive" in July.

This brief review of the events makes clear that Pastor's reply to Kirkpatrick is inadequate. Whatever Somoza's own "corrupt and repressive weight," his fall was aided by a push from the Carter administration. Pastor may wish to argue that Somoza would have fallen even without the push, but that we'll never know. And although many former Carter administration officials and academic commentators sympathetic to the Sandinistas dispute the blanket charge that the Carter administration "lost Nicaragua," most agree that its policies had some part in the overthrow. Richard Feinberg, the Latin American specialist of the State Department's Policy Planning Staff under Carter, has written: "the human rights policy did energize Somoza's opposition and compound his diplomatic isolation. However, on two separate occasions many in the State Department had wanted to ease Somoza out in a controlled transition well before the Sandinistas had become the alternative."[25] The fact that some in the administration wanted to "ease Somoza out" earlier hardly contradicts the claim that the administration helped to topple him.

Lars Schoultz, an academic sympathetic to the Sandinistas, has written:

....I believe the human rights policy of the United States helped to create this opposition [to Somoza]. There are no data to confirm this belief, but in the early 1980s it is widely if not universally held by foreign policy analysts. Popularity is not always the best gauge of an argument's validity, of course, but analysts who rarely found a trace of competence in U.S. foreign policy makers were caught admitting that their human rights policy had encouraged the resurgence of the opposition to repressive Latin American governments. The normally critical liberal weekly *Latin America* noted, for example, that "Carter's policy (albeit unwittingly) undermined the entire *somocista* system in Nicaragua."[26]

Finally, William Bundy finds the Carter administration's responsibility to be every bit as profound as Kirkpatrick argues. He wrote in late 1979: "If Gerald Ford had been elected in 1976....it seems a safe bet that Tacho Somoza would still be in charge of Managua."[27]

The case of Iran is quite different from that of Nicaragua. Far from pushing the Shah out, U.S. policy-makers, at least at the top level, were frightened by the prospect of his fall. An argument made about Iran is that Carter's human rights policy contributed, albeit indirectly, to the fall of the Shah by energizing the opposition and by paralyzing the Shah, the Iranian military, and perhaps even the U.S. government, once the crisis was underway. This is essentially the argument made by Michael Ledeen and William Lewis in their book, *Debacle: The American Failure in Iran*.[28] Stephen Cohen, the official who was responsible for human rights policy toward Iran, has taken the lead in debunking these accusations. "Ledeen and Lewis tell a fairy tale," says Cohen, "because we lost all the battles [within the administration] to apply human rights pressures on the Shah." Cohen adds: "The best you can do...and this is pure hypothesis...is say that because of general rhetoric about human rights spoken by Jimmy Carter in the United States, the Shah felt himself to be under some pressure."[29]

But Cohen doesn't do justice to the case. It is more than "pure hypothesis" that the Shah felt pressure. Sandra Vogelgesang, who served in 1977 as the human rights specialist on the State Department's Policy Planning Staff, wrote in mid-1978, while the Shah still seemed securely on his throne, that "the Shah of Iran...has responded to criticisms from the United States and others by releasing political prisoners, engaging in fewer reported cases of torture, inviting the International Committee of the Red Cross to make two inspections of Iranian prisons, permitting meetings with representatives of the International Commission of Jurists, and continuing to give high priority to such basic human needs as health care and housing."[30]

Nor is it true that *no* human rights sanctions were applied to Iran. At the insistence of Patricia Derian, the Iranian military was denied tear gas and other crowd-control equipment, a decision with which Cohen says he disagreed because it was unimportant.[31] Perhaps it was unimportant, but it was not entirely without consequences. A major turning point in the Iranian crisis was the infamous "bloody Friday" when the Shah's troops fired on demonstrators in

Jaleh Square, killing hundreds. According to Barry Rubin's highly regarded account of the crisis, the Iranian generals "wanted riot control equipment. Many of the deaths that had occurred could have been avoided, they said. If they had had tear gas they would not have had to rely on bullets."[32] Rubin does not assert that the generals' claims were ingenuous. They may of course have been merely self-serving, but they are certainly not implausible.

The argument that Carter's policy served to energize the Iranian opposition comes from an authority, Richard Cottam, who was bitterly opposed to the Shah and on whom Cohen himself relies. Cottam wrote in early 1978, before the Iranian crisis began: "The Carter human rights advocacy has precipitated in Iran the reappearance of public opposition" and, moreover, "there is not the slightest question that the timing of opposition activity is directly related to Carter's pronouncements on human rights."[33]

When the crisis reached full bloom, Brzezinski reports in his memoirs that he tended to favor a coup by the Iranian military in the hope that the armed forces could restore order and authority. That approach sounds draconian, but on hindsight it is possible to say that it might have been a more humane outcome than the triumph of Khomeini. Brzezinski says that he was stymied by the top officials of the State Department who "were much more preoccupied with the goal of promoting the democratization of Iran and feared actions—U.S. or Iranian—that might have the opposite effect."[34] This is in effect confirmed by Vance in his memoirs, where he writes that the "Shah's best chance" was "to share enough power with a coalition government to split the moderate nationalists off from the Khomeini followers."[35] In addition, Brzezinski charges that "the lower echelons of State, on the Iran Desk, were clearly cheering the Shah's opponents."[36] The Iran desk chief to whom Brzezinski is referring, Henry Precht, sent a delegation to Iran in the midst of the crisis, one of whose three members was Stephen Cohen of the human rights bureau. Ledeen and Lewis write that Cohen's assignment was "to ensure that [Ambassador]

Sullivan would continue to remind the shah of America's commitment to human rights and that the Iranians would not be subjected to a savage repression."[37] Cohen denies this, insisting that the primary purpose of his visit was fact-finding, but he agrees that a "subsidiary purpose" may have been to send "send some kind of message to somebody by including me on the team."[38] If Cohen was viewed by others as he was by Under Secretary Newsom, as one of those eager to see the Shah overthrown,[39] then his inclusion in the delegation may have sent a strong message indeed.

There are many who argue that the events in Iran were the work of profound forces on which American policy had only minimal impact, but the above facts make at least plausible the contrary argument put by Max Lerner: "There are no 'inevitable' revolutions. The Iranian revolution...didn't have to take place. The fact that it did was largely due to American blunders and the American policy climate."[40] Lerner may overstate the case, and Bundy may be right in arguing that the American influence on the course of events was only marginal, but the argument that U.S. human rights policy contributed in some degree, probably never measurable, to the outcome in Iran seems compelling. And in his memoirs President Carter seems to concede that his human rights policy contributed to the overthrow of Somoza or the Shah or both when he says that he knew from the beginning that "there would be cases when oppressed people could obtain freedom only by changing their own laws or leaders."[41]

Difficult as they are to measure, the good that the Carter policy did in Argentina, Indonesia, and the Dominican Republic, and the harm that it did in Iran and Nicaragua, are effects that are material. But the more profound effects of the Carter human rights policy may be those that are not material, but "spiritual"—those that exist only in the minds of people. Like the material effects, the spiritual effects include both some that were beneficial and some that were harmful to the cause of human rights.

My main premise here is that a crucial determinant of

the state of human rights in the world is the state of the *idea* of human rights. How widely human rights will be respected depends upon how many people believe that human rights should be respected and upon how deeply they believe it. Will unfree people fight for their rights? What risks will they take? What sacrifices will they make? And will members of elites obey the rules that protect human rights? Will office-holders submit to the rule of law? Will they leave office peacefully when their terms expire? Will leaders of inter-est groups engage in constructive compromise with other groups? Will members of blocs and factions and parties tolerate expression of opinions different from their own? Will intellectuals and artists and educators help to create a climate in which those norms respectful of human rights are rein-forced? These are the questions on which the state of human rights in individual societies and in the world depends.

This way of viewing the problem is in explicit contrast to views that hold that the state of human rights is deter-mined by such "objective" factors as wealth or industrial development or class and race relations, although of course it does not deny that these factors may affect people's thoughts about human rights, as well as other things. Nor does it claim that if the idea of human rights flourishes, the fulfillment of those rights will necessarily follow. As long as there are armed tyrants in the world, human rights must be defended, not only in the realm of ideas but in that of arms, as well. Poland provides a good example of a society whose populace gives every sign that it wants and under-stands and is willing to fight for human rights, and yet is still denied them by a relatively small number of people with guns, mostly foreigners. But, the case of Poland is not typi-cal. In most of the unfree world today, the idea of human rights holds insufficient force over the minds of elites and of the masses, and its requirements are insufficiently under-stood. The goal of human rights policy is to change this.

How, then, did the Carter human rights policy affect the state of *the idea of human rights*? Peter G. Brown and Douglas MacLean argue: "If the policy merely gives high visibility to human rights, but low priority to actions that promote them, it may be counterproductive."[42] My view is the opposite of this. Giving it high visibility strengthens the idea of human rights. The presidency is still a "bully pulpit" and the United States is still the world's most influential country. When the president of the United States emphasizes human rights, as Carter did, this is bound to have a significant effect. Who knows how many people were inspired by it? How many were deservingly embarrassed by it? How many dissidents were encouraged or emboldened by it? How many were sustained or given faith? We will never be able to count the number, but surely there were some, and perhaps many.

After Carter's first year in office, the International League for Human Rights said:

> Within the past year, human rights has for the first time become a subject of national policy debate in many countries. Human rights concerns have been the focus of discussion in international organizations and of greater attention in the world media. A most significant factor in this has been President Carter and the U.S. human rights policy.[43]

And a year later, Arthur Schlesinger wrote: "For all its vulnerabilities, the campaign had significantly altered the international atmosphere. It had placed human rights on the world's agenda—and on the world's conscience."[44] For these reasons I believe that President Carter is justified to claim in his memoirs:

> The lifting of the human spirit, the revival of hope, the absence of fear, the release from prison, the end of torture, the reunion of a family, the newfound sense of human dignity—these are difficult to quantify, but I am certain that many people were able to experience them because the United States of America let it be known that we stood for freedom and justice for all people.[45]

The struggle to strengthen the idea of human rights, however, does not consist only in broadcasting it, of putting it "on the world's agenda." It consists just as importantly in clarifying it and teaching its true meaning. The reasons for this are not pedantic. Human rights and the idea of human rights have powerful enemies in the world today. But nowhere do they announce themselves as such. In other times, the idea of human rights had been explicitly rejected by those who said it contradicted the divine order or historic destiny. But today the enemies of human rights all proclaim themselves to be its most ardent champions. This is most obviously true in all of the vicious dictatorships that go by the name "People's Democracy," but the phenomenon is not limited to the Left: Anastasio Somoza explains in his memoirs that when he was president, Nicaragua was "a free and democratic nation."[46] In this age there is much less danger that the phrase, "human rights," will be forgotten or rejected than that its meaning will be lost. It follows that the highest task in the struggle to strengthen the idea of human rights is to defend it against impostors and to keep its meaning clear. At this task the Carter administration failed; indeed it may justly be accused of having added to the muddle.

Part of this problem was caused by Carter's own inadequacies and part was caused by the policy choices of his administration. In the former category there are a long string of ignorant or impulsive or opportunistic utterances that made his human rights policy look foolish or that did harm in other ways. For example, whether or not the distinction between "totalitarian" and "authoritarian" dictatorships ought to have major operational implications for U.S. human rights policy, the concept "totalitarian" is a valuable one to the cause of human rights because it aids in the understanding of the dynamics of certain forms of oppression. Carter relentlessly debased this term by applying it to America's allies to whom no knowledgeable person, of whatever political stripe, would find it applicable. Thus, speaking of the cuts in aid to rightist U.S. allies, Carter proclaimed proudly: "We are no longer the best friend of every scurrilous totalitarian government on Earth."[47]

Secondly, Carter often made outlandish claims about the effects of his human rights policy that suggested that either he didn't understand much about the world or that he was insincere and motivated by narrow political self-interest. For example, on dozens of occasions he repeated the litany that as a result of his policies, "almost the entire world leadership is now preoccupied with the question of human rights," that there is not "a single leader of a nation on Earth today who doesn't have within his or her consciousness a concern about human rights," that "among almost all the leaders of the 150 nations of the world this year, there is a preoccupation with and a concern about human rights."[48]

Worse still was Carter's penchant for flattering tyrants. Campaigning in Minneapolis, Carter boasted: "We are strong enough now not to have to depend on every cheap, tinhorn dictatorship in the world."[49] But then he told Gierek that he was an "enlightened leader," Ceaucescu that he was a "great leader," Tito that he "exemplifies the eagerness for freedom," and Pahlavi that Iran was an "island of stability" because of the "love which your people give to you."[50]

In addition to Carter's own various faux pas, critical policy choices that guided his human rights policy helped to confuse rather than clarify the meaning of human rights. In order to curry favor with the Third World, the administration embraced the concept of "economic and social rights," a concept whose effect, and probably whose purpose, is not to expand the realm of "rights" but to dilute the concept of "rights." In pursuit of universalism it placed undue emphasis on UN-sponsored international human rights documents which at best are utopian and at worst hypocritical. And out of bureaucratic cautiousness it created a category, "the integrity of the person," which in reality is a category of abuses and designated it instead as a category of "rights." The net effect was to downplay the idea of human rights as it is known in the American, more broadly the Western, tradition, which remains the only tradition that has given the world human rights in practice.

Second, in the name of case-by-case pragmatism, the Carter human rights policy bound itself to no standard of consistency. At times this meant that the policy was erratic or irrational, reflecting accidents of the bureaucratic process or the biases of administration officials. Still worse, the policy reflected a strong emphasis on weak countries ("tinhorn dictatorships") and countries with which the United States had little other important business, thus conveying the impression that human rights was not a matter of principle for the United States, but a slogan of convenience or hypocrisy.

Because of its disdain for consistency and its emphasis on punitive instruments, the Carter policy focused more sharply on rightist than on Communist regimes. This played into the hands of the powerful international propaganda campaigns waged by the Communists, hypocritically in the name of "human rights," the aim of which is to destabilize the "imperialist camp." Worse, it helped to mislead our own people and others about where in today's world the most dire enemies of human rights are found. The emphasis on punitive measures also served to sow confusion about how human rights are achieved, and about the purposes of human rights policy.

Worst of all, by proclaiming and, indeed, attempting to conduct, a human rights policy that stood above ideology, the Carter administration opted out of the very struggle for the idea of human rights. It believed or pretended to believe that either the respect or the violation of human rights was nothing more than a collection of actions performed by governments unrelated to the ideas that guide them. This was not merely foolish, it was dangerous. If Americans and others who now enjoy unimpaired exercise of their human rights ever came to believe that this heritage was merely a bit of random good fortune, rather than the fruits of a painstakingly constructed system of ideas, they would stand in danger of losing those rights, for they would be without any guide as to how to defend them in difficult times.

We can't say how much of one or how much of the other, but the good that the Carter policy did for the idea of human rights by broadcasting it must be weighed against the harm it did by contributing to the miasma that surrounds the term, much of it deliberately stirred up by the enemies of human rights.

NOTES

1. Raymond D. Gastil, "The Comparative Survey of Freedom," *Freedom at Issue*, No. 76 (January-February 1984), p. 5.
2. Interview with David Newsom held in Washington, D.C., June 22, 1982.
3. Zbigniew Brzezinski, *Power and Principle* (New York: Farrar, Straus, Giroux, 1983), p. 129.
4. Interviews with Elliott Abrams, Assistant Secretary of State for Human Rights and Humanitarian Affairs, held in Washington, D.C., Sept. 30, 1983 and Oct. 21, 1983.
5. Henry A. Kissinger, "Continuity and Change in American Foreign Policy," *Society*, Vol. 15 (November-December 1977), p. 100.
6. Ernst Haas, "Human Rights" in Kenneth A. Oye, Donald Rothchild and Robert J. Lieber, eds., *Eagle Entangled* (New York: Longman, 1979), p. 184.
7. "Los Angeles, California," *Weekly Compilation of Presidential Documents*, Oct. 31, 1977, p. 1650.
8. "Opinion Roundup," *Public Opinion*, January 1981, p. 29.
9. "Interview With the President," *Weekly Compilation of Presidential Documents* Aug. 21, 1978, p. 1410.
10. Daniel P. Moynihan, "The Politics of Human Rights," *Commentary*, Vol. 64, No. 2 (1977), p. 20.
11. Carl Gershman, "The Rise and Fall of the New Foreign Policy Establishment," *Commentary*, Vol. 70, No. 1 (July 1980), pp. 13-24.
12. Quoted in Ibid., p. 20.
13. Charles H. Fairbanks, Jr., "The British Campaign Against the Slave Trade," in Fred E. Baumann, ed., *Human Rights and American Foreign Policy* (Gambier, Ohio: Kenyon College, 1982), p. 127.
14. William P. Bundy, "Who Lost Patagonia? Foreign Policy in the 1980 Campaign," *Foreign Affairs* Vol. 58, No. 1 (Fall 1979), pp. 1-27.
15. Jeane Kirkpatrick, "U.S. Security and Latin America," *Commentary*, Vol. 71, No. 1 (January 1981), p. 36. Emphasis in original.

16. "Letters from Readers," *Commentary*, Vol. 71, No. 4 (April 1981), p. 6.

17. U.S., Congress, House, Committee on Appropriations, *Foreign Assistance and Related Agencies Appropriations for FY1978, Part 1*, 95th Cong., 1st sess., 1977, pp. 748-749.

18. Richard R. Fagen, "Dateline Nicaragua: The End of the Affair," *Foreign Policy*, No. 36 (Fall 1979), p. 183.

19. "A Crusade That Isn't Going to Die," *Time*, Feb. 27, 1978, p. 23.

20. U.S., Congress, House, Committee on International Relations, *Foreign Assistance Legislation for FY1979, Part 4, Hearings before the Subcommittees on International Organizations and on Inter-American Affairs*, 95th Cong., 2nd sess., 1978, p. 98.

21. " 'The Twelve:' Nicaragua's Unlikely Band of Somoza Foes," *Washington Post*, July 23, 1978, p. A26.

22. "Western Hemisphere: Nicaragua," *Department of State Bulletin*, May 1979, p. 66.

23. Anastasio Somoza, as told to Jack Cox, *Nicaragua Betrayed*, (Boston: Western Islands, 1980), pp. 311-381.

24. "Western Hemisphere: Nicaragua," *Department of State Bulletin*, August 1979, pp. 55-60.

25. Richard Feinberg, "U.S. Human Rights Policy: Latin America," *International Policy Report*, Vol. VI, No. 1 (October 1980), Center for International Policy, p. 6.

26. Lars Schoultz, *Human Rights and United States Policy toward Latin America* (Princeton: Princeton U., 1981), p. 363.

27. Bundy, "Who Lost Patagonia?", pp. 8-9.

28. Michael Ledeen and William Lewis, *Debacle: The American Failure in Iran* (New York: Alfred A. Knopf, 1981).

29. Interview with Stephen Cohen, held in Washington, D.C., Nov. 7, 1983.

30. Sandra Vogelgesang, "What Price Principle? U.S. Policy on Human Rights," *Foreign Affairs*, Vol. 56, No. 4 (July 1978), p. 823.

31. Interview with Stephen Cohen, held in Washington, D.C., Nov. 14, 1983.

32. Barry Rubin, *Paved with Good Intentions: The American Experience in Iran* (New York: Oxford U., 1980), p. 227.

33. Richard W. Cottam, "The Case of Iran," in Raymond D. Gastil, *Freedom in the World 1978* (Boston: G.K. Hall, 1978), pp. 105, 102.

34. Zbigniew Brzezinski, *Power and Principle* (New York: Farrar,

Straus, Giroux, 1983), p. 355.

35. Cyrus Vance, *Hard Choices* (New York: Simon and Schuster, 1983) p. 331.
36. Brzezinski, *Power and Principle*, p. 396.
37. Ledeen and Lewis, *Debacle*, p. 159.
38. Cohen interview, Nov. 7.
39. See Ch. 1, note 35.
40. Max Lerner, "Human Rights and American Foreign Policy: A Symposium," *Commentary*, Vol. 72, No. 5 (November 1981), p. 47.
41. Jimmy Carter, *Keeping Faith* (New York: Bantam, 1982), p. 143.
42. Peter G. Brown and Douglas MacLean, "Introduction" to Brown and MacLean, eds., *Human Rights and U.S. Foreign Policy* (Lexington, Mass.: D.C. Heath, 1979), p. xvii.
43. Quoted in U.S., Congress, House, Committee on Foreign Affairs, *Human Rights and U.S. Foreign Policy, Hearings before the Subcommittee on International Organizations*, 96th Cong, 1st sess., 1979, p. 9.
44. Arthur Schlesinger, Jr., "Human Rights and the American Tradition," *Foreign Affairs*, Vol. 57, No. 3, p. 522.
45. Carter, *Keeping Faith*, p. 150.
46. Somoza, *Nicaragua Betrayed*, p. xi.
47. "Columbus, Ohio," *Weekly Compilation of Presidential Documents*, Oct. 2, 1978, p. 1623.
48. "Interview With the President," Ibid., May 30, 1977, p. 768; "The President's News Conference of June 13, 1977," Ibid., June 20, 1977, p. 878; "American Convention on Human Rights," Ibid., June 6, 1977, p. 838.
49. "Minneapolis, Minnesota," Ibid., Oct. 30, 1978, pp. 1831-1832.
50. "Warsaw, Poland," Ibid., Jan. 2, 1978, p. 1970; "Visit of President Ceausescu of Romania," Ibid., April 17, 1978, p. 740; "Visit of President Josip Broz Tito of Yugoslavia," Ibid., March 13, 1978, p. 474; "Tehran, Iran," Ibid., Jan. 2, 1978, p. 1975.

EIGHT

A View to the Future: Resolving the Dilemmas

What lessons can be learned from the Carter experience about how the United States should conduct its human rights policy? For all its mistakes and failures, the Carter policy showed the latent importance of the human rights issue. Jeane Kirkpatrick, Carter's most trenchant critic, commented: "not only should human rights play a central role in U.S. foreign policy, no U.S. foreign policy can possibly succeed that does not accord them a central role."[1] This is so because, as Jimmy Carter rightly said, the belief in human rights is the common blood that flows in American veins. Our sense of nationhood flows from the set of principles expressed in the Constitution and the Declaration of Independence. In order for the United States to act in the world with a degree of national unity and with a sense of conviction, our policy must be felt to be grounded in those principles. It is also so because the politics of the modern age are fought not only over territory and resources, and with missiles and factories, but over and with ideas—and human rights is the essence of the American idea.

There are those who doubt that human rights should be a focus of U.S. foreign policy. Some say that it is "wrong" to intervene in the domestic affairs of other countries. But this is not true in a legal sense. The relevant international law, essentially UN law, is a muddle. The UN Charter upholds the sanctity of "domestic jurisdiction" (Article 2[7]), but it also obligates members to respect "human rights and fundamental freedoms" (Articles 55 and 56). The confusion that this contradiction engenders is exemplified by General Assembly Resolution 2131 (XX) which proclaims: "Every State has an inalienable right to choose its political, economic, social and cultural systems, without interference in any form by another State." This seems clear enough, although General Assembly resolutions are not legally binding. But the very next clause of the same resolution flatly contradicts the principle of non-intervention. It enjoins every state to "contribute to the complete elimination of racial discrimination...in all its forms and manifestations." In sum, the most reasonable interpretation of existing law is that *armed* intervention is proscribed, except conceivably in very extreme situations, but that moral intervention on behalf of human rights is permissible.

If it is not legally wrong, is it morally wrong to intervene in the affairs of other nations in order to encourage respect for human rights? Only if the nation, rather than the human individual, is regarded as the ultimate moral unit. But by what logic does the nation have moral standing apart from that of the human beings who make it up? The practical fact is that in the twentieth century especially, but throughout all history as well, nations have intervened politically, morally, and intellectually in the affairs of other nations. If we Americans cherish our human rights, and if we share with America's Founders the belief that these rights are "unalienable" or that they are goods with which people have been "endowed by their Creator," then it is certainly morally permissible, probably even morally obligatory, that we do what we can within reason to help other people to secure theirs.

There are two other arguments against human rights

policy that are much more formidable. One of these holds that Soviet power or Communism constitutes by far the most dangerous enemy of human rights in the world today, and that American power constitutes the irreplaceable shield of human rights wherever they now exist. Therefore any marginal gains for human rights that are bought at the expense of America's power relative to that of the Communists simply aren't worth it—they are likely to constitute a long-term net loss for the cause of human rights.

This argument is only half-true. Communism *is* by far the greatest enemy of human rights, but a human rights policy is not a hindrance to combatting Communism, it is essential to it. Some may prefer the term "freedom" or "democracy" to "human rights"—but whatever the name, the United States needs to have a response to Communism on the level of ideology. The essence of Communism—and the key to the threat that it poses both to American "interests" and to the cause of human rights—lies in the interplay of ideas and violence. Everywhere that Communism exists, it has come by force; nowhere has it triumphed by the force of its ideas alone. But almost everywhere its triumphs of arms have first been prepared by the use of "ideas"—propaganda, agitation, subversion, political maneuver—to enfeeble the opposition. Someone has wisely quipped that, to Communists, politics is the continuation of war by other means. Conversely, each victory of Communist arms strengthens it ideologically, lending plausibility to its claim to represent the future.

To resist Communism effectively, the United States must oppose it both in the realm of arms and in the realm of ideas. To ignore the former would be calamitous—even more directly for the cause of human rights than for the United States as a nation-state. If the United States sharply reduced its military forces and foreswore the effort to exercise global influence, as in the wake of Vietnam many Americans wished, it still might be able to survive intact, behind a relatively inexpensive curtain of nuclear missiles. But the cause of human rights would not survive outside our borders, and,

223

in time, perhaps not within them either.

But if Communism cannot be resisted without adequate arms, neither can it be resisted by arms alone. Arms alone are useless without men to wield them, men with loyalty and conviction. No Third World ruler commanded more and better arms than the Shah of Iran, but when he finally faced a real challenge, they proved of no use. The one democracy in the postwar era whose soldiers have shown real elan is Israel, and the reason is no mystery: they have a strong sense of what it is they are fighting for. In Central America today the United States is in danger of suffering truly damaging military defeats not because it is outgunned, but because its political position is so precarious.

In combatting Communism in the realm of ideas, the United States has many disadvantages and one great advantage. The disadvantages stem from the fact that democracy is ill-suited for "ideological combat." Communist governments possess vast propaganda apparatuses that the United States cannot and will never match. Communists believe that they possess the one truth, whereas democrats believe only in the freedom to search for the truth. In the "war of ideas," open-mindedness is often a poor match for certitude.

On the other hand, the great advantage that the United States holds is the evidence of experience. Our system is lightyears better, more humane, than the Communist system, measured by any standard, including those that Marxism itself proclaims. This is given mute but eloquent testimony by the simple fact that the United States is besieged by people from all over the world trying to get in, while every Communist country in the world posts armed guards and barbed wire to keep its people from getting out. The essence of this difference can be expressed in the words "human rights." And that is why it is powerfully in the interests of the United States to talk about and dramatize human rights, to keep the issue of human rights high on the agenda of public discourse and in the thoughts of individuals all over the world.

The other argument against a human rights policy holds that U.S. foreign policy must be guided by the "national interest" and that such altruistic goals as human rights can play no more than a peripheral part because, as Ernst Haas says: "A consistent and energetic policy in the human rights field makes impossible the attainment of other, often more important, objectives."[2] The critical flaw in this argument is that it is hard to think of any situation where the advancement of human rights conflicts with other U.S. interests. On the contrary, the advancement of human rights almost always serves concrete American interests, both because it is a victory for our system of values and because every country in the world where human rights flourish is friendly, some of course more than others, to the United States.

Destabilizing friendly dictatorial governments may not serve U.S. interests, but it may not serve the cause of human rights either. If a friendly dictatorship gives way to a more democratic government, the cause of human rights will benefit, and the interests of the United States will not ordinarily be harmed. On the other hand, if it gives way to a new dictatorship, ideologically hostile to the United States, that, as we have seen over and again, ordinarily turns out to be a setback not only for American interests, but for human rights as well. In short, the fall of a dictator may or may not be a good thing for the United States or for human rights—that depends on what comes after. The triumph of democracy, however, will almost always be a good thing both for human rights and for the United States. The goal of our human rights policy should not be to destabilize existing governments, but to encourage democratic currents.

Confusion on this score has arisen from the strong association of human rights policy with the use of punitive measures. It is widely taken for granted that cutting foreign aid to dictators is the essence of any human rights policy. But punitive measures, as we have seen, are not very effective in advancing human rights. And, as it turns out, the main impetus behind the growth of punitive measures was the desire not to advance human rights but to diminish American influence. It is not inherently wrong to give aid to dictatorial governments. No ruler in the history of the human race had on his hands more blood of his own citizens than Stalin. Yet who, today, apart perhaps from Solzhenitsyn, argues that it was wrong for the United States to have given aid to his government in the last world war? If punitive measures prove on the whole to be effective in advancing human rights, then it is doubtful that American interests will suffer much from their use. If they prove on the whole ineffective, then their use should be avoided or reserved for special situations.

If we avoid both heavy reliance on punitive measures and avoid destabilizing governments in the face of uncertain futures, then most of the presumed conflict between human rights goals and the national interest disappears. Some conflict perhaps remains. If the United States is speaking loudly about human rights, if it is succoring dissidents and encouraging democratic forces, this may cause some friction in our dealings with dictatorial governments, especially Communist ones. It injures, as Adam Ulam put it about the Russians, their "ideological-national pride."[3] The Russians, our adversaries but partners in SALT, and the Chinese, our semiallies against the Russians, both respond angrily to U.S. talk about human rights. But neither of those governments is willing to abandon for a moment its claim that our way of life is both wrong and doomed, nor is either willing to allow its people to be exposed to our views, although they are completely free to convey their views to the American people, a freedom of which they are not too modest to avail themselves. If we allow their resentment to deter us from speaking out about human rights we will be engaging in a kind of unilateral ideological disarmament. This may possibly avert some friction, but it may just as well have the effect, like other forms of appeasement, of inviting new demands.

A well thought-out human rights policy may not be entirely free from conflicts with other U.S. policy goals (what policy is?), but the harm that may accrue to other U.S. interests will be small compared to the benefits that such a policy can bring, benefits that will serve both our ideals and our interests.

What would be the elements of a well thought-out human rights policy? It would, first of all, appreciate that other cultures are different from ours and that every culture is worthy of respect, but it would not be deterred by charges of "ethnocentrism" from recognizing the special relevance of the American experience to the universal quest for human rights. The yearning for human rights, for individual dignity, for liberty, is widespread and age-old. But the achievement of human rights as a system, a way of life, is America's unique and wondrous contribution to mankind.

Of course, the American system was not cut from whole cloth. It built on many traditions. Nor is the American system the last word in human rights. Other systems of freedom have flowered since ours; some may have improved on ours in some respects. Our system is not and was not perfect, especially in the area of race where our flaws were glaring. But all this said, the largest fact remains that it was the American approach to human rights that made human rights a reality in the world.

This truth is embarrassing, for it sounds so self-congratulatory. But there is an important reason why we must not avoid it. The rhetoric of "human rights" is widely employed. Communists use it. Assorted Third World tyrants use it. Feckless and hypocritical UN committees use it. Plainly, not all of these human rights traditions are equally valid. The approach to "human rights" of the Communist world or most of the Third World or even of the UN has yielded little of value and much that is noxious, while the American approach has yielded nourishing fruit.

The American approach to human rights rests on certain premises about the nature of man and the primacy of the individual over the state; and it emphasizes certain principles— freedom of expression and association, due process of law, government by the consent of the governed. These are the ideas that our human rights policy must try to impart to the rest of the world.

We should work to strengthen and clarify the concept of "human rights." This means resisting the temptation to stretch the term to embrace such seemingly well-meaning ideas as that of "economic and social rights." We should of course be concerned with the economic well-being of people, and probably the amount of foreign aid we give should be greatly increased. This is a matter of basic compassion; to call it a matter of "rights" gains nothing—it will not feed a single extra person—but it endangers something else of great value. We should also cease treating the category of violations of the integrity of the person as if it were a category of rights separable from other rights. Of course we will want to speak more loudly, act more urgently, in response to the rampages of the Khmer Rouge, the homicidal mania of Idi Amin, or the insidious work of the Salvadoran death squads, than, say, to the fact that Jordan continues to be ruled as a hereditary monarchy. But proclaiming special categories of rights doesn't help us to do this; we do it out of common sense and natural revulsion. The only effect of proclaiming special categories of rights is to denigrate other rights.

The UN and its treaties should not be a focus of major attention in U.S. human rights policy. It has often been remarked that a problem with the UN is that it represents governments rather than people. But the problem, insofar as human rights are concerned, is worse than that. The UN isn't made up merely of governments, it is made up primarily of dictatorships. Virtually every violator of human rights in the world has a vote in the UN, but none of their victims has. There are sound diplomatic reasons for the United States to participate in the UN, but as an arena for advancing the cause of human rights it holds little promise. The same may be said for the human rights treaties adopted under UN auspices. We should ratify them if we can find a way, through reservations and the like, without jeopardizing our own constitutional processes, but we should not anticipate that they are likely any time in the foreseeable future to constitute anything more than elaborate monuments to hypocrisy.

This is not to say that we should give up altogether on using international instruments as a means of advancing human rights. Surely the goal of an international regime for the protection of human rights is a noble one. It is worth keeping alive in the hope that it might become more realistic in a post-Communist world. In the meantime, the European and Inter-American human rights conventions are valuable instruments and may offer models for the creation of others. These others needn't be regional, but the key is that they would have to be considerably less than universal, so as to avoid being dominated, as the UN is, by dictators. The United States needs mechanisms that serve to push our "authoritarian" Third World allies toward democratization while simultaneously paying recognition to their moral superiority to the world's totalitarians. Perhaps some international conventions could be fashioned that would serve this end.

A sound human rights policy will strive for consistency of application to all countries. Of course this does not mean treating all abusive governments identically. Some governments are worse enemies of human rights than others. And there are some other legitimate reasons for not treating all situations identically. It is legitimate to take into account a country's progress. Thus, for example, Czechoslovakia during the "Prague Spring" and Poland during the heyday of Solidarnosc were both still one-party states, but obviously the much more impressive fact at that moment was how much they had evolved toward respect for human rights. Common sense directed our attention to how far they had come, not to how far they had yet to go. Common sense also commands us to be mindful of a country's background in determining what we can expect from it. The Pinochet government is the more abhorrent for Chile's democratic nistory; whereas if Tanzania or Mozambique became tomorrow as free as Chile is today we could not help but be very gratified at the progress.

What is *not* legitimate in a human rights policy is inconsistency based on our own self-interest, raising our voice in moral righteousness wherever it seems inexpensive to do so. It is hard to believe that a policy such as this will inspire many people for very long. On the other hand nothing could better impress the world with our moral seriousness than our willingness to stand by our human rights principles uniformly, even where it costs us something. This does mean, as the Reagan administration discovered after a few months, that "if we act as if offenses against freedom don't matter in countries friendly to us, no one will take seriously our words about Communist violations."[4] But the Carter administration showed that it is easy enough to put the squeeze on weak friendly countries. The more important test is whether we are willing to apply our human rights policy to powerful countries resistant to human rights, whether or not they are friendly. The best litmus tests are the Peoples's Republic of China and Saudi Arabia.

Pursuing a consistent policy is much easier if the policy does not involve heavy use of punitive measures. These ought to be saved for special situations, either where violations are extreme, as in Amin's Uganda, or where a single act, such as the generals' threat to abort the 1978 Dominican election, seems likely to have a decisive effect on the status of human rights in a country. The principal medium of human rights policy must be words. As Patricia Derian once said: "The whole of society…is based on ideas, and you do something about ideas with words."[5] If we rely on words rather than punishments, then we should not fear to be even-handed.

Do we have the courage to voice our support for China's democratic dissidents? Or to express our revulsion at the severing of hands of Saudi thieves? What will these countries do to us if we insist on the principle of speaking the truth about human rights as best we can discover it? There is good reason to believe that they will just learn to live with it, probably after first probing to see if they can intimidate us into backing off. The evidence for this comes from our experience with the human rights "Country Reports."

The first set of reports was issued early in 1977, and

evoked an angry reaction from countries that were criticized, including declarations by five Latin American countries rejecting all military aid from the United States so as not to be subject to the reports. Richard Holbrooke, Carter's assistant secretary of state for East Asian and Pacific Affairs, testified that: "I had never participated in any exercise in the State Department that I found more offensive than presenting...written, public, unclassified reports in which we passed judgment on other countries."[6] Other important Carter administration officials, including Jessica Tuchman, the National Security Council staff member in charge of human rights issues, shared Holbrooke's displeasure with the frictions engendered by the country reports.[7] Even Patricia Derian, for all her reputation as a firebrand, testified in 1978 after the release of the second annual batch of reports that she was unhappy with the task. "There is the underlying question of whether we should be writing such reports at all," she said. "There needs to be a better way."[8] By "a better way" Derian indicated she meant turning the country reports over to some quasi-governmental agency outside of the State Department, a proposal that was first raised by Warren Christopher, and which was later spelled out most fully by William F. Buckley in an article in *Foreign Affairs*.[9]

The Christopher-Derian-Buckley proposal never got off the ground, and the State Department produced a more thorough batch of reports during each of Derian's remaining years and during each subsequent year, notwithstanding the Reagan administration's initial ambivalence about human rights policy. The five Latin countries that were so offended in 1977 have since resumed accepting our aid, and although each year the reports grow more detailed and more accurate, they now are greeted with hardly a murmur of protest. The simple fact is that the rest of the world has gotten used to them, or has realized that this is something the United States is determined to continue doing, so there is no point in protesting.

The reports, moreover, have become one of the most valuable components of U.S. human rights policy. Former

Rep. Don Fraser, the originator of much human rights legislation, has said: "In the long run..the most useful provision
in section 502(B) [governing human rights and military aid]
was the requirement that the State Department report on
human rights conditions in each of the countries."[10] Even
with the many criticisms that liberals have of the Reagan administration in the area of human rights policy, the reports
are widely credited for their seriousness and objectivity. The
requirement of preparing the reports serves to draw attention
within the State Department to human rights questions that
might otherwise be passed over quickly. More important,
the reports themselves are a precious resource. The very existence of an up-to-date source, bearing the "authoritative"
imprimatur of the U.S. government, on the state of human
rights in every country in the world is of inestimable service
to the cause of human rights.

One might add that it is unlikely that these reports
would be nearly as good or as useful had the job of preparing
them been turned over to some quasi-public agency. The experience with a range of such authorities, from the U.S. Civil
Rights Commission to public radio and television, teaches
that they readily fall prey to the political biases of their members or staff, sometimes even to an extreme degree. It is unlikely that the reports would be as fair and objective as they
are were it not for the fact that they are prepared in the State
Department itself and those who prepare them know that
they will be held to standards of objectivity commensurate
with their public responsibilities.

Shifting away from heavy use of punitive measures is
desirable, but it is only part of a broader shift in emphasis:
our human rights policy should be aimed less at governments
than at people. Its goal should be to foster democratic currents, to create democrats. The National Endowment for
Democracy will, it is to be hoped, become a vehicle for doing
this. It remains to be seen whether Congress will give the
endowment sufficient support to make significant progress
in this work.

In its first annual report, the endowment outlined the

component parts of its democracy-building program, all of them commendable. These include activities designed to foster pluralism by aiding the growth of independent labor, business, and civic associations as nongovernmental centers of power; education in the theory and practice of democracy as well as practical training in party-building, poll-watching, parliamentary procedure, and the other mechanics of the democratic process; sponsorship of publications by dissidents in and exiles from dictatorial countries; research aimed at identifying some of the causes that explain why democracy has faired better in some developing countries than others; and support for the creation of a new international organization of democratic countries.

Most of the endowment's efforts are of necessity aimed either at countries with fledgling democratic institutions that need strengthening, or at countries whose governments, though dictatorial, tolerate some degree of open communication and activity by independent groups and individuals. A more formidable problem is presented by "closed societies" whose governments tolerate few if any independent communal activities. In such societies, the endowment's minimal goal is to "keep alive the flame of freedom."

Toward that end, U.S. human rights policy should give high priority to providing moral support to persecuted democrats and dissidents wherever they are found, and to focusing attention on their cases. President Carter reports in his memoirs that: "In all my discussions with...dissidents, and with citizens of other countries whose freedom had been curtailed, they always emphasized how important it was for us to continue reminding the world of their plight."[11] Some have argued that publicizing the cases of dissidents serves only to spur their persecutors to greater efforts in order to show their defiance of American pressures. But the clear majority of dissidents reject this argument. And even if there is no way to judge with certainty whether publicity will deter or invigorate the persecutors, there is still a powerful reason for being outspoken. These courageous dissidents have made sober decisions to accept bitter sacrifices for their beliefs. We, alas, often will be able to do very little to ease their physical suffering. But there is something else that we can do for them that may be equally important—we can give them spiritual sustenance to ease their isolation. We can try to convey to them the knowledge that there is a world outside of their prisons, outside of their countries, that knows about their struggles and *believes they are right*. Such key Soviet dissidents as Andrei Sakharov seem always to take pains in their public statements to draw attention to as many individual cases as they reasonably can. Why should we do any less? The Human Rights Bureau should create some regular system, perhaps regular press briefings by the assistant secretary, to publicize current cases of persecuted dissidents.

With respect to those countries, such as the Communist, that restrict the inflow of information, we should, as part of our human rights policy, seek to exploit advances in technology that will help us to penetrate the communications barrier. For example, it apparently is possible to circumvent the jamming of radio broadcasts if we devote sufficient effort and resources to this task. New technologies in telephone and television transmissions may provide other opportunities.

However distant it may seem in many cases, the goal of a human rights policy is the same for all countries—the creation of political systems that are predicated on belief in human rights and that contain built-in mechanisms for their protection. The only political system that does that, though it can come in myriad variations, is democracy. In this sense a human rights policy is profoundly ideological, and should be unabashedly so. True, U.S. policy should avoid one of the things that the Carter administration was seeking to avoid when it insisted that its policy was not "ideological"—the appearance that the United States is criticizing Soviet violations merely in order to gain tactical advantage in a competition the real motivation for which is great power rivalry. But stressing the "ideological" nature of our criticisms of the Soviet system should help to make clear that we are motivated not by ulterior interests but by cherished beliefs. This will be all the more convincing if we dare make the same human rights criticisms of those Communists who are our "allies" that we make of those who are our enemies.

To approach the human rights issue as if it were a matter merely of a series of discrete events—"violations"—is like trying to approach the problem of hunger without taking poverty into account. To say, as Patt Derian said, that human rights violations can occur under any system is true, but it is true in the same sense that it is true that death can come to a healthy person just as it can come to the critically ill. In some systems, violations occur as isolated exceptions. In others, violations are the very essence of the system. The struggle for human rights is not, cannot be, an endless chase after an infinite number of individual events. Rather, it is the struggle to establish a way of life based on respect for human rights.

Two political systems today offer themselves to the world as models—democracy and Communism. Most of the world has already adopted or come to live under one model or the other, while that which remains is constantly pulled between the two. One of these models is predicated on belief in human rights; the other is predicated on their denial. To attempt to conduct a human rights policy that is oblivious to the contest between these two models is to ignore the central human right question of our time.

A constant theme in America's history, although its strength has waxed and waned, is the sense of America's "mission" as the world's first democracy. In this century, that sense has been shaken by several developments: the advent of Communism, a system of more recent provenance than ours and with universal pretensions, that claims to be the true embodiment of the future; the collapse of democratic forms in one after another of the new states that gained independence after World War II; our defeat in Vietnam which called into question our ability to resist the spread of systems antithetical to our own and the wisdom of trying to do so. But the same streak in our national character that leads us at times to give way too much to enthusiasm can also lead us to give way too much to disappointment. Communism may indeed prove to be the model for man's future, but if so it will be an unhappy future. The only thing certain is that the future is not ordained; it will be what men and women make it. That it may look more like our system than like Communism is a goal worth striving for. The experience of the newly independent states only shows us the difficulty of the task. And our experience in Vietnam shows us the difficulty in using our power effectively. The advent of the human rights issue, and the resonance that Jimmy Carter found in it, shows that the sense of mission, the democratic faith, still pulses in American veins. A sound and sustained human rights policy can help to vindicate that faith.

NOTES

1. Jeane Kirkpatrick, "Human Rights and American Foreign Policy: A Symposium," *Commentary*, Vol. 72, No. 5 (November 1981), p. 42.
2. Ernst Haas, "Human Rights," in Oye, Lieber and Rothchild, eds., *Eagle Entangled* (New York: Longman, 1979), p. 169.
3. Adam Ulam, "U.S.-Soviet Relations: Unhappy Coexistence," *Foreign Affairs*, Vol. 57, No. 3, p. 559.
4. William Clark, Deputy Secretary of State, and Richard T. Kennedy, Under Secretary, "Memorandum for the Secretary, Subject: Reinvigoration of Human Rights Policy," Oct. 26, 1981, p. 3, copy in author's files.
5. CBS Television and Radio, "Face the Nation," Dec. 25, 1977, transcript p. 16.
6. U.S., Congress, House, Committee on Foreign Affairs, *Reconciling Human Rights and U.S. Security Interests in Asia, Hearings before the Subcommittees on Asian and Pacific Affairs and on Human Rights and International Organizations*, 97th Cong., 2nd sess., 1982, p. 62.
7. Interview with Jessica Tuchman, held in Washington, D.C., Dec. 29, 1983.
8. U.S., Congress, House, Committee on Appropriations, *Foreign Assistance and Related Agencies Appropriations for FY1979, Part 2*, 95th Cong., 2nd Sess., 1978., p. 437.

9. William F. Buckley, "Human Rights and Foreign Policy: A Proposal," *Foreign Affairs*, Vol. 58, No. 4 (Spring 1980) pp. 775-796.
10. U.S., Congress, House, Committee on Foreign Affairs, *Human Rights and U.S. Foreign Policy, Hearings before the Subcommittee on International Organizations*, 96th Cong., 1st sess., 1979, p. 300.
11. Jimmy Carter, *Keeping Faith* (New York: Bantam Books, 1982), p. 149.

Appendix

Notes and explanations regarding the statistical exercise aimed at measuring the effects of punitive measures.

I. The Freedom House scale contains no measure of "economic and social" rights, nor is there any other scale of these rights that would allow measurements fine enough to gauge changes over the course of a single administration. The Overseas Development Council's "Physical Quality of Life Index" is a creative effort to measure social and economic progress.[1] It is, however, useless for the purpose of measuring the effects of a policy of only a few years' duration because it is not based on data that are available on an annual basis, but rather on data for five-year or ten-year spans.[2] The absence of a scale for "economic and social rights" is, in any event, not fatal to my exercise because, despite its rhetorical emphasis on "economic and social rights," the Carter administration rarely resorted to material sanctions out of its concern about these rights. Rather, the sanctions it exacted were almost always in response to violations of civil and political rights, most often violations of the "integrity of the person," which, in the Freedom House scheme, would be included in the scales of political and civil rights.

II. It may be objected that the scale used by Freedom House reflects a "conservative" political bias. Thus, for example, Lars Schoultz complains that "Freedom House's undisguised hostility toward socialist economies, renders its rankings of human rights performance somewhat inconsistent."[3] Schoultz, who admires the governments of Cuba and Nicaragua,[4] probably disagrees strenuously with the most recent Freedom House rating which gives both of these countries worse ratings than it gives to El Salvador.[5] But even if these objections are well taken, they have little bearing on my exercise which aims to examine changes in Freedom House's ratings of individual countries from one year to the next and does not aim to compare countries with each other. After all it is not just this year that Freedom House gives El Salvador a better human rights rating than it gives Cuba; it has done the same for each of the previous ten years. Moreover, in terms of the change *within* countries, Freedom House shows a slight improvement in Cuba over the past seven years and a deteriorating trend in El Salvador, judgments with which Freedom House's critics would probably agree. As far as I can see, the only sense in which these ideological objections to Freedom House's ratings would create a cogent doubt about the "validity" of my exercise is in the case of a country in which there was a change from a left-wing to a right-wing government, or vice versa, during the years which I am examining. There is only one such case among the 28 countries on which I am focusing—Nicaragua—and its impact is mathematically insignificant.

III. The 28 countries receiving punitive measures were Afghanistan, Argentina, Benin, Central African Empire, Chile, El Salvador, Ethiopia, Guatemala, Guinea, South Korea, Laos, Paraguay, the Philippines, Uruguay, Vietnam, So. Yemen, Indonesia, Bolivia, Haiti, Nicaragua, Zaire, So. Africa, Bangladesh, Mozambique, Somalia, Liberia, Pakistan, and Guyana. This list comprises those countries named in reports to Congress by various arms of the executive branch and, in the case of security assistance, those named by Stephen B. Cohen, the deputy assistant secretary for Human Rights in charge of security assistance, in his article, "Conditioning U.S. Security Assistance on Human Rights Practices."[6] These were the recipients of punitive measures taken explicitly on human rights grounds. Other countries may have suffered decreases in economic or military aid for a confluence of reasons, of which human rights was one or was thought to be one by some of the officials involved in the decision—but there is no record of this. The absence of such cases, if they exist, from the group that I am examining is not fatal to my exercise, because it is fair to assume that if human rights-based sanctions had any discernible effect, it would show up more clearly in the cases where the sanction was clear and explicit than in those where it was ambiguous and inferential.

IV. Under PL480, the "Food for Peace" program, countries defined by AID as having serious human rights problems were not barred from receiving food, because it met basic human needs, but they were required to sign special agreements with AID granting the United States closer scrutiny over the allocation of the food or of any funds derived from its sale, in order to assure that this aid was indeed benefiting the neediest. Of my list of 28, six countries (Indonesia, Bangladesh, Mozambique, Somalia, Pakistan and Liberia) received no sanctions other than being required to sign such agreements. Because this was a formal procedure applied to human rights violators, I have included these six on my list, but, because no aid was actually cut, another observer might find it more fitting to omit the six. This would make no significant change in the figures. Without the six, the average score of the remaining 22 was 11.8 (instead of 11.7) at the beginning of 1977 and 12.0 (instead of 11.9) at the beginning of 1981. If, in deference to the ideological critiques of the Freedom House ratings discussed above, Nicaragua is entirely eliminated from the calculations, the averages are 11.7 at the beginning, and 12.0 at the end, of the Carter administration.

NOTES

1. Morris David Morris, *Measuring the Condition of the World's Poor* (New York: Pergamon Press, 1979).
2. See Roger D. Hansen and Contributors, *U.S. Foreign Policy and the Third World: Agenda 1982* (New York: Praeger, 1982), p. 170, notes 4 and 5.
3. "U.S. Policy Toward Human Rights in Latin America: A

Comparative Analysis of Two Administrations," in Ved Nanada, James Scarritt, and George Shephard, Jr., eds., *Global Human Rights: Public Policies, Comparative Measures and NGO Strategies* (Boulder: Westview, 1981), p. 80.

4. See Lars Schoultz, *Human Rights and United States Policy toward Latin America* (Princeton: Princeton U. Press, 1981), pp. 378-379.

5. Raymond D. Gastil, "The Comparative Survey of Freedom 1984," *Freedom at Issue*, No. 76 (January-February 1984), pp. 8-9.

6. Stephen B. Cohen, "Conditioning U.S. Security Assistance on Human Rights Practices," *American Journal of International Law*, Vol. 76 (1982), p. 270.

Index

243